Praise for Kara Swisher

"Most people in this town stab you in the back, but [Kara] stabbed me in the front, and I appreciate that."
—John McLaughlin, former host, *The McLaughlin Group*

"She has a coffee before bed every night, after midnight. This seems somehow emblematic to me. (In a good way.)"
—Ben Smith, media writer guy and other *reportrepreneur* besides Kara

"I don't buy into the meme of Kara Swisher the ass-kicker who says what she wants, like she's this honey badger who doesn't give a shit."
—Paul Carr, guy who knows from honey badgers

"A force in the industry."
—Meredith Kopit Levien, CEO, *The New York Times*

"It is a constant joke in the Valley when people write memos for them to say, 'I hope Kara never sees this.'"
—Sheryl Sandberg, former COO, Facebook (before it was called Meta, in order to hide in plain sight)

"She's willing to get into the brawl with me."
—Ari Emanuel, Endeavor CEO and well-known brawler

"There she was with a front-row seat to the mining of great intellectual property—using technology, really—as a means of creating value [and] in effect turned the results of her own reporting on herself."
—Bob Iger, CEO of Disney, two times

"Part of the power of her podcast is there's a sense of some-body who has been here the whole time and is kind of fed up."
—Casey Newton, tech journalist (and former renter of Kara's guest cottage in San Francisco)

"Kara has become so shrill at this point that only dogs can hear her."
—Elon Musk, Tesla guy, May 2023

"I mentor a lot of people, and almost every single one of them is worried about losing their place if they step out of line. And I'm like, the only way you get higher is if you step out of line. That's the only way. Seriously. Unless you're un-talented. And then you should stay in line."
—Kara Swisher, other *reportrepreneur* besides Ben

"I have rarely seen evil in as pure a form as Yoel Roth and Kara Swisher's heart is filled with seething hate. I regard their dislike of me as a compliment."
—Elon Musk (who could use a compliment these days), September 2023

BURN BOOK

A TECH LOVE STORY

KARA SWISHER

Simon & Schuster

NEW YORK   LONDON   TORONTO
SYDNEY   NEW DELHI

1230 Avenue of the Americas
New York, NY 10020

First Simon & Schuster hardcover edition February 2024

SIMON & SCHUSTER and colophon are registered trademarks
of Simon & Schuster, LLC

Simon & Schuster: Celebrating 100 Years of Publishing in 2024

For information about special discounts for bulk purchases,
please contact Simon & Schuster Special Sales at 1-866-506-1949
or business@simonandschuster.com.

The Simon & Schuster Speakers Bureau can bring authors to your
live event. For more information or to book an event, contact the
Simon & Schuster Speakers Bureau at 1-866-248-3049
or visit our website at www.simonspeakers.com.

Manufactured in the United States of America

1   3   5   7   9   10   8   6   4   2

Library of Congress Cataloging-in-Publication Data has been applied for.

ISBN 978-1-9821-6389-1
ISBN978-1-9821-6391-4 (ebook)

To Walt Mossberg

You wrote in the first line of your first column on tech: "Personal computers are just too hard to use, and it isn't your fault." Some thirty years later, that remains true, and so is the fact that you have altered the course of my life in ways I can never repay. And it is—thankfully for me—your fault.

Contents

Sheeple Who Need Sheeple

They were careless people, Tom and Daisy—they smashed up things and creatures and then retreated back into their money or their vast carelessness or whatever it was that kept them together, and let other people clean up the mess they had made.

—F. SCOTT FITZGERALD, *THE GREAT GATSBY*

As it turned out, it was capitalism after all.

If I had to pick the moment when it all went off the rails for the tech industry, I'd choose Saturday morning, December 10, 2016, when I was at a farmers market considering some epic Meyer lemons with my oldest son, who liked to cook. It was there in the San Francisco sunshine as the fog burned away up the hill in Noe Valley that I got a tip: The crowned heads of Silicon Valley's most powerful tech companies had been summoned to tromp into Manhattan's Trump Tower and meet the man who had unexpectedly just been elected president and was the antithesis of all they supposedly represented.

"Skulk" was more like it. The only reason I was hearing about the tech summit was because one of tech's top-tier players had *not* been invited due to his "liberal leanings" and "outspoken opposition" to President-Elect Donald Trump. The outcast called me in a lather.

"Sucking up to that corpulent loser who never met a business he didn't drive straight into a wall, it's shameful," he said. "Can you believe it? Can you *believe* it?"

After decades of covering the nascent Internet industry from its birth, I could believe it. While my actual son filled me with pride, an increasing number of these once fresh-faced wunderkinds I had mostly rooted for now made me feel like a parent whose progeny had turned into, *well*, assholes.

My first call was to one of the potentates who was sometimes testy, often funny, and always accessible. Of everyone I had covered, I could count on Tesla and SpaceX CEO Elon Musk to engage with me on a semi-human basis. While Musk would morph later into a troll-king-at-scale on Twitter, which he would rename X, he was among the few tech titans who did not fall back on practiced talking points, even if perhaps he was the one who most should have.

So, what did Musk think of Trump's invitation? The meeting had no stated agenda, which made it clear to me that it had nothing to do with policy and everything to do with a photo op.

"You shouldn't go," I warned him. "Trump's going to screw you."

Musk disagreed. He told me he would attend, adding that he had already joined a business council for the newly elected president, too. When I brought up Trump's constant divisive fearmongering and campaign promises to unravel progress on issues ranging from immigration to gay rights, Musk dismissed the threats.

I can convince him, he assured me. I can influence him, he told me.

Apparently, Musk thought that his very presence would turn the fetid water into fine wine, since he had long considered himself more than just a man, but an icon and, on some days, a god. Good luck with that, I thought to myself as we hung up.

I moved on, calling other C-suiters for comment. The guest list had been compiled by contrarian investor and persistent irritant Peter Thiel, who had made a fortune betting on visionary technologies. Still, his latest vision for the future was his most outlandish: backing Trump. It was certainly a bold bet by Thiel, and it had panned out magnificently.

I didn't even attempt to contact Thiel. The entrepreneur had long since stopped communicating with me, especially after a lengthy video interview in 2007 where we agreed on exactly nothing. After the camera stopped rolling, I pressed Thiel on the need to ensure gays had the same rights to be married and have children as straight people. Both Thiel and I are famously gay, but he argued that gays should not get "special rights," even as I asserted that we had no rights at all. We had exactly nothing in common. And, while we would both go on to get married and have kids (me, twice), it was probably a good instinct on his part to avoid me.

But I talked with other invitees, a few of whom said that Thiel had pressured them to get on board. Others welcomed Thiel's invite and insisted that Trump did not mean the terrible things he had said repeatedly on the stump. Another tried to convince me that meeting Trump "was a public show of truce." Like Musk, many insisted they would bring up substantive issues, except behind closed doors.

"Look, this is obviously a circus," said one person to me. "Everyone in tech just wants to be invisible right now when it comes to this administration but has to participate since we've done it before."

The sticky part was that many of the tech leaders—including Facebook's Sheryl Sandberg, who had been a prominent supporter of Democratic presidential candidate Hillary Clinton—had openly opposed Trump's stances during the campaign. Almost all of them pushed back when Trump called for "a total and complete shutdown of Muslims entering the United States" and announced a plan to severely limit immigration. In fact, two of the invitees—Musk and Microsoft's new CEO Satya Nadella—were immigrants themselves. And most had privately derided Trump to me as a buffoon.

This kind of casual hypocrisy became increasingly common over the decades that I covered Silicon Valley's elite. Over that time, I watched founders transform from young, idealistic strivers in a scrappy upstart industry into leaders of some of America's largest and most influential businesses. And while there were exceptions, the richer and more powerful people grew, the more compromised they became—wrapping themselves in expensive cashmere batting until the genuine person fell deep inside a cocoon of comfort and privilege where no unpleasantness intruded.

When people get really rich, they seem to attract legions of enablers who lick them up and down all day. Many of these billionaires had then started to think of this fawning as reality, where suddenly everything that comes out of their mouths is golden. History gets rewritten as hagiography. But if you knew them in the before times and have some prior knowledge of their original selves, you either become an asset (truth-teller) or a threat (truth-teller) to them.

Still, I hoped even they had some limits and there was a way to view the meeting as an opportunity, an opening to voice one's opinion. I advised the people who called me back to make a strong public joint statement going into the meeting on key values and issues important to tech and its employees.

"Isn't that the point of a democracy?" I urged one CEO. "Let the public know that you're not going to Trump Tower to bend the knee to a king, but to stand up to a bully. You can resist Trump's stances against immigrants, because it is immigrants who built America and immigrants who most definitely built tech. You can defend science, because climate change is a big threat and tech can be a crucial part of fixing it. You can insist we invest in critical technologies that point the way to revolutions in things like health and transportation, and not get bogged down in the politics."

Admittedly, I was monologuing. Even though I started out as a reporter, I had shifted into an analyst and sometimes an advocate. Increasingly, I used my extensive contact list to offer my honest opinion not just to readers, but to these increasingly clownish billionaires.

My advice, of course, was completely ignored. These famed "disrupters" accepted Trump's invitation with no conditions. They gave up their dignity for nothing. Hewlett Packard's Meg Whitman, whom I had tangled with over her opposition to gay marriage when she ran for governor (a stance she later recanted), was the rare exception and was therefore not at the meeting. Despite being a staunch Republican, she had accurately pegged Trump as "a dishonest demagogue" and shifted her support to Clinton in August before the election.

Investor Chris Sacca, who also was not invited to the meeting, likewise seemed to grasp what was happening, boiling it down beautifully. "It's funny, in every tech deal I've ever done, the photo op comes after you've signed the papers," he told me. "If Trump publicly commits to embrace science, stops threatening censorship of the Internet, rejects fake news, and denounces hate against our diverse employees, only then it would make sense for tech leaders to visit Trump Tower. Short of that, they are being used to legitimize a fascist."

Did Sacca change minds where I had failed? Nope. And on December 14, the people—or, more accurately, "sheeple," as I called them in print—who had helped invent the future slipped in through the back entrance of Trump Tower to enable a fascist. Even though the president-elect had openly attacked Amazon and Apple by name, Jeff Bezos and Tim Cook joined many others to compete in a non-televised episode of *The Apprentice: Nerd Edition.*

What none of these CEOs wanted to admit were the real reasons they flocked to the wolf's gilded den: There was a heap of money at stake, and they wanted to avoid a lot of damage the incoming Trump administration could do to the tech sector. As much as tech execs wanted visas, they also wanted contracts with the new government, especially the military. They wanted profits repatriated back to the U.S. from foreign countries where they had been stashing their lucre. More than anything, they wanted to be shielded from regulation, which they had neatly and completely avoided so far.

Normally, sucking up to power isn't news in the corporate world, but Silicon Valley was supposed to be different. In 2000, Google incorporated the motto "Don't be evil" into its code of conduct. At Tesla, Musk insisted that his dedication to humanity led him to make cool electric cars for the mass market and reduce dependence on fossil fuel. Facebook was supposed to be a tool to create "stronger relationships with those you love, a stronger economy with more opportunities, and a stronger society that reflects all of our values."

All these companies began with a gauzy credo to change the world. And they had indeed done that, but in ways they hadn't imagined at the start, increasingly with troubling consequences from a flood of misinformation to a society becoming isolated and addicted to its gadgets. So had I, so much so that I had taken to joking at the end when I made speeches: "I leave you to your own devices. . . . I mean that; your phone is the best relationship you all have now, the first thing you pick up in the morning and the last thing you touch at night."

It always got a laugh, but by the time Trump was halfway through his term, it was much less funny and it was dead clear that I had underestimated how compromised the tech companies would become.

"Facebook, as well as Twitter and Google's YouTube and the rest, have become the digital arms dealers of the modern age," I wrote in one of my first columns after I joined the *New York Times* as a columnist in 2018. "They have mutated human communication, so that connecting people has too often become about pitting them against one another and turbocharged that discord to an unprecedented and damaging volume. They have weaponized the First Amendment. They have weaponized civic discourse. And they have weaponized, most of all, politics."

The tech titans would argue that they were no worse than cable networks like Fox News (true, but a very low bar) and that there was no easily provable causality that they polarized the populace (a nearly impossible thing to measure). Most of all, they often dismissed any weaponization as "unintended consequences."

Maybe so, but it was not an *unimaginable* consequence. French philosopher Paul Virilio has a quote I think about a lot: "When you invent the ship, you also invent the shipwreck; when you invent the plane, you also invent the plane crash; and when you invent electricity, you invent electrocution. . . . Every technology carries its own negativity, which is invented at the same time as technical progress."

Let me be clear: Hitler didn't need Instagram. Mussolini didn't need to tweet. Murderous autocrats did not need to Snapchat their way to infamy. But just imagine if they'd had those supercharged tools. Well, Trump did, and he won the election, thanks in large part to social media. It wasn't the only reason, but it's easy to see a direct line from FDR mastering radio to JFK mastering TV to DJT mastering social technology. And Trump didn't do it alone. Purveyors of propaganda, both foreign and domestic, saw an opportunity to spread lies and misinformation. Today, malevolent actors continue to game the platforms, and there's still no real solution in sight, because these powerful platforms are doing exactly what they were designed to do.

Back on the twenty-fifth floor of Trump Tower, the tech leaders managed to nix the photo op, but not the video op. In the four minutes that have been publicly released, we can see a grinning Trump flanked by Vice President–Elect Mike Pence and Thiel, who Trump awkwardly pats on the hand and praises for being "very special."

Reporters were quickly shooed out when the meeting commenced. Afterward, Bezos called it "very productive," and Safra Catz, Oracle's chief executive and a Trump transition team member, flashed a thumbs-up to cameras. Most other attendees slipped out the same way they had snuck in.

I was not surprised that the tech summit attendees didn't release a statement, either collectively or individually. But you know who did? Trump. His team went public with a list of thirteen topics of discussion with no mention of immigration, even though I'd called around and learned that Microsoft's Nadella had asked specifically about H-1B visas, often called the "genius visa." Reportedly, Trump responded with, "Let's fix that. What can I do to make it better?" Instead, his administration made it worse, eventually issuing a proclamation to suspend the entry of H-1B visa holders. Only successful litigation stopped the action.

It was a massive embarrassment for an industry that had promised to be better than anything that had come before it.

In November 2018, I interviewed Musk for my *Recode Decode* podcast. I reminded him that I had called and warned him about Trump before that tech summit.

"I said you shouldn't go, because he was going to screw you, remember?" I said. "We had a whole—"

Musk interrupted me. "Well, you are right," he said.

"I am right, thank you, Elon. I know that," I replied.

I do enjoy being right, but I took no pleasure in it this time.

The Trump tech summit was a major turning point for me and how I viewed the industry I'd been covering since the early 1990s. The lack of humanity was overwhelming. My minor in college was in Holocaust studies. I studied propaganda, and I could see Trump was an expert at it. I knew exactly where this was headed. I ended my original column that broke the story with this:

"Welcome to the brave new world, which is neither brave nor new. But it's now the world we live in, in which it's Trump who is the disrupter and tech the disrupted. Yeah, you can say it: *Fuckfuckfuck.*"

Maybe "fuckfuckfuck" wasn't the most professional sentence I've ever written, but I was trying to express my deep disappointment. I love tech, I breathe tech. And I believe in tech. But for tech to fulfill its promise, founders and executives who ran their creations needed to put more safety tools in place. They needed to anticipate consequences more. Or at all. They needed to acknowledge that online rage might extend into the real world in increasingly scary ways.

Instead, far too many of these founders and innovators were careless, an attitude best summarized by the ethos on early Facebook office posters: "Move fast and break things." I know it's a software slogan and it would later change (Facebook CEO and co-founder Mark Zuckerberg jokingly changed it to "Move fast with stable infra," as in infrastructure, in 2014), but I still think it reflects a deep-seated childishness. Children like to break things. I'd have initially preferred "Move fast and change things." Or, even more adult, "Move fast and fix things."

But they decided to start with "break," and such carelessness has led to damage around the globe that, in turn, helped me understand what was happening to our own country. In August of 2016, investigative journalist Maria Ressa gave Facebook alarming data about people in the Philippines who were being targeted for graphic online abuse after criticizing President Duterte's drug war. Facebook did not take down the pages until two years after her report.

So, in 2017, Maria contacted me and asked if I could help convince Facebook of the burgeoning threat. "We're the canary in the coal mine, and it's coming to you," said the woman who would later win the Nobel Peace Prize for her efforts to shed light on the murderous reality in her country. "Can you help me stop them?"

As it turned out, as much as I tried to sound alarms, I could not stop them.

Each year since has brought bigger and fresher tech messes. Twitter, stupidly renamed X, has mutated into a platform where the richest man in the world offers his retweet support to racist, sexist, and homophobic conspiracies. AI's deep fakes and misinformation open a virtual Pandora's box, with the potential to unleash troubles to plague humankind faster than any actual plague. Chinese-owned TikTok makes parents feel better by employing safety features for teens, while the site could be extending the Communist Party's surveillance state across the globe, according to increasing numbers of government officials I have interviewed around the world.

Over time, I've come to settle on a theory that tech people embrace one of two pop culture visions of the future. First, there's the "Star Wars" view, which pits the forces of good against the Dark Side. And, as we know, the Dark Side puts up a disturbingly good fight. While the Death Star gets destroyed, heroes die and then it inevitably gets rebuilt. Evil, in fact, does tend to prevail.

Then there's the "Star Trek" view, where a crew works together to travel to distant worlds like an interstellar Benetton commercial, promoting tolerance and convincing villains not to be villains. It often works. I am, no surprise, a Trekkie, and I am not alone. At a 2007 *AllThingsD* conference well-known tech columnist Walt Mossberg and I hosted, Apple legend Steve Jobs appeared onstage and said: "I like *Star Trek*. I want *Star Trek*."

Now Jobs is long dead, and the "Star Wars" version seems to have won. Even if it was never the intention, tech companies became key players in killing our comity and stymieing our politics, our government, our social fabric, and most of all, our minds, by seeding isolation, outrage, and addictive behavior. Innocuous boy-kings who wanted to make the world a better place and ended up cosplaying Darth Vader feels like science fiction. But everything I am about to tell you really happened.

Yeah, I can say it: *Fuckfuckfuck.*

CHAPTER I

Babylon Was

If you fell down yesterday, stand up today.

—H. G. WELLS

I know you came for stories about the tech billionaires like Elon and Mark and Sheryl and Peter and Jeff and Steve and Tim.

Don't worry—you'll get to meet all of them, as I did over my three-decade career covering these moguls. But this is a book about me and tech, a relationship that started as a meet-cute love story then turned sour over time. Be assured, this book is mostly about those guys—and let's be clear, they are mostly guys. But to truly understand my relationship with tech, you also have to know a little about me. I'll keep it short (also like me IRL, at five-foot-two).

The Internet and I were both born in 1962. That year, a scientist from MIT suggested connecting computers to create an Advanced Research Projects Agency Network, or ARPAnet, which became the technological foundation of the Internet. While there are conflicting explanations as to its inspiration— to create a hardened communications system in case of nuclear attack, to allow researchers to be able to access a limited number of powerful supercomputers from across the world, or because it was simply a long-dreamed technological challenge—the push to build a communications network emerged from the fecund brain of J.C.R. Licklider. He was a famed computer scientist who sketched out the idea in a 1963 memo that described an "Intergalactic Computer Network." I always loved this conceptual notion since it was both lofty and a little bit silly. It spoke of a unity among humankind, too, brought to you by the miracles of technology. Many others followed his lead into tech, all with the base intent of bringing humanity together for higher purposes.

My origin was a lot less heady. I grew up in Roslyn Harbor, New York, on the northern part of Long Island, the middle child of three. When I was five, my beloved father died. To say my life changed in the moment he suffered a cerebral hemorrhage without warning would be an understatement.

"Just imagine right now if half of your friends died," I said to an interviewer decades later, referring to a book called *The Loss That Is Forever*, about children whose parents die at a young age. "Your parents, when you're five, are really pretty much your entire world. If one-half of your friends just suddenly died, it would be shocking and devastating, and so I think it also gives you a sense of the capriciousness of life; that life can change on a dime, that bad things happen, and that you survive them just fine. You just keep going."

Actual memories faded quickly and all that was left were analog photos. In every single image, my father looks sunny and hopeful as he beams at the camera. It's clear he loved the life he had built from a modest West Virginia upbringing. A stint in the Navy had paid for college and medical school, and after rising to a lieutenant commander rank, he took his first big civilian job running the anesthesiology department at Brooklyn Jewish Hospital. He used the windfall to buy his first house for his growing family. Then he died before he had even moved in.

Can I articulate such a loss? Hardly. How can you account for what you never had? You cannot. I wrote about this in 1989, after I had my father's body exhumed and moved back to his home state at my grandmother's behest. In the piece, I am clearly beginning to think about what we lose and leave behind. Ironically, this is in contrast to the digital medium I was soon about to cover: the Internet, where everything is essentially indelible.

Not for me, though, as I wrote in the *Washington Post*:

I remember no living face at all, only the one I see frozen in snapshots. I suppose there was a moment when I did that final time, and he answered as always in his languid drawl, "Good night, good night, good night," before turning out the lights. I do remember many nights like that, but not the last one. I try sometimes, squeezing my memories dry, but years ago I just about gave up on it. As I dial the cemetery to make arrangements, it seems as though I will try again, despite the pain all my friends say will undoubtedly come from "unearthing" the past—yes, that's the word one used—an attempting to preserve that which is lost.

He was only 34 years old. Dr. Louis Bush Swisher died from the complications of a brain aneurysm that burst without warning one sunny Sunday morning more than 20 years ago. My room was so dark that when I came out into the hall to help wake him for breakfast, the brightness of the day slapped me back to the shadowy doorway. I watched from there as my brother knocked purposefully on the door of my parents' bedroom to get my father up. The door was locked, and Jeffrey turned the knob round and round and hit the door with his hip. He just didn't give up, though no amount of shoving was going to open it, I remember thinking at the time. That was me, the practical one, with the unlikely childhood understanding that some things just aren't ever going to move.

We both thought my father had fallen into a deep sleep in there while writing a speech he was to give the next day. So, my older brother Jeff kept kicking the door and smacking it and making such a noise that my mother finally came up, knocked impatiently and said, "Bush, Bush, open up the door right now; you're making Jeff very upset." But he did not wake.

After that, it was quick: The firemen coming to ax the door to splinters, the ambulance and stretcher with all sorts of things hanging off of it. And the extraordinary silence when it was over. I went back into my cocoon of a room, well before they carried my father out, and only imagine now the gurney with him on it, the white sheet, the hysterical cries of my mother following behind, saying, "What is wrong with him?" I stayed in my room, where it was quiet, and fell back asleep. I never did see my father again. He lingered for weeks through January and finally died after two horrible operations. They buried him on a very cold February day. I didn't go to the funeral.

Heavy, right? And it got worse. After Dad died, my family moved to Princeton after my mother remarried. Her choice for a second husband was the polar opposite of my kind and merry father, who was, I always thought, too good for this world.

One of the first things my stepfather did was to take the house my dad was so proud of and sell it. He also gave away my father's dog, a basset hound named Prudence. Erasing all those parts of my father seemed a weird flex, and my mother—whose own life had gone off the rails so abruptly—did not resist. He provided a very comfortable upper-middle-class environment and then ruined it with a cavalcade of casual cruelties. We had a tennis court, but he locked access to it. I had a phone in my room, but he bugged it (and found nothing, as I was perhaps the dullest of teens, with no interest in drugs or drinking). Dinners served by a cook were an ongoing series of exhausting mind games and tests of knowledge for me and my brothers.

But don't feel sorry for me, and if you want to play a game of Thorns and Roses, there was a plus to being raised by someone I came to think of as a villain—I became extraordinarily fast on my feet. My stepfather also taught me to play backgammon and Risk, games of both luck and boldness, which helped me become a very good tactical and strategic thinker. I lost a dog but got very good at gamesmanship and general mindfuckery.

It helped that I was smart, reading and doing math well above my grade level, a whiff of early genius that would not last past seventh grade when everyone else caught up. Still, like many in tech, I got bored easily in school. In second grade, I walked out of class one day, so the teacher sent me to the principal's office. My mother was called in and asked why I had left and I answered: "I already read the material." Clearly, I was already prepping for the obnoxious arrogance I would later cover.

My attitude toward school barely changed through college,

which I largely thought was a huge waste of time, a sentiment I seem to share with Peter Thiel, God help me. I attended the School of Foreign Service at Georgetown University, which was not my first choice. That was Stanford, where my brother Jeff had gone and where I did not get in. Back then, Georgetown was a backup school and attracted a lot of middle-level students, especially from Catholic schools. I was Catholic, too, though quite lapsed. I got confirmed for my beloved grandmother when I was thirteen, and that was the last time I walked into a church for any religious reason.

Despite the Jesuits' influence, my college classmates liked to get shit-faced drunk every weekend and fornicate badly. I still did not drink and was a closeted lesbian, which made Georgetown the absolutely worst fit. I watched angrily as the school waged a contentious legal battle with a student group called Gay People of Georgetown University. Not only did it fight the funding of the organization, but it also didn't even want gay people to meet on campus. The irony, of course, was that many of the priests who ran the school were obviously (but, fine, allegedly) closeted. Years after I graduated, Georgetown invited me back to give a speech about my experience. I outlined their hypocrisy in detail, which they took pretty well, considering I called them out strongly for their perfidy.

Back then, though, it was difficult to breathe. So, as a freshman, I applied to transfer to Barnard. I was admitted and made plans to move to New York City in January. But sometime later that fall, I ran into a junior named Roberta Oster, who worked on the student newspaper. She'd read some of my work and promptly told me, "You're not leaving. You're going to write for me and be a star." She eventually persuaded me of my pending journalistic genius, so I let the Barnard spot go and started reporting for the school paper called *The Hoya*. My voice-heavy columns covered topics from how to get along with different kinds of roommates (mine partied in the extreme, of course, and I still loved them) and wanting to get a tattoo, to the town-and-gown clashes between students and area residents.

By the end of my freshman year, I had won the student journalism award—the Edward B. Bunn Award named after Father Bunn—that was typically given to a senior. "Best Bunns," I crowed to the pissed-off seniors. It was obnoxious, but I loved journalism and was indeed good at it from the get-go. I'll also admit that I loved the attention and acclaim it brought.

Because Georgetown was in D.C., I read the *Washington Post* every day. I revered the paper until one day they wrote about something on campus that I cared about—a speech by a notorious military murderer from El Salvador. I also covered the speech, along with the student protests. To my surprise, the short *Post* story was rife with small errors.

Even though it was just eight inches long, I was furious that a news organization that I admired could be so sloppy. I decided to call the paper on my dial-up phone and was so irksome in my desire to correct the record that I managed to get then Metro editor Larry Kramer on the line. I told him that I was disappointed in their inaccuracies.

He challenged me to come down and say that to his face and asked me if I thought I could do better. I would, and I could. I took the bus from campus to the *Post*'s headquarters on 15th Street NW. When I appeared, Larry and I continued to debate the crappy story he had published. Exasperated by my insistence that it was an embarrassment, even for a very short story,

Kramer hired me on the spot as a stringer for the paper. My beat was to cover Georgetown, which I did for several years, gathering clips and invaluable experience.

Working for the *Post* was much more fun than school, except for my history courses. My focus was on propaganda and how groups like the Nazis used media and communications tools to twist facts, radicalize their populace, and demonize the targeted populations. Obviously, Hitler and his henchmen had conducted a master class in evil. But what struck me was how easily people could be manipulated by fear and rage and how facts could be destroyed without repercussions.

I think about that college version of me a lot. I was subjected to much propaganda about my own self, as the general public's understanding of what being gay was like was quite different than the actual experience. Media was central to this warping of reality. I was particularly attracted to Vito Russo's 1981 book *The Celluloid Closet,* which surgically traced the way gays and lesbians were portrayed by Hollywood as compared to how they were treated in real life. Movies were filled with tragic suicidal dykes, conniving gay men, silly fops, and butch aggressors. Those depictions were not a fair reflection of me or anyone I knew. But these were the tropes that needed changing.

So strong was the prevailing negative attitude toward gays that I did not pursue the life I had long considered. My dream was to follow my father into the military and work as a strategic analyst there or at the Central Intelligence Agency. I have long been a firm believer in the most vaunted parts of the American experience and wanted to be part of protecting that against the darker forces of our national DNA. But pushing against the antigay tide was nearly impossible at the time, and the ferreting out of gays in the military continued for over a decade. Even the 1993 Clinton-era "Don't Ask, Don't Tell" rules were atrocious. The problem was I didn't want anyone to be forced into the closet. I wanted them to ask, and I was compelled to tell.

With my first-choice career path blocked due to discrimination, I fell back on becoming a journalist. I applied to the top school at the time, the Columbia University Graduate School of Journalism, and got in. Looking back, I wish I had taken that tuition money and bought Apple stock, which was then languishing. The Columbia program was run mostly by quaint professors who had lived in a very different era of media. Computers were scarce and learning how to write headlines using a pica rule seemed like a waste of time. While the basics of journalism remained important, the medium was about to become the message—a famous line of Marshall McLuhan's—on steroids, and how to navigate that gap was not part of the curriculum.

To be fair, it was the early days of digital, and the use of computers at the time was rare. After graduation, I applied to a spate of newspapers and was roundly rejected (often and ironically by people who later tried to hire me). I returned to D.C. and began freelancing. As luck and a purge of editors would have it, I showed up at the *Washington City Paper* right when its pugnacious new editor, Jack Shafer, was without a staff.

Shafer hired me to be a deputy editor, but I immediately felt out of my depth. Despite his obvious editing skills, Shafer was not exactly the mentoring type. I'd been hired for a role I wasn't qualified for, and I don't think I did a very good job. Well, I know I didn't, because Shafer fired me within a year, and I don't recall feeling that it was deeply unfair.

In fact, I'm not one of those people who finds life deeply unfair, but I do remember thinking that while I was not more experienced than these guys were, I was going to be bigger than them. In those early days, I'd see some of the decisions my bosses made and think, This is how I'd do it. I was beginning to get an inkling of my own tastes and judgment. I just didn't have the certainty and maturity to act on it. Once, I interviewed for an internship at the *Washington Post*, and the editor said I was "too confident." I've since come to understand that this is something men say to women to shut them up and undercut them. I was not going to let that happen. And so, I replied: "I'm not too confident. I'm fantastic. Or I will be." I have always, always been like this. It's hard to neg me. Those who do only encourage me to try to win even more.

My next boss was John McLaughlin, of the famed and pioneering TV scream fest *The McLaughlin Group*. I mostly ghostwrote his column in the *National Review*, with him adding in the right-wing invective. I also worked on his show, a precursor to reductive cable news that oversimplified complex policy for entertainment. I was a liberal, obviously, but most of the staff were suck-up McLaughlin acolytes who considered him a very big deal because he'd written speeches for Richard Nixon. That was his power.

McLaughlin was also a truly awful human being. He was abusive to the staff in the broadest and strangest ways. He would demand that everybody make him toast buttered in a specific way. Even his chief of staff had to make him toast. So, I wasn't surprised when one day he called me into his office to ask, "Would you make toast for me?"

I told him, "No, I'm not making you toast. I have a graduate degree in journalism and that means no toast-making of any kind, even rye."

He did not take the hint.

"Everybody on staff makes me toast," he continued. "And if I ask and you don't, then you will be fired."

"Well, I'm not making you toast if you ask," I replied. "So, you're going to have to fire me when you do that."

He repeated the threat. "Just so you know, if I ask you and you don't make it, I'll fire you."

"Okay, I got it," I said, nodding.

Part of me wanted him to ask me so I could leave. But he never did. Not once.

When he was planning his annual party, McLaughlin—or Dr. McLaughlin as he preferred, thanks to a dusty PhD in philosophy—kept most of the staff waiting as he figured out whom to invite and whom *not* to invite because of some perceived slight. He truly believed that not getting to attend his party would cause someone pain. I rolled my eyes visibly as he regaled the room with his plans to ding some undersecretary of whatever in the then Reagan administration. He noticed my disdain immediately, since I was the only one not nodding in violent agreement.

"Well, young lady, aren't you impressed by the *collective* power of the people I am assembling in that room?" he thundered at me in his patented stentorian voice. "They are coming to see me and pay homage!"

I paused and held my tongue. Then I thought, What the hell, Kubla Khan, and forged ahead. "Listen, Dr. McLaughlin, I was in

Greece this summer at a temple and there was some writing on the wall. I asked the guide what it said, and he told me it read: 'Babylon was.' Which means, I think, that every major power falls at some point no matter how they strive and struggle. So, someday soon enough, that means I'm going to be really powerful and you're going to be, like, in a wheelchair in an old folks' home being fed stewed apricots or something."

McLaughlin looked at me like he was going to erupt and fire me on the spot. Then he burst out laughing. "Right you are," he said, before addressing his other more terrified employees, all of whom thought I was about to be ritually sacrificed. "She *gets* what power is!"

So did he. As it turned out, he was also a sexual harasser and eventually started bothering a woman on staff who was my friend. I accompanied her to report his behavior to his chief of staff, who told us we "must be lying." I quit on the spot. Later, I would be deposed in a lawsuit of another woman that McLaughlin grabbed in some desperate clinch to avoid the inevitable demise that was coming for him. When he settled and that case did not go to court, I didn't want him let off the hook, so I talked to a features writer named Eric Alterman who was working on a *Washington Post* magazine piece about McLaughlin. The 1990 piece was called "Pundit Power" and included this quote from a twenty-eight-year-old former staffer:

> "I think that sexual harassment is like pornography," Swisher says. "You know it when you see it. People can tell you look nice and there will be no menace to it. With John McLaughlin, there was menace."

Letting the *Post* print my full name was considered brave, but it was a professionally stupid thing to do. I felt compelled to speak on the record because journalists wouldn't quote anonymous victims and I could, at least, bear witness. As I later told another interviewer: "I essentially called him a pig, with my name attached. You have to stand up and not be embarrassed or victimized." It was a value that would never change in me and a characteristic to which I owe a lot of my career.

I found my way back to the *Post*, first as a copy aide, then working my way up to a news aide and, afterward, an intern. At the newspaper I learned more about power and who wields it, with exhausting machinations that were a typically pointless and time-wasting exercise to me. I decided very early to never try to run anything too big.

And there were other ways to advocate for change, as I did when I listened to editors who wanted to print erroneous and hateful antigay statements. When I pointed out that the statements were both inaccurate and disingenuous, I was warned against being an "advocate" and "emotional." Another time, *Post* editors wanted to publish an egregious photo that perpetuated an old gay trope. Again, I objected, reminding them, "We contain multitudes." (I love Walt Whitman's "Song of Myself": "Do I contradict myself? / Very well then, I contradict myself. / (I am large, I contain multitudes.)")

Did those all straight, all white, mostly men grasp the meaning of the quote or even know Whitman? They did not and insisted on using the photo. As a lowly news assistant, you know what I did? There was no digital photography back then, so I swiped the actual physical photo off the design desk and stuck it in my desk drawer. They had to pick another photo, which, fortunately, wasn't an insulting caricature.

Do I regret my subterfuge? Not for one fucking second. Then and there, I decided that was the best way to go through life—not caring about the consequences of saying or doing what I believed was right.

Around the same time, the Style section sent me to cover a party. A few minutes after I arrived, I spotted McLaughlin across the room. This was after I'd been quoted in the *Post*'s "Pundit Power" piece, and I thought maybe he'd try to avoid me. But no. He was a very tall and imposing man and he strode right over to me with massive puffed-out chest in full plumage.

"Kara Swisher," he said loudly, as if he were on a TV set. "Kara Swisher, most people in this town stab you in the back, but you stabbed me in the front and I appreciate it." Then he let out a giant laugh.

In some ways, I admired McLaughlin for that. He was a nasty old goat, but he understood the terms of the battle. I looked him right in the eyes. Reticence and subtlety were definitely not going to be my style, especially when accuracy and honesty were so effective. And so, without hesitating, I shot back: "Anytime, you son of a bitch."

McLaughlin guffawed at that, too, since it was clear he had taught me well. It was such a moment of fantasticness for me—for someone I considered an evil person, I got along with him rather well, one of many rogues I would spark with. Then, he said goodbye and that was the last time I ever saw him. What I did not say to him before he left, except in my head afterward, was this: "You can't die soon enough for me, *Dr.* McLaughlin."

I wish I had. In years to come, I would not miss those opportunities. Life is far too short, as I had learned at five years old. I did not have the time to waste.

Neither did McLaughlin. That year, 1990, was the peak of his career. From that point on, he became less and less relevant until he finally keeled in 2016. By that time, I was right where I had told him I would be—and so was he.

Babylon *was*, indeed.

CHAPTER 2

Before the Gold Rush

Only connect! That was the whole of her sermon. Only connect the prose and the passion, and both will be exalted, and human love will be seen at its height. Live in fragments no longer.

—E. M. FORSTER, *HOWARDS END*

Al Gore *did* invent the Internet. Kind of.

As most probably know, the former vice president was widely pilloried for claiming this distinction in a 1999 interview on CNN. His exact words were: "During my service in the United States Congress, I took the initiative in creating the Internet."

Absolutely true. As a senator from Tennessee, Gore crafted and pushed through the "High Performance Computing and Communication Act of 1991," aka the "Gore Bill." This legislation funded initiatives like the game-changing Mosaic browser and was critical to the commercialization of the now indispensable medium.

I met Gore in 1989 while reporting a story about his efforts to limit the use of chlorofluorocarbons that were depleting the ozone levels. He was right about climate change, too. Really, even though he sounded like an idiot when he said he invented the Internet, we should probably thank the guy for all he's done and for being one of the few in D.C. who took an interest in the tech at all.

The other person who oddly enough deserves some credit is then Speaker of the House Newt Gingrich, who blocked a dunderheaded amendment by then Nevada senator James Exon to the Communications Decency Act of 1996. Although Gingrich has since morphed into one of the more ghoulish political figures in the Republican Party, he was an important character in pushing back early and aggressive political attempts to stifle an open and free Internet. *Mother Jones* even credits Gingrich with saving porn, which feels apt these days since he now defends the most porny president in American history. Well played, Newt!

With access to federal support, the first Internet companies started forming in the early 1990s. The *Washington Post* gave me the space to report on a broad range of digital topics, largely because no one else would, and having just turned thirty, I was the "young" person in the newsroom. In fact, I was also already hooked. During a short fellowship at Duke University, I'd had a revelation. I was sitting in front of a computer and logged into the nascent World Wide Web and experienced firsthand its awesome power to deliver content. So, what was the first thing I did?

I downloaded a *Calvin & Hobbes* cartoon collection. Did I care even slightly that I managed to jam up the computer network doing it? I did not. But the system administrator—a young man already sporting a proto-techie-slash-seventh-grader look—was pissed.

"You clogged up everything," he said, chastising me.

"But I downloaded a whole book, pretty much by just pushing a button," I said to him. "A whole book, for fuck's sake!"

"Big deal," he said, flashing me that girls-can't-code scowl I would come to know so well. I definitely could not code, but I knew something that this geek did not seem to grok: A book could be *all* the books, and a song could be *all* the songs, and a movie could be *all* the movies. It was right then and there that I came up with the concept that would carry me for decades hence and still does to this day:

Everything that can be digitized will be digitized.

If "God said, let there be light: and there was light" is the most important tech concept ever—and let's be clear, no golden geek, however much they think so, has topped that one as yet—this idea of being able to turn the analog into the digital is at the heart of the promise and the challenges we still face today.

That day in the cramped computer lab in Durham, I realized that we were at yet another critical turn in history, when technology ushers in a new age. I was witnessing the dawn of the printing press, electricity, the light bulb, the telegraph, the radio, the telephone, or the television. It was obvious to me that this innovation was the next great content and communications delivery system. Most of all, I knew I had struck gold. I was fully on board for the Internet age, and however it evolved, I wanted to cover it.

And why wouldn't I be riveted? I happened to be in the same state where the first powered flight had taken place ninety years earlier, at Kill Devil Hills near Kitty Hawk, North Carolina, on December 17, 1903, piloted by Orville Wright. The *Wright Flyer* was aloft for just 12 seconds, during which it traveled 120 feet at 6.8 miles per hour.

Was I going to be the person standing on the beach who looked on, underwhelmed and unimpressed, complaining that the flight should have been longer and higher and faster? Would I have been the one to catcall the Wright Brothers, taunting them that their plane was lame and needed better wings? Can you imagine me there on my big-wheeled bicycle, screaming into the wind at the handlebar-mustached tech bros (some things never change), "Can't you get it up?" Someone might have done that, but I would not, because of one important fact: *A man flew.*

Once I had downloaded *Calvin and Hobbes*, I was eager to see how much more this new technology would revolutionize media. Early content was far from world-shaking. A university in England set up a coffeemaker and those who were interested could dial into the web site and watch an electronic photo of the percolator updated every second. It was also the first time that coffee could put you to sleep. Another web page offered instructions on how to explode a grape. In this new world, the "cybercast" of Pope John Paul II's Mass at Camden Yards in Baltimore—which I chronicled as if it were the moon landing—passed for exciting.

Just as the gold prospectors had needed pans and pickaxes, web site builders also needed tools to get to the good stuff. Internet service providers (ISPs) popped up in the D.C. area, which was the site of one of the four big Internet hubs called MAE-East (another big hub, *hahaha*, MAE-West, was in Silicon Valley). That included PSINet and UUNet, which were run by prescient entrepreneurs. These services were different from the old-school database technology that had served the federal government for decades and was run by the so-called "Beltway bandits" who charged a lot and innovated nothing. The new guys were a much different breed.

I once interviewed PSINet's Bill Schrader in his office as he munched on pretzels out of a big plastic barrel. Through bites, he energetically explained to me the seismic change we were witnessing. "Don't you see that this is just beyond anything we have ever done?" he told me like a geek John the Baptist, after he had locked the door.

Wild-eyed, I thought to myself, Will he kill me and shove my remains in the plastic pretzel barrel? I didn't use that in my story, but it was clear he was nearly religious about the Internet. The company Bill cofounded went public in mid-1995, and by July, he was worth $105 million. And, like all such fever dreams, there were also bad endings. By 2001, PSINet had declared bankruptcy.

I was riveted by that part, of total domination followed by utter collapse. (Babylon was, over and over again.) My colleagues thought I was crazy when I affixed my relatively new email address to the bottom of my stories to solicit ideas. "What do you want to do that for? Readers will be able to write you anytime," one told me. Exactly. Instant communication would become my guiding light. Often, I had to explain what digital meant, as if I were trying to explain a tree to a child.

"The Web is like a landscaped subdivision on the wilder, more primitive Internet. It brings a semblance of order to a vast and unorganized mass of electronic information by dividing it into 'home pages,' each with customized data banks that can contain text, graphics, voices, music and even video," I wrote in one story.

In another breathless one, I reported from the front lines of putting @ symbols on business cards. "At first, the symbols on the business card look like ancient hieroglyphics, difficult to decipher for the uninitiated" was my lede.

It was a big deal, for example, when I wrote that Discovery Communications, which was located in the D.C. area, had spent $10 million to . . . build a web site. As I observed then, "The new mantra: You're nobody if you're not somebody.com."

For the first time, I pointed out issues that remain problematic today, including hacking, con jobs, satellite snafus, misinformation, and privacy violations. I covered the debut of the Sony PlayStation, which was exciting then but seems rote now. I was also chronicling the many come-and-gone technologies, like CD-ROMs (compact discs with Read Only Memory), that were heralded as the "multimedia killer" but would soon be killed themselves.

My prediction about the end of media through the decimation of classified ads in newspapers started to come true. In 1995, a quirky entrepreneur in San Francisco named Craig Newmark started emailing friends a list of local events, job opportunities, and things for sale. Less than a year later, he turned Craigslist into a Web-based service and started expanding all over the country and, eventually, the world.

Seeing that, I became convinced that newspapers were going to die off, and I told everyone who would listen to me at the *Post* that we needed to put all the money, all the people, and all the incentives into digital. I insisted that the bosses had to make readers feel like digital was the most important thing. Of course, the bosses never did because the game was always in newspaper. At the *Post* and later the *Wall Street Journal*, marketers would ask in endless meetings: "How can we get young people to make us a daily read?"

And I would respond, "You know what? I have an idea."

And they were like, "Great, Kara has an idea."

And I said, "Let's tape a joint between every single page."

I was definitely being a nuisance, but my point was that younger readers did not want to subscribe to an analog paper. They wanted another thing altogether. I had always advocated for the idea of offering people news in the way they wanted to digest it, even if it meant printing it on salami. Plus, I just could not ignore the importance of being able to download that first book. As prolific tech pioneer Douglas Engelbart, inventor of the computer mouse, early iterations of the graphical user interface, and more, once mused: "The digital revolution is far more significant than the invention of writing or even of printing."

He was right, and even more so when he said: "The better we get at getting better, the faster we will get better."

But where I was working, it was definitely not fast enough. It was glacial. I related my worries about the turtle pace of digital change many times to the Washington Post Company's affable CEO Don Graham, the son of legendary publisher and surprisingly entertaining badass Katharine Graham. How much I loved these owners, I cannot underscore enough, for their bravery and steadfastness and decency and, really, their commitment to excellence in a less-than-excellent world.

Don Graham was also inexplicably humble and even sheepish about his power. He never once made me feel nervous, as I published story after story about the death of local retailers. I knew my work had upset big advertisers who had made him and the *Post* rich. But I never felt the pressure he was getting, even after I wrote this lede in 1990 about the bankruptcy of a local shopping institution:

> First, an answer to the somewhat vulturous question on everybody's mind yesterday after hearing about the closing of a longtime D.C. department store called Garfinckel's: The sale starts Wednesday, as plans now stand. That means everything must go. But how do you get rid of pounds of Godiva chocolate? Dozens of Hermès scarves? A plenitude of pairs of panty hose with the name GARFINCKEL'S boldly printed on the package? Tons of French crystal? Boxes and boxes of bridal registry information?

The very worst thing that Graham—always apologetic for having interrupted me—would say to me was "ouch." Then he would saunter away from my desk with a jaunty wave. What's the opposite of publisher pressure? That was Don. And he displayed the same kind of patience when I started in on him on digital issues, suggesting that he dump AT&T's Interchange—and its dopey publisher-heavy deal—and invest in a then-small online service called AOL instead. He argued that AT&T was tops in tech. I countered that just because they could run a giant bully of a telephone company didn't mean they could be either nimble or innovative in digital media. Interchange, in fact, eventually shuttered as the telco giant shifted to just selling Internet access and the *Post*'s *Digital Ink* and other newspapers moved directly to the Web.

And while Graham was interested when I talked about what

Craig Newmark was doing, he laughed when I told him that Craigslist would wipe out his classified business.

"You charge too much, the customer service sucks, it's static, and most of all, it doesn't work," I lectured him about the business that was crucial to his bottom line. "It will disappear as an analog product since it is a perfect target for digital destruction. You're going to die by the cell and not even know it until it's over and you're dead on the ground."

Don smiled at me with a kindness I certainly did not deserve at that moment. "Ouch," he said.

Years later, Graham would lean into tech and became an early and much-needed adviser to a young Mark Zuckerberg of Facebook and even passed on a chance to grab Facebook shares in order to placate a VC who wanted more equity. "I offered Mark $6 million for 10 percent of Facebook in January of 2005," Graham wrote me. "Unsurprisingly, Accel Partners offered (I think) $15 million. I thought of matching but knew [Accel's Jim Breyer] would raise it; it was simply worth more to them than to us (since we would never be raising money for another round, and a big success would be priceless to them)."

Graham was not dumb, obviously, and his attitude was actually quite typical. In the early 1990s, part of the problem was that tech seemed far too techie and niche. Home computers were not yet household products. Laptops, such as the Apple PowerBook and IBM ThinkPad, were used largely for business, and the modems used to dial up these services were agonizingly slow. And Wi-Fi? It did not exist.

The difficulties of using the new online tech were clear from the moment I crashed Duke's system. Fortunately, I was dating a woman named Lisa Dickey at the time and she was an early and savvy adopter. While working at an international organization in Washington, Lisa had used various chat and technically difficult text and bulletin board systems to communicate abroad. When she moved to Russia in the fall of 1994, I wanted to stay in touch via something other than snail mail and phone calls. That's when Lisa introduced me to email, suggesting I sign up for an AOL account.

I had already dabbled in writing about the sector, starting in 1988 when the Library of Congress announced they would add software to their collection. "It does seem a little odd that the Library of Congress—the place where public relations officers answer the phone, 'Hello, the library with the most books'—is going to start collecting software programs," I wrote.

And while I was not yet on the tech beat then, I did hit the main theme perfectly, adding the analog keening of a librarian named Sandra Lawson who saw the revolution coming. "'It would take a stack of books to achieve what this could do in a second,' said Lawson about a research program loaded on a computer. Is the library of yesterday, with its piles of books, musty smells and never-ending aisles, on its way out? 'I think people will always love the feel of books,' she said wistfully."

But I was not even slightly sentimental, and soon I was trying every service or gadget that I could get. In 1993, I tested an early version of virtual reality, writing a piece titled: "See Me, Feel Me, Touch Me." It was the first substantive piece I would write on tech. And, it was, of course, about online sex.

I tried on the device at one of the least sexy locations on Earth—a Best Buy store in Shirlington, Virginia. The upbeat techie walking me through told me:

"This helmet could take you to Paris." I said, so could Air France, and it throws in cocktails. He told me I could "float through space." That sounded nauseating. Obliquely, we were approaching a certain tantalizing truth, circling it warily, each waiting for the other to strike first. He caved. "Well," he said, conspiratorially, "there is adult entertainment." Ahhh. Cyborgasm. The dirty secret of tech's real potential.

In real life, tech was less exciting but more practical. For work, I was using a variety of connected computers, such as the "luggable" Kaypro with two double-sided floppy disks and WordStar, and the TRS-80 Model 100 (the Trash-80, as it was dubbed) that used phone couplers allowing it to fit over the mouth and ear parts of a public telephone.

But my biggest obsession, by far, was mobile phones. They were too expensive for individual use, but the *Post* had purchased one of the new Motorola bag phones for the newsroom. I borrowed it often despite its ungainliness and persistent lack of connectivity. No one else was interested in it, so I kept it for days at the time, lugging it to all kinds of places to try to make calls, with mixed success. Not long after, I got hold of a Motorola MicroTAC, which was the inspiration for "flip" phones, including the clamshell StarTAC, which hit the market in 1996. I bought dozens of modems, CD-ROMs, and drives to run the silvery discs and all manner of storage gadgets. Most of these devices would become extinct soon enough, due to the growing popularity of the World Wide Web.

W3 or www launched in 1990, introducing itself on the first web site at CERN (the European Organization for Nuclear

Research) as a "wide-area hypermedia information retrieval initiative aiming to give universal access to a large universe of documents." This was a convoluted geek way of saying: All of human knowledge is linked to each other in an endless and ever-evolving chain of *everything*. This critical concept and the terms that were coined by techie Ted Nelson were, as the very simple CERN page noted, "not constrained to be linear."

Translation: It would be everything, everywhere, all at once. And, most importantly, *always*.

The ability to scale infinitely was unprecedented, and to those for whom this truly massive idea clicked, it was elegant and profound. Crucially, the Internet needed all kinds of new digital tools to make it work—suggesting an entirely new industry where none had existed before. These tools included browsers, a piece of software that would allow you to better ride this new "information superhighway," as it was called often back then.

In 1993, I tried out the Mosaic browser, created by Marc Andreessen and Eric Bina while they were grad students at the National Center for Supercomputing Applications at the University of Illinois at Urbana-Champaign. I got to know Andreessen later, for better and worse (much worse as time went on and he became odder). His original browser was fast and able to display images and quickly made him a legend. He decamped to Silicon Valley, co-creating Netscape with a high-profile serial entrepreneur and frequent tech loudmouth named Jim Clark. The company went public in August of 1995, and the Netscape browser completely dominated the market, becoming the first Web company to make a fortune.

And why not? The technology was expanding drastically just as it was intended to do. In mid-1993, there were only 130 web sites, with only 1.5 percent having commercial ".com" designations. A year later, there were close to 3,000. And, by the time I met Steve Case at AOL in 1994, there were ten times that—and then a hundred times again soon enough.

As I sat in a bland office building behind a car dealership in Tysons Corner, Virginia, I took notes. Case was dressed in a button-down Oxford shirt and khakis and perched behind a cheap desk as he launched into his plans to "change the world."

"We're going to be bigger than Time Warner someday," the moon-faced young man said grandly, as if taking down the most powerful media company on the globe was going to be as easy as all that. "This is going to be the next great revolution in technology, and we are going to be the most important company in the space." What a lunatic, I thought. What he was saying was not a little crazy, but a lot, especially given the sketchy history of the company he now headed and its precarious grip on, well, existence. Case had started off as a marketer, figuring out popular toppings for pizza and whether dry shampoo towelettes were ever going to be a thing, so, this extravagant assertion—which he jokingly denies today—seemed like classic product hype.

It's notable as the first, but definitely not the last, time that I would hear this "change the world" speech from a souped-up entrepreneur. And, as it would turn out for many of them, too, the young CEO of America Online was correct. He *was* going to change the world, and although I couldn't have known it at the time, he was also going to change my life. And, in between his razzle-dazzle marketing pronouncements, Case managed to stick an earworm in my brain that day. He and all the AOL executives I met did so by repeating a version of the same word: "Connect."

"Connect" is all over my early notes and seemed like such a simple and basic idea. But with the exponential nature of the medium, that take turned out to be naïve. As futurist Jaron Lanier would later tell me—the biggest experiment in human community also turned out to be the most disastrous. But I was already hopelessly all in on this world, even if switching to cover these nobodies making things no one understood was a backward step in my trajectory at the *Post*. Forget vaporware— a term for software that wasn't all there—tech reporting was a backwater to a backwater, filled with dull geeks and technical who-cares. But, to me, the field was explosive and the possibilities felt infinite. That directionality of digitization domination was the point. It had first hit me at Duke, and then again when I heard Case waxing on.

"Everyone will be able to reach everyone and say anything, know anything, be anything," Case said in a later interview with me.

As I looked down at the cheap carpet the first time I met him, I remember that Case planted his shoes on the battered desk. Then he leaned back in his chair with arms behind his head, looking already like the mogul he'd become within a decade. The big talk, which seemed comical in that moment, wasn't hype. Using AOL's soaring stock, he would indeed manage to get control of Time Warner in the span of less than a decade in the so-called "deal of the century." Case would eventually become the proverbial dog that caught the car. But in that dingy office, he was just a startup guy with a lot of confidence and a company made up of misfits and outsiders that I took to calling the "Bad News Bears," after the 1976 movie.

I remember driving back from AOL to the *Post* that day, traveling down Route 66 in my VW Rabbit convertible and thinking that I could not wait to start covering Case and the rest of those supremely odd but compelling people. As soon as I got back to the newsroom, I went straight to David Ignatius, my boss at the time in the Business section. He had been the one to suggest the meeting to see if I wanted to focus on this sector. I told him I wanted to get in on this tech stuff, *stat.*

"You sure you don't want to cover politics?" he said. "It's how you get to the top here." His extraordinarily bushy eyebrows arched in a way that made a reporter question themselves and their work (always a good thing). The canny Ignatius knew that getting to cover the White House and Congress was the inside track at the *Post* if you wanted to succeed. So why would I turn my back on all that? Why cover some guy who thought he could best the entrenched powers that be and own the world, when I could write about the people who actually *did* own the world?

What Ignatius correctly clocked was that I had exactly zero interest in that back-slapping mess of compromise for even the best journalists. As an assistant in the Style section, I had to buttonhole the grandees of D.C. to get quotes to make quick and tasty dishes of nothing that were lapped up by the chattering class on the Potomac. I hated it. More to the point, I hated their entitlement and certainty that the future belonged to them. In my heart of hearts, even just seeing the tiny flashes of what these techies were making, I couldn't shake the idea that those who invented and innovated would be the ones who mattered. I thought of the quote from Mary Poppins, who when asked by the

Banks children how long she would remain, answered, "I'll stay till the wind changes."

The wind had definitely changed, and to me, it was an easy choice between attending more soul-crushing D.C. parties or standing on that beach in Kitty Hawk, watching something remarkable glide by. Ignatius already knew what my decision would be and said what turned out to be the understatement of all time: "This Internet thing seems pretty cool."

By 1996, I had spent months at AOL working on my first book, *AOL.com: How Steve Case Beat Bill Gates, Nailed the Netheads, and Made Millions in the War for the Web*. I had done some final interviews in New York, and as I walked out of a building on Park Avenue on a sparklingly blue-sky day, it all became clear: If I was really going to do this, I had to leave the suffocating East Coast. I needed to move to California.

Maybe I was like the people who wanted in on the Gold Rush. I always think about those who were content to stay on the East Coast or stopped in Pennsylvania or Ohio. They only went so far before settling. Not me. I had transformed into one of the nuts who kept going. I had to be there to fill a vacuum, since nobody who was there was really covering the business side. The reports mostly came from techies, who focused on chip speed, and the gadget fanboys who wanted free stuff. When I told people at the *Post* that I wanted to head west, they were confused because I didn't know about engineering. I said to them: "Don't you understand? This is not about technology. This is about everything else *but* the technology."

Only one person fully supported my move. Walt Mossberg was already the most famous of tech reporters for his popular *Wall Street Journal* column, "Personal Technology," which debuted in 1991 and opened with the single greatest lede about tech: "Personal computers are just too hard to use, and it isn't your fault." I had introduced myself to the goateed guru while writing my AOL book, and he graciously agreed to an interview. Walt and I instantly became close, bound by professional kismet and a tech mind meld.

I began asking him questions about everything and discovered that he knew everything and everyone. I loved hanging in his office at the *Journal*, which had a "computer museum" that included, as one profile of him enumerated, "a Timex Sinclair 1000 (his first computer), an Apple IIe, a portable Apple IIc, a first-gen Macintosh, a Radio Shack TRS 80 Model 100, a Palm Pilot, an Atari 800." We spent hours geeking out together, and Walt could see me straining at the smallness of my little D.C. pond. At a basement lunch place on Connecticut Avenue NW where we were eating French dip sandwiches and talking tech, he could see that I was eager to swim in a larger ocean, the Pacific one. Walt looked me straight in the eye and said: "Go West, young woman."

And that is *exactly* what I did.

CHAPTER 3

California, Here I Came

Go West, young man, and grow up with the country.

—HORACE GREELEY

In 1997, the *Wall Street Journal* had no dedicated reporter covering the Internet, and Walt was convinced that the paper needed to hire me to be its first explorer of this new world. So, Walt called top *Journal* editor Paul Steiger and basically ordered him to hire me. Walt had that kind of pull since his must-read tech review column raked in tens of millions of dollars in advertising annually at the time.

That's why Walt was also the most highly paid editorial staffer at the *Journal*, and deservedly so. He had the highest standards of journalistic integrity, never becoming a slobbering fanboy like so many. In fact, Walt chose to live in D.C., far away from Silicon Valley, in order to maintain the distance needed to judge the products fairly. While Walt was often on the phone with Bill Gates or Steve Jobs or the many moguls who wanted his ear, he always kept the relationships professional. He didn't want to hang with them on weekends or send his kids to school with their kids.

At the same time, Walt wanted a colleague who could cover these techies up close, calling them out for their mistakes and making sure they knew they'd be held accountable. The leap was still easier said than done for me. D.C. felt like home. I had a tight network of friends, an apartment I owned, a really great girlfriend, and a supportive workplace. But the idea of creating an entirely new beat was impossible to resist. In my final days, I ran into *Post* owner Don Graham and he asked why I was leaving. Once again, I launched into an explanation about lower publishing plains, rising rivers of information, and the weakening of the relationship between the readership and advertisers. As always, the perpetually affable Graham chuckled gently as I went on and on like a jackass.

"The flood is coming," I warned him, sounding more like AOL's Steve Case than I cared to. "So, I'm seeking higher ground."

"You better stay dry then," he joked. "And it looks like I'm going to need a bigger boat."

Noah's Ark, I thought, which I mercifully kept to myself. Thus, at thirty-four years old, I left the *Post* and joined the *Wall Street Journal*. I packed my car with all my belongings and headed across the country to a state I barely knew. And like the forty-niners a century earlier, I was excited to stake my claim. Walt had just one more piece of advice for me before I left. "Parachute in with your cleats on," he said. "They'll never know what hit them. Be fair but cover them hard since they're going to run the world."

I rolled into San Francisco on a perfect California day: blue skies, bright sun, seventy-eight-degree weather, a light breeze blowing in from the bay. I was looking forward to the ever-present smell of eucalyptus trees that calms me in ways that I still cannot explain. It's a visceral and earthy scent, like the deepest of woods on the rainiest of days. Unfortunately, sweaty leather was the first major odor that hit me on that particular day, due to the thousands of people jamming up the street and blocking me in traffic. They were attending the famed Folsom Street Fair, an annual BDSM and leather subculture event that takes place in San Francisco's South of Market district. Arriving at this moment in my Subaru Outback was kind of a perfect cliché for a lesbian entering her new life.

I was intrigued by the sight of so many people living their lives out loud, presumably proud, in ways that no one back East seemed able to for very long or with any energy. That was a personal plus for moving west, where anything went. That was definitely not the case professionally, and I quickly discovered the same lack of excitement over this new digital age at the *Journal*, where much of the New York staff didn't know what to make of me.

"I guess you'll be covering CB radio," the paper's hopelessly arrogant media reporter told me. Media reporting was considered the hottest beat for up-and-comers. After all, these journalists got to cover corporate behemoths, like Time Warner, Condé Nast, News Corp, and Disney, that controlled everything humanity saw and heard. It was no surprise that the media reporters acted like the grandees they covered, preening with the unmistakable air of being frequently wrong but never in doubt.

The reporter—whom I will not name out of professional courtesy, since he now works for an online publication, pontificating on digital topics, as if he knew from the get-go that this was the way it was going to turn out—did not know at all that this was how it would turn out. This was why he referenced citizens band radio, the late-1970s mobile communications system used mostly by long-haul truckers, which became a fad due to movies like *Smokey and the Bandit* and songs like "Convoy." Suddenly, everyone had a CB radio. And then, just as quickly, that fad was over and out. The reporter thought this was the best dig ever, since most media reporters viewed the emerging digital sector as a flash in the pan. He was also fond of describing early digital startups as "a Ponzi scheme" and "a Potemkin village," which many definitely turned out to be.

"You won't have much to cover when they all go out of business," he informed me with a snark that stung. There was still a big dollop of old media in me, which questioned the possibility of digital domination. I thought about saying nothing and just letting that one go. After all, I wasn't the ambassador from Techlandia.

Instead, because I am controlled by id and not superego, I decided to match his self-righteous dismissiveness. "The Internet is going to grind down all of media into dust," I retorted, taking his bait. "The media as you know it is dying by the cell, so everyone should lay down now." He laughed at me, perhaps one of his last. I couldn't have cared less that the most ambitious reporters at my new outlet thought the Internet was a dead-end beat.

Obviously, computer and chip makers, as well as a variety of database and infrastructure companies, were critically important to the tech ecosystem. Paying attention to these massive businesses was an important part of the *Journal*'s coverage. But to me, that was like focusing on the inside of the mechanical watch—an assortment of gears, calipers, and gaskets few people understood or cared to know about. The Internet was different. I was determined to tell people not how the watch worked, but what time it was.

One of my first stops was Netscape, which had then secured 75 percent of the browser market. Tech wunderkind Andreessen was utterly brilliant in mind but hopelessly juvenile in spirit. Dank humor was the Andreessen style of in-your-face joking that was a lot less funny than he imagined. He was in his mid-twenties but seemed more like he was eleven or twelve years old. At the time, he struggled to clock social cues easily and never tried hard with social niceties. And he would often see disagreements as an attack rather than an opening to learn something. I was equally obstreperous, of course, which made for one of the most interesting relationships I had in the early days of my time in Silicon Valley.

Today, part of Andreessen's brand is to rail at the media, but there was a time when he always picked up the phone for me, at all hours. It was the same with texts—all of which I saved in a "Marc" file, because I had a sense even then that these boy men would try hard to reinvent themselves and erase their former selves. Texts from Marc were indicative of a restless and vaguely disgruntled mind. They typically included a range of funny observations, smart takes, casual insults of foes (and also friends), and a whole lot of GIFs on every topic from Microsoft to Sarah Palin. (No comment on that, but suffice it to say, we both found her simultaneously appalling and curiously fetching and we hated ourselves for that. At least I did.) In other words, Andreessen, like many Internet moguls, loved the media until he hated it. He has since blocked me (as well as many others) and refuses to respond, almost as enthusiastically as he once texted me at all hours. In all likelihood, he probably thinks I have become a harpy. This is not ideal professionally, and personally, I will admit that I miss his quirky and tetchy personality. He was a jerk but an enjoyable jerk. Now he's a tiresome and aggrieved jerk, who has joined the grievance industrial complex as a permanent citizen.

In truth, Andreessen was always a little sour and dystopian, which many reports have attributed to problems he had with his family, though he never discussed it with me. He felt like he was born fully a geek god, and the arrogance was part of the armor. I did not mind, since he did not try to shine me on as others did, hiding their true natures. That's why I enjoyed conversations with Andreessen the most, even though they often took place at Hobee's, a local chain of forgettable comfort food that the Midwestern-born Andreessen preferred over the much better food in the Bay Area. He told me then that he was a creature of habit and liked to keep his choices simple, so it was always eggs. Lots of eggs.

Favoring comfort was a sentiment that was echoed by those who copied him. That meant sloppy clothes, soft furniture, burritos as fine cuisine, and work as home, with all luxuries from haircuts and exercise to dry cleaning provided for. Indeed, the Netscape campus in Mountain View was an adult version of a kindergarten. There was prepared food at all hours, games of all sorts, beanbag-style chairs, and fleece hoodies. It was a weird boy wonderland, not unlike Pinocchio's Pleasure Island, except no one minded the transformation from human into donkey. Instead, they relished it. Driving to Netscape HQ in the always-warm California sunshine, I felt that I was already far too old for this—ancient, in fact—in my early thirties.

To bring these man-boys into line, Netscape's board put the world's nicest daddy ever in charge, installing an affable and very experienced telecom exec named Jim Barksdale as CEO in January of 1995. Born and raised in Mississippi, Barksdale had all these Southern aphorisms. My favorite was: "Remember to keep the main thing the main thing." I liked Barksdale immediately and found him to be the kind of leader I wished there were more of. Highly ethical, but with a love of young techies, he exuded decency at every turn. And one thing stood out: Barksdale never lied to me, as Andreessen did so many times that I stopped counting. (In reply to one text from him that was flatly untrue, I simply wrote: "Pants on fire.")

Sadly, Andreessen was the norm. I can't say I was either shocked by this or even upset. As a journalist, I came to realize that rather than lying to me, these entrepreneurs were more often lying to themselves. Maybe they felt it was necessary in order to suspend reality and create a new industry out of nothing. Thomas Edison did this constantly, of course, famous for turfing rivals like Nikola Tesla via nefarious tricks. Too often, inventors are painted as heroic, with their faults glossed over in our accepted narrative. Most are damaged in a significant way, usually from early in their lives. Tech is littered with men whose parents—typically fathers—were either cruel or absent. By the time they grew to be adults, many were unhappy and often had some disgruntled tale of being misunderstood before they were proved triumphantly right. Most of all, the damaged ones shared one sad attribute: They all seemed achingly lonely.

I came to realize that many tech titans' warped self-righteousness fueled them more than money, power, and the growing legions of obsequious enablers on the payroll. It inevitably curdled their souls, creating an arrogance that masked what was a deep self-hatred and anger. I have never seen a more powerful and rich group of people who saw themselves as the victim so intensely. Which is why, by nature, they insisted on re-framing every failure and mistake they made as an asset—even when it was a failure and, sometimes, a very damaging mistake. Of course, they loved quoting Edison's quaint trope: "I have not failed. I've just found ten thousand ways that won't work." But this declaration leaves out a lot about who's responsible when things go terribly awry and real people get hurt. And because of the reach and amplification of tech, that hurt scaled quickly and continues to this day.

But failure was not what was happening to Netscape at that time. Barksdale's "main thing" was up and to the right and soon the Netscape crew were the new kings of the Valley. Netscape quickly went public, mounting an extremely successful IPO on August 9, 1995. The stock was set to be offered at $14 per share, but it doubled the IPO to $28 per share. That value soared to $75 during the first day of trading, which shocked investors and set the tone for many tech offerings to come. By the end of the first day of trading, Netscape had a market value of almost $3 billion. "I don't think anybody had an idea of how big this thing would be," Barksdale told me. "Unlike a lot of passive mediums, this is a network that the mere mortal can affect, can jump on and ride to anywhere."

So could Andreessen, who was worth almost $59 million post-IPO. Soon, he became the embodiment of a boy genius on magazine covers. In the most famous, he sat denim-clad and barefoot on a red velvet and gilt throne for *Time* in 1996. The headline: "The Golden Geeks: They invent. They start companies. And the stock market has made them INSTANT-AIRES. Who are they? How do they live? And what do they mean for America's future?" Thankfully, "Instantaires" never caught on, but the other questions were what drew me to Silicon Valley.

After Netscape, my next stop was Yahoo, which went public in 1996 with a market cap of nearly $900 million. That number quickly doubled. Just as young and puckish as Netscape, Yahoo was founded in 1995 by Jerry Yang and David Filo, while they were graduate students at Stanford University—the famed school from which many of the top players would emerge. Originally called "Jerry and David's Guide to the World Wide Web," which was created in 1994, as the portal grew popular, it was renamed Yahoo, an acronym for "Yet Another Hierarchical Officious Oracle."

Along with Netscape, Yahoo became the hot place to work. Of the two, Yahoo was more consumer focused, with its jaunty lettering, irritating exclamation point, and air of youthful wackiness. Yahoo took what AOL had pioneered and put it directly on the Internet. It became the most important web site that was a directory of other web sites, all listed by hand by a group of human Web crawlers. Yes, one at a time, by a group that I dubbed "the Internet bouncers."

I laughed about this with Andy Gems, whom I interviewed in a very dark room at Yahoo's campus in Sunnyvale, California, for one of my first articles at the *Journal*, headlined "The Gatekeeper." Previously, Gems had worked at Borders Books and Music in downtown San Francisco, and he was now one of the roughly sixty Yahoo employees who controlled admittance to the popular directory. Accompanied by a pet tarantula that ate live crickets at his desk, Gems had one of the most powerful jobs on the Internet, deciding with sixty other surfers what got accepted and what did not on the early Internet's most important guides. Even then, issues of moderation were problematic. The only sites Yahoo did not add to its critical directory were those that promoted illegal activities such as bomb making and child pornography. But sites for many controversial topics were listed, often in the "Society and Culture" area. Sites that promoted the Ku Klux Klan and other hate groups made it past the gatekeepers with Gems insisting to me that he was not a "censor."

Sound familiar?

That aside, Yahoo was the new gateway to the Internet, and it's quaint today to think about the artisanal nature of its business. The future began to unfold over time as Yahoo added all kinds of digital bells and whistles like email, personalization, commerce, and news, as well as its flagship guide. As with Netscape, the marketing of Yahoo was relentless. Yang was the front man and Filo was the tech guy. Filo was so terse that it was a small victory when I could extract even a one-word answer out of him. Later, Yahoo brought in more professional executive leadership, like Tim Koogle and later Hollywood's Terry Semel, but originally the brand was built around Yang and Filo and their leap from the computer lab to the stratosphere. In one cover story, they exuberantly exploded out of a purple Yahoo Mini. In another, Yang, who named himself "Chief Yahoo," rode a surfboard with a computer on his head.

Internet people loved to do things like this, since it gave them an air of "I don't care for corporate formalities," which appealed to the audience they were aiming at and made good copy. Much of it, of course, was performative, signaling to the public that these inventors were going to seize power and have a good time doing it. I even wrote a story about the "lies" of Silicon Valley, which holds up rather well a quarter century later. "No wonder, then, that self-congratulation and self-deception are now a part of the Valley's ethos, right up there with fearless risk-taking, maniacal effort and programming genius," I wrote, listing lines like:

"It's not about the money." (It was!)

"It's not about the fame." (It also was!)

"There's no dress code/no special parking spaces/no fancy offices here, because we're not hung up on status symbols." (They were, just different ones.)

"No one is really in charge here." (Ahahahaha.)

"It's not about a product, it's about changing the world." (It was about the product.)

"We have no competition/We have a lot of competition." (Sigh.)

Even then, I found this PR theater tiresome and obvious. That was certainly the case when I visited Yahoo's rival Excite, which had six young founders. On a tour of the open-plan headquarters, which featured a faux garage door as a reference to the old trope of startups and their humble beginnings as backyard tinkerers, one of the six—I honestly can't recall which—excitedly showed me a twisty red children's slide installed between the company's second and first floors. "Go ahead and slide down," he urged me, presuming that finding your inner child was key to unlocking my entrepreneurial spirit. "We make all our partners do it."

"No," I said, since I was not their partner and tried to maintain some grumpy dignity. "I didn't like slides when I was five years old and I definitely don't like them now that I am an adult." He was crestfallen.

But the slide feint was not uncommon. Most of the headquarters of the various Internet companies had bouncy balls, scooters of all kinds, skateboards, and always places to nap. It was as if preternaturally large three-year-olds had gotten hold of vast piles of money and realized they could have an endless supply of candy and toys. I did eat the candy, but I avoided the toys. Later, my sons would love to come with me to work when they were *actual* kids since there was always a go-kart somewhere. What this aggressive and performative playfulness had to do with innovation, I never quite grokked, although I did see the importance of breaking free from the confines of cubicle culture and endless meetings. But tech took it one step further, aiming for childlike and then veering into childish pretty quickly. And conformity, too. Once companies like Yahoo and Netscape instituted these silly environments, everyone copied them, and their indulgent VC parents went along for the ride.

It was obviously silly. Who was I to argue? These new developments seemed to be working. Few tech leaders had learned the most potent lesson of the sector yet: The young inevitably eat the old. The manic nature of the industry has to be seen in this dichotomy, in that every single tech company is on its way to something else, and power does not last in ways that it did before. It felt very ephemeral at the time, which was one of its assets (change!) and one of its greatest weaknesses (wait, too much change!). As was inevitable, by early 1998, Netscape's #1 browser status was slipping fast. Under attack by Microsoft,

Netscape mulled the sale of whole or part of itself. By the end of that year, Netscape was acquired by AOL and Marc Andreessen had shifted over to become its employee as chief techie, which was quite pathetic (which he realized and so left as soon as he could).

Still, the good times were still rolling, as company after company went public with stunts and come-ons and much less moneymaking than would eventually be needed. And why not? At the time, the basic laws of gravity did not apply to these wondrous tech gods. In truth, it became ridiculous quite quickly. In one case, a well-known investment banker called to pitch me a story about a company whose share price was going to hit the sky after going public and was "pre-revenue." While I was used to lack of profitability, that one hit me hard. "I'm looking out the window of my office right now and there's an old lady on the corner," I said. "Why don't you cut to the chase and just mug her and take all her money? It'd be faster." The banker told me I was hysterical, and not in a good way.

Being the skunk at a garden party led to a lot of crinkled noses and accusations of being overly negative, which would be the go-to insult of the press. While that was sometimes warranted, I maintained that part of my job was to make that stink and write about where it could all go wrong. I got particularly fixated on an online grocery delivery company called Webvan, which had thirty-five hundred employees at its peak. They kept raising rounds of funding, but after crunching their numbers, I could tell that the math was not mathing. Along with many others, I kept reporting on that pertinent point. No one cared for my analysis and the party went on. (For three years at least— which is when the startup filed for bankruptcy.) Another perfect example was Kozmo.com, an early one-hour delivery service that had raised $250 million from a range of top venture firms and in 1999 turned in revenue of $3.5 million with $26.3 million in losses. While I loved the idea of online married with real-world commerce—I had been a retail reporter for seven years, after all—and felt the marriage was inevitable, this seemed problematic. It was. Within two years, Kozmo was failing.

That's why I turned down a series of job offers from basically all of these companies. "You'll make $100 million quick," said one startup CEO to me, dangling a job as editorial director for a site that had exactly no editorial at all. Over the years, I got job offers from every major Internet company and a whole lot of minor ones. I always turned them down, because—well—just because I liked reporting. Many journalists did jump during the boom, but I never did. Such a move seemed soul crushing. Maybe I also knew that I was far too much of an irritant to survive until my shares vested.

That included yet another vague editor-in-chief job that was dangled by Ted Leonsis of AOL, the company where my tech career began. That got a hard no from me, too, even though AOL's influence had morphed. So much so that in a *Journal* column at the end of 1999, I suggested that AOL—now as dominant as Case had predicted—merge with "a big traditional media company, which would offer a variety of distribution and content arms." I had named Time Warner as a guess, but my editor removed it as too far-fetched. To me, it seemed like an obvious move to make with all the funny money before reality set in. The rules of the bubble are different, until it pops. Within a month, AOL announced its merger with Time Warner, which was really a complete takeover. It would be the peak moment for the Internet's first revolution, before the businesses all came crashing down for most of them.

But when it was announced, techies were joyous at the AOL–Time Warner deal and saw it as a rout of the old guard. "You won, Kara," I was told by a fellow tech reporter who also could not stand old-media arrogance, even as it was about to undergo a radical shift. While the Internet certainly was not CB radio—I was right about that—the entire deal made me nervous from the start. While everything had changed irrevocably, I could not shake the feeling that there was an earthquake coming, much sooner than later.

CHAPTER 4

Search Me

Ask, and it shall be given you; seek, and ye shall find; knock, and it shall be opened unto you.

—MATTHEW 7:7

I've always hated the phrase "speak truth to power," because it assumes all power is bad. It should really be "speak truth to power when the power is false or damaging—or even just plain bizarre."

In the bizarre camp was when I found myself staring at an ice sculpture of a woman whose breast was oozing White Russians, a Kahlúa and cream concoction. I was a guest at the baby shower party for Google founder Sergey Brin and his wife, Anne Wojcicki, who were expecting their first child in 2008. Naturally, they decided to celebrate with a huge party in the factory district of San Francisco. Before you could lift a glass to the icy nipple to get a sip, guests had to brave a jungle of dangling baby photos of Sergey and Anne at the door. The club's entrance was manned by the kind of preternaturally ebullient and hyper-organized women that always seemed to surround the rich of Silicon Valley.

"Would you like a diaper? Or a onesie?" asked a young woman with amazingly swingy blonde hair and a very sincere smile, as if the question were not even slightly fucked up. But we were in San Francisco, after all, where such happenings were apparently popular among its citizens. I try not to judge, even when I am absolutely judging.

To be clear: I was judging *hard*.

But this was worse than a simple case of sexual preferences. This young woman was asking my baby-wear preference, because that was the "fun" part of the night. Guests either got to wear a diaper with an oversized comical pin, a ruffled baby hat that came with a rattle, *or* adult-sized footy pajamas accessorized with a teddy bear and a sucker. I declined it all immediately, which made the swingy hair stop swinging and the smile shift to a frown. "Everyone has to wear one," she insisted. "Everyone *is* wearing one!"

Not me! I ran into the party before she could lay a talcum-powdered hand on me and found some of the most powerful people in tech and media—all decked out as newborns. Brin wore a onesie as he roller-skated around the room. Wendi Deng, then the wife of News Corp titan Rupert Murdoch (whom I had taken to referring to as "Uncle Satan"), had chosen a diaper and sucker combo. Deng quickly asked me how she looked, which was disturbing since she was wearing some kind of leather pants and stiletto boots under the giant Pampers, and that was a freaky disconnect I preferred not to be experiencing at that moment (or, frankly, ever). Thankfully, Uncle Satan was not in attendance, so I got to miss that particular visual. And, just as thankfully, over in a corner, then Mayor Gavin Newsom, who had grown close to the Google founders, was wearing a normal suit.

"How'd you get out of wearing the costume?" I asked the tall and handsome pol, who had legalized gay marriage in San Francisco in 2004 and would take office as the governor of California in 2019.

"I knew you'd be here and take my photo and put it all over the Internet and my political career would be ruined because I was wearing a diaper at the behest of an Internet billionaire," said Newsom, whom I liked because he always got the ridiculousness of these people. "How did you get out of it?"

"Dignity," I answered. "Shall we toast to that?"

And with that we each raised a glass to catch the liqueur-flavored milk from the icy nipple, dignity be damned. It was, of course, delicious.

My journey to this surreal moment started in 1999 when famed venture capitalist John Doerr pointed out the startup to me. Doerr had invested $12.5 million in an early Google funding round, along with $12.5 million from Sequoia Capital's Mike Moritz. That the pair of major VC rivals had cooperated was unusual, and they both joined Google's board of directors. I had grown fond of talking to the whip-smart Doerr, even though he'd often call me up close to deadline on a scoop related to one of his many investments and say: "Are you *sure* you're right?"

I *was* right—I was terrified not to be—and his tweaking of a journalist's natural insecurity over accuracy made me laugh since he was really one of the more earnest and self-effacing of the lot. He certainly could have been more arrogant, given he had a legendary record with investments that included Amazon, Intuit, and Netscape. So, when he made recommendations, I listened, even though his bets did not always pan out. But Doerr was insistent that I meet Sergey Brin and Larry Page, the pair of

Stanford PhD students who had started the company at the university in 1998. "They're a little odder than people you've met so far," said Doerr, "but they are really special."

I was dubious at first since I had covered a number of search efforts that had died quick deaths. Google's key idea of Page-Rank, which measured the importance of web pages, seemed especially geeky. Relevance was the key determinant, and Google had noted in a statement that their offerings were "computed by solving an equation of 500 million variables and two billion terms."

"It's different," insisted Doerr. "Trust me on this one." So, he made the intros to the young entrepreneurs, whom I immediately nicknamed "the twins" even though they were not anything alike. Page was terse, while Brin never stopped talking. Page was grave, while Brin was the comic relief. Page was sharp-tongued, while Brin aimed for sweetness. Both were indeed odd, as Doerr said, but profoundly so. At one point, Page had taken to wearing a pollution monitor around his neck all the time to make sure he was not inhaling whatever might kill him from the atmosphere. In contrast, Brin was always dressing as if he were about to go surfing or join a yoga class at any moment. In fact, he sometimes launched into a downward-facing dog yoga move when you were talking to him.

Still, the two founders shared a quirkiness in habit and speech, and both embraced a classic entrepreneurial narrative, having moved their startup to the nearby garage of a house that was owned by a junior marketing executive at Intel. Her name was Susan Wojcicki. She charged them $1,700 a month for the space, although she first asked for stock options. The twins declined for the rent, but she got a pile later when she became a full-time employee. Wojcicki, who looked like the soccer mom she also was, would soon quit Intel and join Google as a marketing manager. This was fortunate for me since she became the "normal" person at Google who could explain to me what was happening inside the carnival show that the company quickly became. It was also a welcome relief to have a woman—there were, in fact, many more at Google than anywhere else—in a position of relative power.

Within months, Google had outgrown her garage. After a short stint in a small office in downtown Palo Alto, the fast-growing company with thirty employees would then move to 2400 Bayshore Parkway in Mountain View. Wojcicki negotiated the lease for the forty-two thousand square feet that would eventually spread and become the HQ of the famed Googleplex, which would expand to millions of square feet across the globe. It was at Bayshore where I first met the twins, having driven my Honda minivan down for lunch at their tiny cafeteria. Though small, Google had still managed to hire Charlie Ayers, the former chef for the Grateful Dead. (Ayers made tens of millions from the stint when he, too, received stock options.) The food Charlie made was indeed delicious, and the founders were extraordinarily awkward, especially Page, who as CEO did not seem to relish the idea of being the forward-facing executive. Brin filled the silence, attempting to make a series of silly jokes that landed about 46 percent of the time. Wojcicki stopped by to say hello, and it was, as I recall, a moment of sweet relief to have a functional conversation.

I was trying, as all reporters do, to find any kind of purchase to mount a big feature story for the front page. A bunch of colorful exercise balls and scooters strewn about an office was not going to cut it. I was looking for anything special to convince my editors that a story on the twins was worth it, but their inability to play even the most basic of PR games was apparent. Obvious brilliance was bristling off the pair, for whom every idea was possible, even if some were utterly wacky. Over the years, they'd imagine a lot, from putting ski lifts on the hills of San Francisco to help citizens get around, to building giant windmills in Hawaii to produce energy for cars that hovered. They imagined barges in San Francisco Bay that would serve as "an interactive space where people can learn about new technology" and turned that one into a reality from 2010 to 2012.

Still, it would hardly matter what they made after that first and most important product, their famed search engine. I thought of it as a database of human intentions, a description that came to me when I was waiting in the lobby of one of their buildings, as I watched a lighted scroll of terms being searched at the moment (they took out the porn-related ones). I tried to grasp what each person making a request wanted. One time, the words "horse," "swimming," and "picnic" whooshed by, and I thought of a person somewhere trying to plan a lovely summer day. Google also had a spinning digital globe on a screen, with streams of various colored lights—each representing a question someone on Earth had—that exploded up like klieg lights depending on how many questions were being asked. It also became immediately clear as the globe came around that far too much of the world could not search since they lacked connectivity, even as others were bathed in light. "We need more Internet in Africa," Brin observed to me once as we both stared at the pulsing globe. "We need to get on that."

There was a strain of tech religion to both Brin and Page, for whom money never seemed to be the driving force then, even if it soon would be. Once they built the very best search engine to which they would later marry online advertising in an innovative auction platform, they created an explosively profitable business. Among the many Internet companies being created at a furious pace, that massive profit would soon set Google apart.

Another smart move that only a few companies made at the time was to bring in professional management. In 2001, Google recruited well-known tech leader Eric Schmidt to essentially be the adult in the room. A former Sun Microsystems executive, Schmidt had become a star there, but foundered at Utah-based Novell, out of sight and definitely out of mind as the software maker saw its proprietary protocols being supplanted by open ones. Schmidt's loyal PR guy had often tried to convince me to travel to Provo to talk about Novell, which was a very hard no for me and the *Journal*. But when Doerr and Moritz connected Schmidt with the twins, sparks flew. Schmidt recognized that forming a troika with Page and Brin was the chance of a lifetime. He joined Google first as board chairman in March of 2001 and by summer was named CEO.

Although Provo was a nonstarter, I was happy to travel to Mountain View to interview the canny Schmidt, who could be both a Silicon Valley sotto voce insider and somewhat of a blowhard about big topics. Schmidt exuded competence and assurance, painting himself as the one who could tend the delicate flower geniuses and bring order to the chaos. Page and Brin got nice titles, as president of products and president of technology. It was the smart move. Google did it right from the start, employing a simple but jaunty brand, intuitive usability, and total efficacy. Most importantly, they had a killer product from the start. This was precisely why Page joke-whispered to me, "Don't tell them," as I looked up at a growth chart that was plastered on the walls of the office.

He was referring to a two-year deal that Google had struck with Yahoo to power the search engine for the ascendant Web portal that did not have algorithmic search capabilities. Yahoo, as well as AOL, had once tried to buy Google. Those deals never happened, and Google wisely chose to rent out its tech instead. As part of the vendor arrangement, the Google name, with its primary color letters, was prominently featured on the much-visited Yahoo web site. This boneheaded phenomenon of a tech brand building itself on another brand's site had happened before. AOL rode along on CompuServe's growth by buying ads on the service. Yahoo itself had drafted off the popularity of Netscape's home page. It was as if Coke let Pepsi put their name on cans, and the new economy acted like this was no big deal.

But it was a big deal when Yahoo selected Google to be its default search provider in mid-2000, to add to its directory and navigational guide. "Google's search services help individuals find the information they're looking for on the Web with unprecedented levels of ease, speed, and relevancy," said Page in the press release. "Through this relationship, Yahoo!'s vast audience will now benefit from increased accuracy and rapid return of high-quality, relevant search results."

And how. Because while the growth of "Yahoo search powered by Google" surged as a result, the more massive numbers on the chart were for Google.com and its iconic and infectiously charming "I feel lucky" button. Google delivered exactly what you were searching for, all via the magical PageRank algorithm. The service was fast, correct, and totally useful. As I looked up at the charted growth for the main Google brand plastered on the walls of the office, it was immediately apparent that there was a fast-moving shift of Yahoo customers to Google.

"Do they know?" I asked Page. It was so obvious what was about to happen I could not imagine that Yahoo did not see it. It was also, for me, a very good story.

"I don't think so," he said, flashing a sly grin he sometimes let break through his typical poker face. Despite his physical awkwardness and stilted manner, Page was a smooth operator and, really, a killer. He looked at me dead in the eyes and added: "But don't tell them." Of course, that's the first thing that I did. When I got to my car in Google's parking lot, I called up Yahoo cofounder and Chief Yahoo Jerry Yang, with whom I had developed a spiky though friendly relationship that was not unlike two bickering siblings. I did not often warn companies, but I had seen this so many times before that I could not keep it to myself. "You need to get them off your platform," I said regarding the dangerous licensing deal. "They look harmless, but they'll kill you."

Yang laughed at me, as he often did. He told me Yahoo was making a ton of money with the additional search for the small fee that it paid for Google's services. Obviously, the company would cut the search firm loose or buy them whenever it became a threat. It also helped that Yahoo had acquired a pile of Google shares—5 percent of the young company—as part of the search deal and felt it was in the dominant position. After all, Yahoo was the most important consumer company, and Google was a simple box on the page that could only serve up tech for companies with stronger relationships with customers. Yang was right to feel confident at the time and ignore my paranoia. By now, he was a billionaire. And while Yahoo stock had been dinged along with all the others in the downturn, CEO Semel was turbocharging the company's media aspirations. In comparison, Google must have felt like a geek mouse.

Still, Page's ambitions felt endless. As I often said about the most brilliant of the Silicon Valley entrepreneurs, he seemed to be playing Spock chess while others were playing checkers. By 2002, Google's home page had one-third of all search referrals globally, climbing from only 1 percent in just two years. At the same time, Yahoo had dropped from 46 percent to 36 percent. Yahoo's leadership did have an inkling that they needed to control their own technology fate. By late 2002, Semel, who had no tech skills to speak of, understood the challenge and bought Google's search rival Inktomi for $235 million. Inktomi had made its business selling its unbranded search technology to Amazon, Microsoft's MSN, and eBay, but it was still struggling against the Google onslaught. Inktomi also had paid-inclusion technology that ranked the pool of advertisers by relevance to a search by a user. Yahoo had been working with a company called Overture, which had a pay-for-placement approach that ranked search results by who paid the most, which made it more profitable to investors, but less attractive to consumers. To further lock in the advantage, Yahoo also paid $1.63 billion to buy Overture, largely because online ad spending—basically banner ads—was eclipsed by online search ad spending.

Unfortunately, Google had already run away with the market, launching AdWords in 2000, perfecting its profit-gushing cost-per-click auction model in which marketers bid for that click. AdSense followed and allowed targeted ads on sites. On top of that, Google was fast building an irresistible consumer offering, too, having launched an automated news page that become quickly popular. A lot more was on the way, like email, mapping, photos, video, and blogs. And content, with a big push into downloading books and other media into the exploding Google database. Anything that can be digitized would be, I thought many times. That included when Page showed me a room at Google HQ full of televisions and explained that Google was experimenting using the text from closed-captioning to translate video into a searchable form. "Do you own the rights to the shows? You need to own the intellectual property to do that," I said to Page. He looked at me blankly and walked on.

In truth, Google was becoming a Borg that would suck in all the world's information and then spit it out for profit. And, eventually, resistance would be futile in every media. In late summer 2003, for example, Page, Wojcicki, and my then wife, Megan Smith, flew to New York to meet with the major publishing houses about Google's plan to scan all the world's books, starting with those out of print. They were looking for cooperation and were greeted by near total disdain, followed by total rejection. In an odd twist, there was a major blackout in NYC that day, and Page and Wojcicki could not get to their hotel rooms on the high floors of the skyscrapers. They ended up joining Megan and me at my mother's ninth-floor midtown apartment, where they camped out on the floor.

Page was both disappointed and confused that the publishers had not jumped on Google's proposal to help get their content digitized. I tried to explain why IP was so important to media companies and that you could not just take it without consequences. And once Google did this, no one else could afford to digitize the material, so content makers and their work would eventually be held hostage by the technology and access to it. Google would dominate all content without having generated anything but the delivery system. To Page, this seemed illogical. He and many at the company were relentless about the idea that all information needed to be vacuumed up and sorted by the Googlers to bring illumination to the human race and distribution to all. (Google would later be sued by book publishers, as well as many others in media, cases that the search giant eventually won under fair use.)

Page actually fretted about a lot to me, which made me admire him more despite his decidedly rougher edges and a tone that could turn brainiac dismissive quickly, an affect that would increase over time. Unlike others in tech, he had little interest in fame, and it was always my impression that he wanted more to disappear than become more prominent. He also worried about the impact of Google's pending IPO in 2004 that would change everything and turn them all instantly into wealthy elites. At a TED conference in early 2002 in Monterey, California, five months before the offering, we sat at a table in the conference center late at night and talked about the future of Google. Page was much more open and reflective in those days and, as smart as he was, knew what was coming was something he did not quite understand. While Schmidt loved the attention of being at the hottest tech company of the moment—glad-handing just about anyone who passed him in the tony crowd and forever flirting—Page avoided such gatherings and only appeared when he had to. He had nearly no filter.

So back then, we talked a lot since he often did not understand all the moves he would later learn well. And I needed to understand from the man who really was most critical to creating Google what he had been trying to make and what problem he was solving. At that moment he was sorting through how to go public with some modicum of integrity, as he seemed to loathe investment bankers and all the Kabuki theater that went with an IPO. Google would later go public via an unusual "Dutch auction" that involved collecting bids from interested investors to determine the highest price at which it could sell its shares. In a 2010 *Harvard Business Review* piece titled "How I Did It: Google's CEO on the Enduring Lessons of a Quirky IPO," Schmidt explained the theory: "I know this may sound like baloney, but we settled decisively on the Dutch auction after we got a letter from a little old lady—or at least someone who claimed to be a little old lady. She wrote something along the lines of 'I don't understand why I can't make money from your IPO the way the stockbrokers will.'"

Page was wary of it all, although he told me he knew he had to do it to allow loyal employees to cash out. But he also thought going public might ruin everything and even expressed a desire to keep the company private. Even then, Silicon Valley was already littered with look-at-me narcissists, who never met an idea that they did not try to take credit for. Not Page. It was also no surprise that he and others at Google insisted on establishing a set of corporate values that the company could adhere to as it headed into the stratosphere. The founders decided to use the motto "Don't Be Evil," a concept that had been introduced earlier internally by engineers and was also a dig at competitors like Microsoft, which Googlers criticized for not being transparent with users.

That software company was in the midst of a major antitrust trial and had become a bogeyman to Silicon Valley, which often decried Microsoft as a company that dominated by controlling.

What was ironic is that Google would soon dominate by becoming the de facto and indispensable crossroads of everything. But at the time, Google saw itself as the scrappy Han Solo to Bill Gates's Darth Vader.

I was still surprised when Page called me and asked for help in trying to write an essay of these sentiments, including the idea of "Don't Be Evil," and explaining to Wall Street just how different they were. Presumably, he made the request because I knew the company well. My then wife, Megan, worked there and had earlier gone to Space Camp in Huntsville, Alabama, with the twins, and also a very young Elon Musk and his then wife, Justine. We had even spent time with Page and his then girlfriend, Google executive Marissa Mayer. Google was a place where personal and professional mixed a lot. At one point early on, it felt like everyone there was dating someone else there, a situation that would become a problem later. I guess Page must have figured I was a friendly or, even, a friend, though I was neither. I was a beat reporter covering the company, and writing this essay would be inappropriate. I begged off quickly. Later, as my spouse got higher jobs at Google, I had to insert links to long disclosures on my stories. Eventually, I stopped reporting on Google altogether.

I also thought the whole idea of "Don't Be Evil" was both arrogant and naïve. *Look at us! We're quirky!* And the evil part was an overly dramatic framing: Did no problematic actions made by tech fall somewhere between benign and heinous? Page did find another and more friendly journalist to help him hash out the essay, which appeared in Google's IPO prospectus in a letter from the twins, reading in part: "Don't be evil. We strongly believe that in the long term, we will be better served—as shareholders and in all other ways—by a company that does good things for the world even if we forgo some short-term gains." Yes, I know, the ironies of what was to come between Big Tech and data privacy and how the power of Google to know everything began to appear more menacing. In the years to come, Google would undergo increasing scrutiny about its monopoly-like power over search and its ability to crush upstart competitors. There were additional worries about its hegemony over future tech like artificial intelligence.

Not evil, perhaps, but decidedly creepy. And quick. Several years later, Google tried to take over Yahoo's search, which came after an unsolicited attempt by Microsoft to buy Yahoo for $45 billion in early 2008 as it sought to goose its own Bing search service. Yahoo managed to push back Microsoft CEO Steve Ballmer in a contentious but forgettable battle that I covered closely. By the end of 2007, Google clocked 63 percent of world-wide queries, with Yahoo limping along at just under 20 percent. To recover, Yahoo tried to run into the arms of Google to strike a search ad partnership. This outsourcing would have essentially allowed Google to control the search ad business and, really, all of search. I was adamant that this near monopoly not happen.

"And while it might be a long-cherished dream of Google's to take over Yahoo search—and also get the chance to return to the scene of the crime, since Google got its first big push from doing Yahoo search, before Yahoo wised up too late—there is simply no way this will be allowed by regulators, nor should it," I wrote on my *All Things Digital* site. "Still, you have to almost admire the chutzpah of the search giant in making this move, if the sheer and unadulterated arrogance of it wasn't so distract-ing." I noted then that Google had almost none of the obvious menacing aggression that characterized Microsoft when it thoroughly dominated tech. Still, Google was headed toward the same kind of monopoly that it had decried less than five years earlier in its manifesto.

"It is bad for advertisers, it is bad for consumers, it is bad for innovation, no matter how well-intentioned Google is," I wrote, also noting that at least Microsoft executives knew they were "thugs." Perhaps that went a little too far, which is what prompted one of the troika of Schmidt, Brin, and Page—I honestly cannot recall which one—to call me with hurt feelings. I do remember one telling me not to worry about their burgeoning power over all the world's information.

"We're good people," he said to me. It's true they were nice, and it's true that they did not start out in that simple garage to be the gods of information, as well as the richest and most powerful people on the planet.

"I'm not worried about the good people in charge now," I replied, my history education still acute. "I'm worried about the bad people later." You know, the evil ones. Since, unlike the people I covered, I had studied history and I had zero doubt they would show up soon enough.

CHAPTER 5

The Mongoose

Never trust anyone who has not brought a book with them.

—LEMONY SNICKET

Larry and Sergey were not the only "information thieves"—a spot-on term that Walt Mossberg coined for the data-rapacious moguls who were building their empires bit by other people's bytes. Up in Seattle, a short and energetic man was lousy at hiding his vaunting ambitions, masking them behind a genuinely infectious maniacal laugh, a curiously baby-fat face, and an anodyne presentation of pleated khakis, sensible shoes, and blue Oxford shirt. Still, from the start, I had no doubt that Jeff Bezos would eat my face off if that is what he needed to do to get ahead.

"Feral," in fact, was the first word that jumped into my head when I met Bezos in the Seattle area in the mid-1990s. He brought me to an industrial area near the airport, and I watched as he skittered around a warehouse like a frenetic mongoose. Bezos explained how and why he had picked this part of the U.S. for his headquarters. Seattle was cheaper than Silicon Valley, full of tech talent because of Microsoft and Lockheed, and ideal for shipping across the world. Bezos told everyone that he had driven across the country with his wife, after leaving a swank job at Wall Street's D. E. Shaw. He grasped the potential of the Internet and wanted to make magic before he regretted not jumping in.

It was, of course, a perfect narrative, redolent with the mythology of the pioneers combined with the smarts of the financial wizards and the enthusiasm of a very energetic puppy. Unlike the less sophisticated startup dudes, Bezos came across like he had just emerged from a management consulting meeting for Up with People. A science kid, he'd been his high school valedictorian, and his graduation speech touted the benefits of living in space. Of course, Bezos graduated summa cum laude, Phi Beta Kappa from Princeton with an electrical engineering and computer science degree. His first job was in telecommunications, but like many smart young men of the late 1980s and early 1990s, Bezos soon landed in the financial sector, working at a New York hedge fund where his math skills helped him rise to senior vice president by age thirty. But as comforting as a future of Hamptons summers and Park Avenue apartments must have been, that was not the path Bezos wanted. And so off to the Pacific Northwest went Bezos and his then wife, MacKenzie Scott.

When he initially set up the company in 1994, he had called it Cadabra—yes, as in Abra. He then settled on Amazon, which connoted bigness and—*bonus!*—it began with the letter A, which would place it near the top of any list of Internet companies. At least, that's the adorable founding story Bezos foisted on me and many other reporters, along with the factoid that he used doors as desks at the office to save money. Tech leaders loved to dole out these origin tidbits for color, and the often-hungry media ate them up with gusto. I checked and it appears that I never reported on the door anecdote, largely because desks were already pretty cheap and it seemed painfully performative even for a painfully performative crowd. And at the time, there was no one more performative than Bezos. While I could catch flashes of irritation and even anger under his mannered breeziness, he disguised it well. Then again, I was a prominent reporter on the Internet beat at the *Wall Street Journal*, and his company lacked status beyond other startups then proliferating. So back then, Bezos was always available for a chitchat and spent a lot of time working the room at conferences and events.

Unlike the Google founders, who were born in the 1970s, Bezos was born in the 1960s and wasn't an engineer by nature, so he approached the problem of Web commerce in an analytical way. He made a list of items that could be easily sold online and settled on books, not because he particularly loved them, but because they were a global product. Books were cheap and titles were plentiful and could be traced easily. He was pretty bloodless, even then, despite the affable image. To Bezos, everything was dedicated to the higher purpose of pushing Amazon forward. This would manifest in a tougher work culture than the coddled tech playpens of Silicon Valley. From inception, Amazon had a driven ethos that would roll on through, not unlike the kind of dyspeptic and often secretive company that Bill Gates had built at nearby Microsoft in Redmond. But while Gates was outwardly difficult, Bezos kept his bare-knuckled characteristics in public check.

Since I was also more coldly business minded than the average reporter, it was a relief to talk to Bezos. He had none of the awkward social deficits, and while he was more obviously venal, I appreciated that he never spewed the "I'm changing the world" craplets that had become de rigueur among the tech set. He had truckloads of enthusiasm about his business, but Bezos never was breathless about any of it. His harder-edged persona was in stark contrast to MacKenzie, a serious but unfailingly warm woman who was often with her husband at industry events. It was my impression then that she was a key adviser to him and a sounding board, bristling with intelligence and creativity.

She was impressive by herself, a promising novelist who was a favorite of Toni Morrison when she studied under the author at Princeton. When Scott talked about her writing back then, it felt wistful, as if she knew that her own career would be stymied by her marriage as Bezos's purview over publishing got stronger and more controversial. But whenever he started to get testy with me in ways that seemed oddly sensitive, I would often look to her more evenhanded nature. I thought better of him because of her. Coincidentally, it was the same with Bill and Melinda Gates. One time, Bill and I were backstage at one of our events, watching Melinda being interviewed by Walt Mossberg. We both marveled at her cogent answers, and I turned to Bill, who was always tetchy about something, and said: "I like you 10 percent more because you're married to her." I am sure he felt the same about me.

As it turned out, neither the Bezos nor the Gates marriage would last . . . and neither would mine. But it definitely was nice to see a softer side of these relentless men. Not that the relentlessness ever went away. With these entrepreneurs, almost every encounter became a wrestling match. Bezos and I got into it a lot, including at a TED conference where we sparred over the hypocrisy of pay-to-play placement on the Amazon site. I thought it was wrong to accept money from product makers to place stuff in a way that insinuated it was the best choice for a consumer. Bezos disagreed and compared it to what retail stores did all the time. Nor did he hide his displeasure when his company was struggling and Barron's dubbed his endeavor "Amazon Dot Bomb." I thought it was unfair, too, at the time, but his venting was persistent.

With hindsight, we know that most of the criticisms in the piece—that Walmart or small bookstores or Amazon's own burgeoning expenses would sink the company—were utterly wrong. Still, it irked Bezos that the media did not understand the scale of what he envisioned or respect the aggression and work ethic that would allow him to make it so. If Page and Brin were whimsical brainiacs, Bezos personified muscular ambition. Using a small slug of money from his parents, he debuted the clunky-looking Amazon web site in mid-1995, with the grandiose tagline: the "world's largest bookstore." This claim would help Amazon seem bigger than it was. It would also lead to a lawsuit from Barnes & Noble in 1997 for false advertising, which was quickly settled with no impact on Amazon.

Visiting the Amazon offices, located in a seedier part of Seattle in the early days, felt anything but grandiose. Still, Bezos and his talented CFO Joy Covey, who died in 2013 in a tragic bicycling accident, would talk my ear off about Amazon's fast growth (true) and the coming profitability (not true for many years) and the fact that few analog retailers understood what was happening and could make the needed changes to their business models (also true). While Amazon was small, Bezos thought big. He was most interested in systems and distribution, which he understood were the key to what he wanted to build. Having been a retail reporter, I could see that what he was selling had less to do with tech chops and more to do with how automated and data-driven Amazon could become. "You're not a tech company, you're a souped-up logistics company," I said to him once. He responded with that maniacal laugh.

My assessment became ever clearer on every visit to Amazon HQ. Its revenues rose with Bezos adding more and more products to the site, growing it into a marketplace for everything. Revenue rose to close to $16 million in 1996, which was impressive, except when compared to the $148 million the company made the next year and the $610 million it cleared the year after that. Despite concerns about lack of profitability and increasing pressures from analog retailers over not paying sales taxes (which Amazon finally did nationwide in 2017), it was obvious that Bezos had the kind of momentum that was needed to dominate the e-commerce sector. He was the pioneer in making online shopping a thing. There had been many attempts at doing this, including AOL's creation of a shopping product with all kinds of retail partners. It failed. Yet Bezos succeeded, carefully adding feature after feature after getting the first thing right. Layering delivery systems into the process was the most important part of the equation, as was employing the mathematical modeling he had used at the hedge fund.

As with Walmart, math always seemed to be at the heart of what Amazon was doing, and Bezos's focus on data was a critical element of this marriage of analog and digital. Unlike the Google guys, Bezos was dealing with real physical things, which made his challenge much harder. Clever marketing, low prices, and convenience clicked with consumers, and the stock of Amazon reflected its popularity, rising high on expectations that Bezos had yet to meet. This phenomenon was goosed in late 1998 when CIBC Oppenheimer analyst Henry Blodget raised his price target for Amazon.com, from $150 to $400.

"An investment in the shares clearly requires a strong stomach and a great deal of faith," wrote Blodget, who had expressed a shruggy it-could-happen attitude when I called him to ask how he could support such a call given Amazon's dicey spreadsheet. I was used to a suspension of real fundamentals by this time, but was gobsmacked nonetheless when the stock soared that day by nearly 20 percent and then on to $400 just weeks later. Blodget would later be permanently banned from the securities industry as part of an unrelated fraud settlement, but he was right about where Amazon was headed. It was like me to be the Eeyore of the digital age, but the math was not mathing for me, as it had not at AOL. I did not have the fake-it-until-you-make-it mindset that was clearly the only way to play this.

Amazon was headed up and to the right under Bezos's firm and strategic leadership, as he built moat after moat to stave off competitors old and new. Dynamic pricing always seemed to beat out other vendors. Then, eventually, Amazon's data could anticipate what you wanted before you did. As customers clicked the "Buy Now" button, warehouses spread around the world, while the technology inside those warehouses picked, packed, and addressed the goods with increasing efficiency. These moats protected what would become an impregnable castle. In fact, one of Amazon's many headquarters was an old hospital atop a Seattle hill that looked both foreboding and dominant. It was in that building that it became harder to get to the formerly always available CEO. Since Bezos was not as deeply insecure as many tech types, even if he was just as narcissistic, he had no problem cutting ties with anyone he did not need once the momentum got going.

Not that he did not strive to craft an image. Bezos was indeed changing, starting to shift from the finance and systems nerd to craft a wider-ranging image of a man with his finger on the pulse of the future. He rode around on a Segway at the TED conference. He pontificated on all manner of subjects. He met with smart men and invested craftily in the early rounds of companies, including putting $250,000 of his own money in Google at four cents a share. Most importantly, he started a business to realize his dream of putting humanity in space. This had been Bezos's obsession since he was in high school, when he reportedly imagined space colonies orbiting earth. By 2000, as he was flying higher financially, he quietly founded Blue Origin, a space flight company, to develop all manner of rockets and landing systems. And, presumably, space colonies orbiting Earth.

Rivals were soon legion. While still watching all the portal, communications, and software-focused companies, I found myself spending a lot of time tracking the explosion of e-commerce sites hot on the heels of Amazon's success. Money poured into startups like RedEnvelope, eToys, and Boo. Most of these ventures would prove to be ill-fated, incinerating the cash shoveled into them with astonishing alacrity. While Amazon and Bezos definitely skated close to the edge, most of the rest skated right into the crevasse to be lost forever. The decline of Boo, a British online retailer, was particularly striking. Boo ate up $135 million of VC money in only eighteen months. It finally launched in 1999 and was in bankruptcy within a year.

The immense greed combined with the overwhelming stupidity was a sight to watch.

But some got out alive. I was particularly happy for an online greeting card service called Blue Mountain Arts that exploded onto the scene with huge numbers of users sending cards digitally. Bluemountainarts.com had hardly any outside funding, advertising, or major distribution deals, and was an extension of a physical greeting-card business started in 1971 by Susan Polis Schutz and Stephen Schutz. Soon, Blue Mountain Arts attracted the attention of numerous suitors (including Amazon), with acquisition prices veering toward $1 billion. I had met its founders in 1998 while reporting on a profile of the company. The pair were unlikely Web types, with hippie personas and a lot of chill. They had started their business out of the back of a Volkswagen van in Colorado and didn't pay much attention to the fast-moving sector. Susan was particularly uninterested in the now frantic online markets and viewed them as so much silliness.

"The whole thing confuses me," she would often tell me, even though her son Jared was more savvy and hard charging. The family reminded me of the fictional Keatons in the 1980s hit *Family Ties*. I was not surprised that Susan called me for advice when she got a firm offer for Blue Mountain Arts from Excite at Home—which itself was an unholy merger of the second-string portal Excite with an Internet access scheme cooked up by venture capitalists. The offer was substantial: $430 million in shares and $350 million in cash. I rarely gave advice to anyone I covered and reminded her that I would have to report this business deal. Still, I had a soft spot for the sweet entrepreneur who had managed to catch the raging Internet tiger by the tail and was riding it merrily. Susan just wanted to draw sentimental cards and make the world happier by it. So having seen Blue Mountain's weak financials compared to its soaring valuation, I made a recommendation.

"Take as much cash as you can get," I told her. "Then, run fast for the hills." And that is just what she did, cashing out along with her family, including Jared, who created flower, candy, and cookie businesses as an adjunct to the online card business. Decades later, he would parlay his net worth of almost $125 million and savvy into a successful run for Congress and, later, the governorship of Colorado. My cut for my short career as an investment banker? For years, Susan unfailingly sent me a big box of cards, lemon cakes, and inspirational doodads, a gift which I would leave on the doorstep of whatever Internet executive I wanted to tweak that holiday.

I also spent a lot of time talking to other commerce-related companies that would thrive in the years to come, like Zappos, the online shoe retailer whose founder and CEO was an unusual entrepreneur named Tony Hsieh (who would later die in a fire under tragic circumstances related to drug use). With purchases of goods moving online, customers needed a better way to pay for them, and several tech companies popped up to respond to that need, including PayPal, which was founded in 1998, and its rival X.com, an online bank. One of X's founders was a quirky young man who had scored $22 million from the sale of his first company, an online yellow pages type business that he had ultimately lost control of. His name was Elon Musk.

No one had ever heard of Musk then, and he would be far down the tech hierarchy compared to Bezos, although later they would become fierce rivals in the space race. Musk did not initially clock in with me, and I hardly wrote about him when X merged with PayPal, a company filled with more promising entrepreneurs, like Max Levchin and Peter Thiel. At the time, Musk was just one of so many prospectors who had rushed into Silicon Valley in search of Internet gold. The only thing I can recall clearly about him at the time is that he liked cars. A lot. And he wanted to buy a pricey one when he cashed in.

As the nines in 1999 rolled over to zeroes, there were vague but headline-grabbing worries of Y2K disasters. The *Journal* even sent me to spend the turn of the century at Yahoo and E*Trade in case it all collapsed. Exactly nothing happened, of course, except I got to spend perhaps the least fun December 31 of my life drinking warm beer with taciturn Yahoo cofounder Dave Filo, a quintessential computer engineer who continued to enjoy *not* giving me any colorful quotes. I totally understood since we both wanted to be elsewhere.

The times were heady for stars like Steve Case, Jerry Yang, and most of all, Bezos. And for me, too. I was now regarded as one of the leading chroniclers of these larger-than-life figures of the new age. In 1999, *Industry Standard* magazine named me as "the writer who has most influenced public opinion about the Internet economy." I started getting huge offers from both news organizations and also Internet companies, which I turned down even though the Web ones would have made me extraordinarily wealthy. When I think back on it, I cannot easily explain why I did not cash in. I mean, I like money and did have a taste for entrepreneurship. But if I had to put my finger on it, it was because I did not want to work for anyone to whom I would become beholden. It was impossible for me not to say what I thought, which made me a bad employee. Going to work early for say, Amazon, would have been a prescription for disaster. That said, that $100 million would have been nice.

More to the point, there was something I valued more than making the next dirty dollar, and that was having kids. My professional and personal life were about to change, as I contemplated having a baby before my thirties ended. I've always wanted to have children, even though for most of my life, it was nearly impossible to imagine getting married and having children as a gay person in America. It wasn't that long ago that the raft of difficulties and discrimination was huge and the support among friends and family for creating my own future family was exactly nil.

Still, I cannot forget to this day being a college sophomore at Georgetown University and driving my powder-blue Volkswagen Bug convertible to an outlet mall deep in Virginia to buy some Christmas presents. While browsing at a Carter's discount store, I saw on the rack a striped, red-and-white onesie that I could not stop coming back to because the thought suddenly entered my brain that a baby I'd have someday would wear it. So, I paid $8.99 and took the onesie home and kept it with me in a small box, tags on, until Louie Swisher was born twenty years later. It fit him perfectly.

Oddly enough, at a party at gay portal PlanetOut in 1999, which my then wife, Megan, was running, I ended up having a long talk with Bezos about babies. He was excited about becoming a father for the first time, and it was nice to talk to someone who got it. While I doubt he remembers it, he was very thoughtful on the topic and peppered me with questions about how lesbians had children. While it seems quaint today to be that naïve, it was a bit of a unicorn endeavor then, so I ended up explaining the whole process, which was not as messy as most straight people thought. I walked him through sperm donation and insemination. To his credit, Bezos was not even slightly embarrassed, as many men were, and seemed to find the whole process fascinating. Logistics, I guess.

At one point, he asked me why I would use an anonymous donor versus someone I knew . . . like him. It was in no way an offer, but I joked back that while he was rich, certainly an attractive trait, he was too short and bald for my needs. Of course, he broke out into his famous laugh, and his chortling attracted the attention of the entire party. People turned and asked what we were talking about. I must have jokingly responded that Jeff had volunteered to be the donor of my child. We all had a good laugh. It was less funny when the first news of my pregnancy in late 2001 appeared in the *New York Post*'s Page Six gossip page, under the title, "Columnist Quiz: Who's Daddy?" The item was presumably leaked by someone at the party, speculating that the father of my child was some Internet mogul, and it specifically mentioned Bezos. It was typical of the kind of tasteless dreck that Rupert Murdoch's media empire churned out, always eager to get the words "lesbians" and "turkey basters" in the same sentence.

When the gossipmonger had called to confirm my fecundity, he asked who the father was. I replied that, as a journalist, I could never accept any donation over $25, so it was impossible that I was having a baby with anyone I covered. I offered that it was more likely one of Rupert Murdoch's sons. I mean, the sperm donor was anonymous, so it *could* have been. This was a silly and bizarre moment, of course, although it personally struck me for the first time that traditional media titans like Murdoch would find increasing reasons to attack the newer potentates.

There were signs everywhere of that, and such a narrative was helped by Bezos's relentless marketing, especially of himself and no other Amazon executive. From his humble beginnings only five years earlier, Bezos had gone on to be named *Time* magazine's Person of the Year in 1999. The cover featured a decidedly creepy shot of his smiling face encased in a box filled with packing peanuts, with text that declared, "E-commerce is changing the way the world shops."

Whether it was Amazon or Google—and later Facebook and Netflix—the business sides of traditional companies were fully aware of the looming threat, though they could not quite grok the disruption headed their way. It arrived like a nuclear blast with the twenty-first century, when Steve Case realized the dream he had spoken to me only years earlier. On January 10, 2000, AOL forked over $182 billion of its highly inflated stock and debt to buy Time Warner. The media giant owned Warner Bros., HBO, CNN, TBS, and Time Warner Cable, as well as *Time*, *People*, and *Sports Illustrated* magazines, while AOL had just 30 million subscribers to its largely dial-up service. Later, this acquisition would be dubbed by me as "the heist of the century."

No matter. The energy had so drastically shifted from the old to the new, personified by business leaders like Case and Bezos. What I did not foresee, even though every other column I wrote seemed to have the word "frothy" in it, was that it was always lightest before the dark. In the two years between the turn of the century and 2002, almost eight hundred Internet companies went belly-up as the so-called "dotcom bubble" burst. In

Amazon's first letter to shareholders after going public in 1997, Bezos had focused on the company's "established long-term relationships with many important strategic partners, including America Online, Yahoo!, Excite, Netscape, GeoCities, AltaVista, @Home, and Prodigy."

They'd all be dead or dying soon enough, except Bezos, who was feral enough to survive the coming cataclysm.

CHAPTER 6

The End of the Beginning

*If you do not change direction, you
may end up where you are heading.*

—LAO TZU

On January 11, 2000, the *Wall Street Journal* ran a story detailing how young upstart AOL swallowed the august media behemoth Time Warner. I like to call these types of articles "merger porn" since, like porn, they offer juicy details and extreme close-ups of two entities coming together.

The connection between this merger and sex was even more explicit when Time Warner's major shareholder and colorful entrepreneur Ted Turner declared that he had thumbs-upped the deal "with as much or more excitement and enthusiasm as I did on that night when I first made love some forty-two years ago."

Sounds awkward! Most importantly, the article nailed the situation in a way that I doubt was intended at the time. "Whatever happens, the deal has a powerful out-with-the-old feel and seems to represent with rare clarity one of those infrequent dividing lines between an industry's past and its future," it declared. See how the *Journal* reporters did that with a maximum of portentous clichés? Out with the old! In with the new! A dividing line between the past and the future! With the benefit of hindsight, all these years later, let me cut to the chase: The merger was a clusterfuck from the get-go.

In fact, I wrote a book about this entire debacle called *There Must Be a Pony in Here Somewhere*. While it was hundreds of pages, I can give you a quick synopsis: The Internet had bamboozled Time Warner, which had unsuccessfully spent years trying to figure out a digital strategy, and decided to trade it all for what would turn out to be nothing.

As I noted in the book's first chapter:

> The problem was AOL's business was soon to crater as that boom turned to bust, and its once lofty stock would become almost worthless. In this simplistic scenario, the trade of the century soon became known as the worst deal in history.
>
> This is most certainly the tale that has taken up residence in the stony prison of conventional wisdom: A wheezing and increasingly desperate traditional media company, scared of inevitable death (or worse still, irrelevance) in the hot swirl of a digital revolution, marries itself to the young, sexy and possibly sleazy starlet of the new-media society.
>
> Disaster ensues.

And how. At first, the aging media giant attempted to expand into cyberspace all by itself. Pre-merger flops included set-top boxes that consumers rejected as too complex; a highly touted and much fiddled with Pathfinder web site that debuted in 1994. The site was supposed to take over the Web the way Time Inc.

magazines like *People* and *Sports Illustrated* dominated. But Pathfinder had so many strategic changes that it culminated in a feeling of desperation that led executives to make some very bad choices.

But first, Time Warner made a good one. After losing tens of millions of dollars, the company announced the unsurprising news that it was shutting down Pathfinder in April of 1999. Still, Time Warner refused to admit defeat or even failure, trying to reassert, "This is an evolution, and it follows the way consumers have been using our sites," about what the *New York Times* called "its pioneering outpost in cyberspace." A dead planet is more like it—think Mercury, but glummer. And the planet was ruled by old media executives who perhaps lacked the DNA to make anything substantive happen. Over at News Corp, Rupert Murdoch had stubbed his toe many times. That included a particularly bad site called iGuide done in partnership with telco MCI that got "repositioned" in 1996. And the less said about Condé Nast's CondeNet the better.

So, I thought to myself: What awful idea was now populating the brain of hyper-competitive Time Warner CEO Jerry Levin, to try to pivot, as the millennium dawned and his kingdom was under siege by tech upstarts? Let me be clear, I love a good pivot, and one of my favorite things about covering Silicon Valley is the ability of tech entrepreneurs to move on from failure without a care.

That's because inside all kinds of failures are hidden successes to be found. My favorite example of this came from General Magic, which in 1994 released the Magic Cap (Communicating Applications Platform) operating system, offering concepts that were later incorporated in both the Apple iPhone and Google Android. I once compared Magic Cap's brilliant failure to inventing television in the 1880s. The shows were not there yet.

A spate of search engines died so that Google might thrive. If you squinted, AOL was an earlier Facebook, all about getting together, being together, delivering news. And on and on. Most of the failures were too early, supplanted because of timing or sometimes for not being creative enough. I have always maintained that the people who ultimately succeed are the creative ones. Microsoft was beating Apple in the early innings, but creativity is what kept Apple in the game.

Unfortunately, the AOL deal with Time Warner was about consolidation, not creativity. The executives envisioned a company that could handle all your digital and analog needs, whether it be media, communications, distribution, or commerce. As the holidays hit, AOL's Case and Time Warner's Levin were cuddled up—from a deal perspective—probably enjoying a toasty cup of hot chocolate in anticipation of the blockbuster announcement in ten days.

When the *Journal*'s editor Paul Steiger called me on Sunday, January 9, and told me that a merger was afoot and being run down by ace deal reporters, including Steve Lipin, I was surprised but not shocked. He asked me to check my sources at AOL for news, so I fired up my AOL software and started directly writing them via AIM, its instant messenger service. Since the top leaders followed me and I followed them back, I could see that they were all online, even though it was already late in San Francisco and the middle of the night back East. "We know," I typed into the boxes to them, figuring it would be more effective to bluff them into a confession rather than pussyfoot around. Immediately, there was the loud series of digital door slams, which was AOL's noise when someone closed out their IMs.

Luckily, one exec wrote back: "How did you find out?" This person offered no further details, and the response was by no means a confirmation the paper could use. Still, it did feel like doors closed that night as new ones were about to open. Thankfully, other (better) *Journal* reporters nailed down more details.

Which brings us to timing, which could not have been worse. Right as the group was high-fiving, the merger caused a major reflection by Wall Street and investors that perhaps the numbers underpinning all this were, to use a software term, vaporware. Soon enough, the deal would be followed by a wholesale decimation of the tech industry, as it became clear that the delta between valuation and financial performance in Internet concerns was far too wide to sustain and, really, laughable. AOL Time Warner's stock dropped 75 percent within two years of the deal's completion. It didn't help that executives on both sides warred and AOL's sometimes dicey accounting issues got more scrutiny by reporters and regulators.

Turner had much postcoital regret and would call Levin a "liar and a thief" after the CNN founder lost $7 billion in stock value by the end of 2002. (To quote Don Graham: "Ouch.") At one point, Turner showed up at the Time Warner offices, turned his pants pockets inside out, and declared, "I was robbed." On the fifth anniversary of his $1 billion pledge to the United Nations, he even said, "I went from no money to a pile of money, just as big as the World Trade Center . . . Then—just like the World Trade Center—Poof! It was gone."

I have no words for this crass analogy, but I wrote in my book that "this was, in short, a bad deal in search of a big scapegoat." Soon, repercussions rippled through the entire tech ecosystem as startup after startup closed down, stocks of tech companies limped, and the stars of the sector started to look a lot less starry. Frothy attitudes fell flat as venture firms pulled in their horns and cut and ran from the man-boys they once coddled. The fantastic parties, of course, ended abruptly. I remember thinking that a now long-dead startup probably wished it had not splurged to hire 1980s rock band Devo for a company mixer. Whip it *real* good.

Industry Standard magazine—aka the "newsmagazine of the Internet economy"—became the actual visual standard for the industry's contraction. Their issues on my shelf went from two inches thick at the height of the Web 1.0 boom to what looked like a very thin newsletter. It was a big jolt to a magazine that had sold more ad pages than any other in the U.S. in 2000. The year before, its editors had tried to hire me for an ungodly and undeserved salary—I think it was $1 million—and, despite the dizzying number, I thought the offer was an indication that the economics of the tech world had become untethered, and this was going to end badly.

I found myself weirdly disconcerted by the sudden drop, too. The column I wrote about the tech sector was called "Boom Town," which, meant as a joke, now felt painful. "Been watching the NASDAQ. Think we should change the name to 'Busttown'?" *Journal* managing editor Dan Hertzberg emailed me on November 30, 2000. Nice one, boss! But the mood was soon reflected in my annual end-of-year prediction column, one year after I guessed correctly that an Internet company would buy a media company:

Here's a rock-solid prediction for the Internet in 2001: Jeff Bezos will not be selected *Time*'s Person of the Year. Was it only a year ago that the founder of Amazon was beaming from the front of that magazine, an icon of the New Economy that had taken the world by storm? The choice of Bezos as a cover boy made complete sense at the time. He and other Young Turks on the Web had overturned the old order, sparked an electronic revolution and become impossibly rich.

Impossible, it turns out, was the operative word. Since then, the euphoria (and market capitalization) of the industry has been cut to shreds and some of its most prominent companies are in extreme distress. Few could have imagined that many of the brightest lights of Silicon Valley would lose most of their luster so suddenly.

Many of those old media types inside Time Warner were thrilled by the Web's stumble, and too many yammered on about how people were going to end their love of digital and return to the old and more normal ways. But there was no normal anymore. Even in those anti-digital times, I was still a believer in the essential idea and promise of the technical innovations that had burst on the scene at the end of the last century. I went full Churchill and dubbed the crash "the end of the beginning." Most importantly, it was in the ashes of this bust that the really important companies of the next era would emerge. The AOL–Time Warner deal was indeed a kind of Internet Rubicon: It stopped the stupid boom that needed stopping and ushered the nascent industry into maturity with a rough shove.

I was going to keep the faith and not declare tech dead,

unlike so many who did. Who cared if just-in-time delivery service Kozmo sucked? Someone would figure it out eventually. Music and movies and books and all the rest would still be relentlessly digitized. And the mix of technology and media that would someday enable consumers to gather information anytime and anywhere was still inevitable, even if delayed by the incompetent leaders of Time Warner. Over? Not a chance, and that was right when I decided to jump into the entrepreneurial pool myself and hoped not to drown.

Every metamorphosis in my career started with some bellyaching, and I'd already been bellyaching a lot to Walt about how the way I was working as a columnist was not working. While having a column in a major publication was the goal for most journalists, I felt trapped in a prison of expectations from a medium I barely believed in. Weekly ruminations by me seemed quaint. I wanted a daily soapbox to expectorate in small bursts and without the onerous exhaustion of numerous editors weighing in with often pointless changes.

I wanted to write what I knew based on careful reporting, the network of sources I'd built, and the expertise I'd acquired. I started calling it "reported analysis" to distinguish my take from the ill-informed punditry that had been littering the media landscape. "Reported analysis" meant I needed to break away from the "to be sure" conundrum that plagued me at the *Journal*. Editors were always asking me to get someone else to say in a quote what I could say on my own based on the reporting. In addition, they wanted me to always add a "to be sure" statement, in which I explained that even though my querying and number-crunching showed that some startup gave Ponzi schemes a good name, I needed to hedge by noting "to be sure, not everyone is so negative that this was an obvious flaming trash heap." Even when I *was* sure it was a flaming trash heap.

I also started dreading all the rote reporting work, like writing up earnings reports. I kept wondering why a computer couldn't do that work—which later happened; thank you, AI—and let humans focus on stories that readers did not know yesterday. I started opening the paper and circling the news that was not already widely known by the morning. The circles got ever fewer, with the *Journal*'s typically excellent longer features and investigations being the exception.

I continued to be testy at meetings in which well-meaning editors would discuss how to get "young" readers to read the paper, even as the *Journal* continued to downplay digital and planned a Saturday print edition. I kept thinking if it were up to me, I'd dump the printing presses and go fully digital. But our audience skewed older and whiter and liked their broadsheet. I hated our broadsheet and let it pile up in my living room, opting to consume as much information as I could online. I realized, in short, that I was and would always be a great reporter and a less good employee, which led me to the obvious conclusion that I wanted to have control of my work and my destiny. I longed to decide what to focus on and not spend time chasing or fending off the flood of bad ideas from those who had a stake in the old world. What I desired most boiled down to one thing: the ability to say no.

I also needed to deal with disclosures about my then wife, Megan Smith, who was a high-ranking executive at Google. I even suspended my column due to the issue and started writing another called "Home Economics" about all kinds of home gadgetry, like vacuums and digital toilets. And while I loved anything having to do with tinkering, and a hardware store is my safe space, the column was only a way station as I tried to think up my next route. Since Megan and I had placed an elaborate wall between us on our work, I wanted to offer an explicit disclosure that would explain that in plain English. I also wanted to give my readers the chance to respond if they had questions or concerns. The *Journal* was still caught in a one-way communication with its audience that I thought was long over. In many ways, the consumer had taken control of the content and was not inclined to give it back.

So, I called Walt and said we had to start something fresh and new. "When do we break out?" he asked.

To say I love Walt for that—and so much else—does not begin to express what his enthusiasm meant to me and how easy it would have been for him to stay where he was. But he had just undergone open-heart surgery for vascular issues that plagued his family—his father had a heart attack at fifty years old and Walt had one at fifty-one. This experience, combined with my own you-could-keel-over-at-anytime attitude, meant we both knew one thing clearly: We did not have the time to wait, and no one has that kind of time, in truth.

So, we had to break out. Or in, as it turned out. The landscape of digital content making at the time was still bloggy, with weak publishing tools and no real way to distribute beyond links on Google and Yahoo. As for ad sales and building an easy subscription business, forget it. That would come a bit later. In addition, the idea of raising money for our own digital-only content company seemed hard during what was a major downturn in the economy. We did not relish having to ask for money from the venture capitalists we covered. We had valid concerns that most

VCs would not respect the sanctity of real journalism when the going got tough. And the going always got tough.

Also, Walt had risen to become the most famous tech journalist of the era, and he and his platform were still wedded strongly together. As we noodled, we realized our first and best move was to use Walt's considerable clout to push the business leaders of the *Journal* to let us launch our new venture as an internal skunkworks.

That term comes from tech and refers to a tight group of innovators who steal away from a mothership and create a smaller, faster-moving pirate ship. Our hope was to create a crack team of mouthy malcontents willing to innovate news delivery and host live events. We wanted to launch a digital-only publication with attitude and personality, and without all the meddling from those who love to meddle in a news organization. Our chief concern was that while Internet investors would be more tolerant of losing scads of dough, a reliably profitable company like the *Journal* was not.

Walt and I kept plotting and soon decided that we would flip our script and start with events first. It seemed easier to make money in that business since events only required a deposit on a hotel space and our Rolodex. Plus, events could profit from one of the more resilient facts we relied on: Techies like to gather and swagger. And we hated what the competition was doing, including events that the *Journal* had put on, which felt either like fanboy gatherings (complicit) or sponsor-driven pitches (conflicted). Worst of all, these conferences were boring. This was an arena that needed disruption. Walt and I approached our event as "live journalism," where you could see what we did in real time and remove the mystery that journalists tended to like more than they cared to admit. Another bonus of being live was it was harder for us to be disrupted by digital.

We toured the Dow Jones empire and consulted the powers that be and then mostly sidelined them, except for the ad staff that was eager to have a new product to sell. As a contractor we hired our invaluable producer, Lia Lorenzano-Kennett, who had run the most important tech event at the time, called Agenda. Then we added people she worked with, including Jill Pendergast and Meg Burns, both of whom would stay with us for two decades. Luckily for us, Steiger loved the idea and protected us on the editorial side. Our plan was to launch in 2002, but the economy was still bad enough that the *Journal* delayed our late May outing out of an abundance of caution.

I might have objected, but the timing was good for me, too, since I was pregnant, with a May 15 due date. Louie arrived exactly on time and Pink's "Get This Party Started" became his theme song. Playing that upbeat song on a loop, I combined breastfeeding and making plans for total journalism tech world dominion from my bed, since an unexpected C-section laid me up for weeks. I later strapped Louie into a car seat, as Walt and I drove to Rhode Island to visit TED (Technology Entertainment Design) conference creator Richard Saul Wurman for advice. TED was our touchstone as the most creative, fun, and revelatory event we'd ever attended. Richard listened to our plans and asked if we had a name for the venture. Walt and I had thrown around some possibilities but hadn't landed on something we loved. Fortunately, Richard fixed that. "Just call it 'D,'" he said flatly, as Louie played nearby. "It stands for whatever you want. Delightful. Demanding. Disruptive."

We liked that last one a lot and went with *D: All Things Digital*, with our conference being called the same. While it seems obvious now, the idea at the time was not. Outfits like the *New York Times* (which would later create events copying ours) criticized our gathering in an article saying that it was wrong to invite speakers to an event and then charge the audience. To my mind, that is exactly what a newspaper did: Please let us interview you for our paper . . . and then charge readers for that.

We also set strict rules to protect our journalistic integrity. We would not pay any speaker or provide for their travel. We would not share questions in advance or pull our punches. We would not apologize for pissing off sponsors or give them any purchase onstage for their money. No one could hide on our stage, including us. As a result, the *ATD* conference (which later would be renamed Code) quickly became the place to prove your mettle as a tech leader.

We also thought a lot about our own compensation and the changing nature of being paid for entrepreneurial efforts. It was hard to move *Journal* managers on these issues, since deep down, they felt that every reporter was fungible—even if it was not true. Our first conference made a $1 million profit easily. And while it had sprung directly out of our heads and was our initiative, *Journal* management hardly acknowledged the achievement. The publisher told me it was part of my job and that it would be impossible under budget constraints to get a larger salary based on our massive contribution, given the company's then razor-thin profits.

Obviously, hosting events was not part of my job, and I called Walt and asked: "Did you at least get the flowers?" There were no flowers, so we decided not to organize and host again unless the *Journal* shared profits, which finally happened in the third year of *ATD*. The *Journal* agreed to a one-third split for Walt, me, and Dow Jones. In retrospect, giving me a raise would've been a much less costly business move by the nation's leading business journal.

Remarkably, the company was more concerned with jealousy from other staffers than encouraging more innovation. They never stopped grumbling over giving us money we had generated ourselves. In post-event polls, speakers and audiences consistently said they came for us and not the brand, which ranked near the bottom of every single survey. Walt and I already knew this intuitively and we didn't care who it pissed off. We took to calling some executives who had been resistant at first but then later took credit for our successes "The Weasels." One even dubbed himself the "Father of D," which was the source of endless mockery from us, since he was not even a distant cousin once removed.

As with the tech industry, this was the end of the beginning for us, too. In high school, I was not much of a science student, but my biology teacher once tried to make me understand it with one simple rule: Everything is always on its way to something else. And so were we, persistent in our goal of shaking up journalism regularly. We had both been bitten by the innovation bug that required that we think different.

This is why it made sense that one of our very first guests onstage for the inaugural conference in 2003 was Apple founder Steve Jobs. Often bored by the typical questions he was asked, Jobs welcomed the chance to mix it up in our soon-to-be famous red chairs, which we actually debuted at the second *D* event in 2004. And he always gave as good as he got. Sometimes he obfuscated and even fibbed (denying he was working on a phone when he was right in the middle of doing so, for example). But Jobs was a charmer and came back year after year, enjoying the heat and the challenge. In 2007, he shared our stage for a historic joint interview with his longtime nemesis Bill Gates. This extraordinary meeting of tech's two greatest pioneers revealed both their deep rivalry and enduring respect. It would turn out to be one for the ages.

And it almost didn't happen.

CHAPTER 7

The Golden God

For the past 33 years, I have looked in the mirror every morning and asked myself: "If today were the last day of my life, would I want to do what I am about to do today?" And whenever the answer has been "No" for too many days in a row, I know I need to change something.

—STEVE JOBS, STANFORD UNIVERSITY
COMMENCEMENT SPEECH, 2005

Here are two things to know about Steve Jobs: First, he was always acutely aware that life was finite; second, he could never resist a chance to tweak Bill Gates.

I'll admit I enjoyed both things about him—that is, until I was standing backstage at the *ATD* conference in 2007. Jobs was doing a solo interview onstage with Walt Mossberg, and just like that, Jobs' patented smirky smile (or was it a smiley smirk?) was on full display. Uh oh, I thought, something was about to go down.

Walt dove into how Jobs had pulled Apple from the brink of bankruptcy a decade earlier (with an important financial assist from Microsoft's Gates, by the way). Since then, Jobs' company had become one of the most important creators for the Seattle software giant's products, which prompted the following exchange.

Walt: So, that makes you an enormous Windows software developer.

Steve: We are.

Walt: How does that make you feel?

Steve: We've got cards and letters from lots of people that say iTunes is their favorite app on Windows. It's like giving a glass of ice water to somebody in hell.

Ice. Water. In. Hell. The moment those words came out of his mouth, I had just one thought: Steve Jobs just fucked us.

"There's that Steve Jobs humility," said Walt, looking slightly stricken. I knew exactly what was going through Walt's head. Months earlier, we had managed to put together the interview of our lives, convincing Jobs and Gates, tech's most iconic pair, to appear together on the same stage. Now we were just hours away from that historic event and Jobs was not playing nice. Incredibly, other than at marketing events, Jobs and Gates had never sat together to chew over their deeply complex and competitive relationship that had defined the modern digital landscape. Their joint struggle with the world and each other was arguably the story of tech, as each took a different path to introducing consumers to the digital universe.

Walt had carefully laid the groundwork to get the pioneers to sit for a joint interview, and it was no small effort. Jobs and

Gates shared a longtime antipathy. Gates thought Jobs to be precious in his approach, and Jobs thought Gates had little respect for product excellence. But the two also shared an obvious admiration for each other. Gates had built Microsoft into a business colossus that Jobs was indeed jealous of. And Gates had never reached the status Jobs had as the golden god who melded art and science, creativity and utility, beauty and design. Jobs was what passed for a cool kid in Silicon Valley terms, while Gates was a geek's geek. If both died on the same day, one observer told me, Gates's obituary would begin by noting that he was "the world's richest man" while Jobs' would begin with the words "tech's greatest visionary." In short, Gates had spent his life being the world's wealthiest Goofus to Jobs' elegant Gallant.

That's why Walt approached Jobs first, knowing that Gates would jump at the chance, while Jobs would play hard to get. More than any other journalist, Walt had developed deep relationships with both, especially since he essentially had become an important arbiter of the products they released. Once Jobs said yes first, Gates quickly followed. *ATD* did not typically put out press releases, but as soon as both were in, we did, figuring that once the news of the event was public, it would be harder for either to back out.

In addition to the joint appearance, we offered separate solo interview blocks to each company. Steve Ballmer, who had become CEO of Microsoft in 2000, grabbed their slot. Jobs fronted the Apple session since only he could talk about new products and business specifics. These nuts-and-bolts interviews would allow us to focus the joint interview on loftier and more forward-looking questions. Our hope was to avoid some of the internecine squabbles that the pair had become well known for over the decades. Big thoughts and big ideas and no trash talk, we had joked to Microsoft's Frank Shaw and Apple's Katie Cotton, the comms pros who had the unenviable job of wrangling these titans.

But now, by Jobs, during his solo session, referring to Microsoft as "hell," he was basically implying that Gates, who ran the joint, was Satan. Of course, the dig immediately got back to Gates, who skulked into the green room in an agitated state. Jobs had publicly pantsed him once again and he did not like it one bit.

After Walt wrapped up the one-on-one, Jobs headed to the green room and entered with a "hey what's up?" attitude and a shit-eating grin. Walt and I had scheduled a short meeting for the six of us to go over how we envisioned the upcoming joint session—without flagging the possible questions, which we never did for any speaker, even for these two. As we discussed format, Gates glumly limited his responses to yes and no, while Jobs took jaunty to an obnoxious level. Walt, Katie, Frank, and I traded looks of concern that this was going to be a disastrous interview. We persevered and asked Gates a question about some small detail. Suddenly he blurted out: "Why would I know that? I run hell."

We all froze. Except Jobs, who was holding a very cold bottle of water that was drenched with condensation. He extended his hand with the water bottle toward Gates. "Let me help you," Jobs said playfully. And that, thankfully, broke the very ice that he had made.

We had finished our backstage confab when I asked the two to take a joint photo. That year's conference was sponsored in part by Kodak, which was using new tech and capturing each speaker in high resolution. Despite some resistance, Gates agreed to pose with Jobs. "This is for history," I said to both. The image is indeed iconic, with the pair appearing from the sternum up. Gates stands on the left with messy hair, wire-rimmed glasses, and a button-down striped shirt. Jobs is on the right, a couple of inches taller, hair trimmed, in his wire-rimmed glasses and black turtleneck. Gates is smiling, showing his teeth, while Jobs' lips are closed in a familiar smirky smile.

Minutes later, the two walked onto the conference stage and the audience broke into a standing ovation. Both Jobs and Gates reacted with surprise and even became emotional. I think neither had deeply thought about how closely aligned they would be for all of eternity. But not yet, since Jobs could not resist the tweak. Early in the interview, I threw a softball, asking them both: "What's the greatest misunderstanding about your relationship?" The smiley smirk again curled at the edges of Jobs' mouth, as he deadpanned: "We've kept our marriage secret for over a decade now." The crowd loved it, although Gates looked uncomfortable, caught between wanting to roll with the obvious sexual undertone "hey we're gay" joke in order to not seem uncool and being, well, uncool. Jobs laughed along with the audience. Gates did not.

Gates did muster up some sweetness later. Despite always having a hard time with the heartfelt parts, Gates gestured to Jobs and noted: "It's been fun to work together. I kind of miss some of the people who aren't around anymore. People come and go in this industry. It's nice when somebody sticks around and has some context for all the things that have worked and not worked." While Gates had always been overly aggressive in business and pushed Microsoft in ways that would attract much-deserved scrutiny, one of his most enduring character-istics was a deep love of learning. This admirable trait would come to define the next chapter of his life, which he dedicated to charitable endeavors related to health and climate change via the Gates Foundation. Gates and I had a prickly relationship through most of the time that I covered Microsoft's weak-sauce Internet-focused efforts, but once he stepped away from the company in 2008, he became much more willing to listen than overtalk. He grew to understand the much longer game he was in and could impact.

Jobs almost never lost the idea that this was a very short life and that eternity was very long. And now, despite making a remarkable recovery from a cancer scare years earlier, he had mortality on his mind more than ever. He looked directly at Gates and took stock of their long history. "You know when Bill and I first met each other and worked together in the early days, generally, we were both the youngest guys in the room," Jobs commented. "I'm about six months older than he is, but roughly the same age. And now when we're working at our respective companies—I don't know about you—I'm the oldest guy most of the time. That's why I love being here."

Jobs then looked at Walt, who was eight years older and already white-haired. The audience laughed and Jobs joined them. Always a good sport, Walt responded, "Happy to oblige." Jobs continued speaking about his relationship with Gates.

And then, he delivered his famous one-more-thing. "I think of most things in life as either a Bob Dylan or Beatles song," Jobs said in perhaps one of the more wistful moments I ever saw him in. "And there's that one line in a Beatles song, 'You and I have memories longer than the road that stretches out ahead.'" He paused for exactly the right amount of time, the consummate performer, and then added: "And that's clearly true here." He gestured to Gates with a little wave. The audience broke into an audible "*Awww*," and then began applauding. Gates's eyes darted around, avoiding eye contact with all of us. Walt and I stood to signal that was the (perfect) end to the interview. Gates and Jobs shook hands and then stood together.

As the *ATD* crowd again rose to its feet, none of us in the room knew that Jobs would be gone less than five years later. His death would resonate in ways that are still being felt, and I don't say that lightly. Jobs was no angel, and both his personal and business lives were littered with examples of a man of many faults. Those who covered him earlier and more closely than I did, labeled this "the reality distortion field" that Jobs was able to weave over the company and himself. Still, he represented a consistent excellence when it came to making products, a prescience into possible negative consequences of what his company was making, a regard for design as an equal to tech, and a critical ability to envision the future in terms of both promise and problems. Jobs deserved the many kudos he got, especially as one Internet mogul after another showed through moves both petty and venal over time that they always fell short.

Unlike a lot of journalists, I was not a Jobs fanboy. We often argued about things and disagreed intensely. Once, he came up to me at an event in San Francisco in 2010 after he had debuted the Apple's Ping social network. He had described the network onstage as "sort of like Facebook and Twitter meet iTunes," a confusing launch that concluded with Chris Martin of Coldplay singing a trio of songs including "Viva La Vida," whose lyrics are about a king admitting regret. Afterward in the demo area, Jobs asked me what I thought of Ping. "It sucks and it's going to be a failure and, most of all, Chris Martin hurts my ears," I replied. He grimaced. Martin was a friend of his. But after a few back-and-forths, Jobs said, "You're probably right." He acknowledged that Apple was following in the social space and not leading, a fact he hated as much as he hated Facebook and Myspace.

I can tell you very few figures in positions of power like Jobs ever admitted even the slightest mistake to me that readily. Maybe it helps that he didn't have to do it that much. His career had very few duds and a nearly unblemished record of spot-on product choices. In the half-dozen public interviews that Walt and I did with him from 2003 until his death in 2011, he touted many of these inventions, often well before they were in the hands of consumers. Ping was the outlier. Most Apple products are well made, meticulously designed, and work beautifully. Some tech innovators focus on the product and others focus on the consumer. Jeff Bezos, for example, approached Amazon with an astonishing consumer sensibility. He'd do anything for the customer—almost to a fault. But Jobs pushed Apple to be more of a product-driven culture.

Other companies didn't seem to care about either the consumer or the product. It sucks when people settle for an uninspiring product. Facebook comes to mind. These companies tend to see themselves as utilities. We all need electricity, so it doesn't have to be beautiful or delightful. That's why the electric company gets away with draping ugly wires all over beautiful cities, ruining the view. But I truly appreciate and enjoy my Apple products, which almost always contained both a chip and an idea. Of all the ideas Jobs touted, mobility and wireless were the most significant.

In 1998, I had a revelation about the next move in the technology revolution: "I snipped my copper umbilical cord one sunny weekday not long ago," I wrote in the *Wall Street Journal.* "Canceling my land-line phone account, cutting off service to my home for good, and rendering the telephones that had long sat on tables in every room as useless as my closeted bread machine, I took the final step in a lifelong attempt to free myself from the wires that tethered me. Casting my fate to the heavens, quite literally, I decided to go wireless. Completely wireless. All wireless, all the time, everywhere." That was easier said than done, of course, as I fiddled through a series of mobile devices that were not quite ready to navigate the ecosystem of programs and services to which I needed to be connected. Apple had also missed the boat with its ill-fated Newton personal digital assistant device that debuted in 1993 and was DOA soon after. Jobs dumped the Newton when he returned to the troubled company in 1997, eleven years after his initial ouster at Apple by a board that did not believe in him.

But by 2001, Jobs had made a big splash with the iPod and then begun to ruminate on the iPhone. The original concept started out as a tablet with a stylus, which is what a lot of companies were working on at the time. At the 2010 *ATD* conference, Jobs divulged to Walt and me that "I had this idea of getting rid of the keyboard and asked my folks if we could." As Jobs put it, "We said if you need a stylus, you've already failed." The team came back with a reimagined tablet—basically an early iPad—which Jobs promptly tabled. "I thought, my God, we could build a phone out of this," he said.

My God, indeed. Within a month of our Gates-Jobs interview, the first iPhone would be released to the public for $499 and a two-year contract with AT&T. Jobs had announced its arrival on January 9, 2007, at the MacWorld keynote in San Francisco. "We're going to make some history together today," he said. It was not an overstatement, although it would be twenty-four minutes into the presentation before he unveiled the stubby little device. "After today I don't think anyone is going to look at these phones in the same way," he said. He was right, even though up until that announcement, Jobs had repeatedly denied that Apple was even working on a phone. At *D3* in 2004, I had jokingly told him to cook me up an "iPod phone," and he replied, "Well, that's a hard problem," to which I said, "You're smart," to which he said, "Isn't it funny a ship that leaks from the top?"

Obviously, Apple was already working away on a phone, but Jobs kept up the canny cat-and-mouse act. He was nothing if not an entertaining fabulist, telling Walt onstage at *D6* in 2006 that he had absolutely no plans to create a mobile phone. Jobs explained that one obstacle was working with a telecom company, which required jumping through hoops. "I don't like going through orifices," he joked, comparing telco giants to sphincters. A year later, he had managed to pass through the orifice in a major deal with AT&T. When we pointed out his deception, Jobs shrugged. So, we shrugged, too. Because nothing mattered but the phone he held in his hand, which was about as perfect as it got. While many have argued that other companies, from Samsung to Microsoft to Nokia, could have made this critical mobile leap to app-driven smartphones with multi-touch screens and a real web browser, no company had the combination of personality, design sense, and pure pushiness that would make Apple the dominant global hub technology.

By 2010, Apple's market valuation would surpass Microsoft's, a major milestone. A week later, Jobs was back on the *ATD* stage and I asked him if he had a thought or two about that. "For those of us who have been in the industry a long time, it's surreal," he responded. "But it's not why any of our customers buy our product. Remember what we're doing and why we're doing it. Sometimes you just have to pick the things that look like they're going to be the right horses moving forward. We're trying to make great products. Have courage of our convictions . . . [Customers] pay us to make those choices. If we succeed, they'll buy them, and if we don't, they won't."

This was an utterly different attitude than most companies, who valued the ability to pivot endlessly, too often reaching for ideas that were determined not by quality but by hierarchy. "The best ideas have to win," Jobs insisted over and over to me. He utterly rejected the idea of speed (move fast) and destruction (break things). He believed in working for as long as you needed to get the design and technology right, which was one of Apple's persistent characteristics.

Former Apple chief design officer Jony Ive reminisced about how Jobs operated, at my final Code conference in 2022. "One of the huge challenges particularly amongst large groups is that when you're talking about an idea, often the thing that is easiest to talk about—that is measurable, that's tangible—are the problems," Ive said. "And he was masterful at keeping people focused on the actual vision of the idea. He had a wonderful reverence for the creative process."

Jobs was also at the forefront of media, having bought Pixar in 1986 from George Lucas. Jobs was also deeply interested in newspapers, music, books, and more. At the 2005

ATD, Jobs turned to the audience and asked, "How many of you have heard of podcasts?" Guess how many people raised their hands? No one. Jobs continued, "Okay great. So let me start at the beginning and tell you what this is all about. Podcasting is a word that's a concatenation of iPod and broadcasting. Put together—podcasting." The best he could do at the time was to describe podcasting as *"Wayne's World* for radio." He explained that anybody could record a show and broadcast it out on the Internet for fans who would download the show from their computer to their iPod. Jobs concluded, "It's getting very exciting."

And, unlike most CEOs in Silicon Valley, he contemplated the impact of technology and new media on society. He liked journalism—at least in theory, although in practice he was a master manipulator of the press. Still, take Jobs saying this: "One of my beliefs very strongly is that any democracy depends on a free healthy press. We all know what's happened to economic businesses. News gathering and editorials are important. I don't want to descend into a nation of bloggers."

Compare that with Elon Musk—who might have been the natural inheritor of Jobs' status—tweeting on March 23, 2023, that all press inquiries to Twitter, the microblogging site he bought, would receive a poop emoji in response. (More on Musk later. Obviously.) Suffice it to say that this is something Jobs never would have done and, in fact, would have abhorred. I am also certain Jobs would have despised Musk in his current incarnation.

Perhaps most importantly, Jobs thought a lot about privacy. This quote is from the 2010 *ATD* conference, which I tried to trim down, but gave up because it's worth reading in its entirety:

> Silicon Valley is not monolithic. We've always had a very different view of privacy than some of our colleagues in the Valley. For example, we worry a lot about location in phones. Before any app can get location data, we make it a rule that they have to ask. We ask: "This app wants to use your location data; is that all right with you?" Every time they want to use it, we ask. We do a lot of things like that to ensure that people understand what these apps are doing. . . . A lot of people in the Valley think we're really old-fashioned about this, and maybe we are. But we worry about this. Privacy means people know what they're signing up for in plain English and repeatedly. That's what it means. I'm an optimist. I believe people are smart and some people want to share more data. Ask them. Let them know precisely what you're going do with their data. That's what I think.

To my mind, this kind of thinking made Jobs the most consequential figure of the modern tech age, as he daisy-chained his way from the desktop computer to the laptop to the iPod to the iPhone and to the iPad. Jobs did not just transform tech devices; he transformed music and movies and communications and photography. He envisioned then oversaw the creation of a series of tech that was intuitive, while gliding on innovations that were inevitable.

But, over those critical years—perhaps the most productive

of his life—Jobs was dying. It was in that interview in 2010 that I decided not to ignore what was apparent to everyone in the audience: While he had rallied, Jobs was now declining physically in a much more dire way. But as rail-thin and sallow as he was, he still exuded excitement over what was to come, even as he stressed the immutable values he would never abandon. I recall being struck that Jobs was so full of life, even as it was visibly seeping away from him, that I had to ask: "What do you imagine the next ten years of your life is going to be about?"

He was quiet at first and I could feel the crowd hold its breath, not quite believing I had asked a dying man such a question. "Um, you know . . ." Jobs said and paused. And then, much to my surprise, he addressed an issue we had previously clashed about: how he had manhandled a media organization when it got hold of an iPhone prototype. I had thought Apple's actions were vaguely thuggish and had told him so, while Jobs regarded the journalist as a thief.

"This is probably a bad example, but I am going to use it. When this whole thing with Gizmodo happened, I got a lot of advice from people who said, 'You gotta just let it slide. You shouldn't go after a journalist because they bought stolen property and they tried to extort you. Apple's a big company now. You don't want the PR. You should let it slide,'" he said. "And I thought deeply about this and I ended up concluding that the worst thing that could possibly happen as we get big and we get a little more influence in the world is if we change our core values and start letting it slide. I can't do that. I'd rather quit."

Jobs was just building up a head of steam on this topic, which was more about him as a human and as an entrepreneur than about a stolen phone. "We have the same values now as we had then. Maybe we are a little more experienced and certainly more beat up. But the core values are the same. We come into work wanting to do the same thing today as we did five or ten years ago, which is build the best products for people," said Jobs, noting that getting emails from satisfied customers fueled him daily. "That's what kept me going five years ago and that's what kept me going ten years ago when the doors were almost closed. And it's what will keep me going five years from now whatever happens. So, I don't see why you have to change if you get big." In other words, I won't go changing to try and please you, which is a piece of advice I would think about for myself and my career many times after hearing it from him. Changing, for sure, but with certain values and mainstays that would never alter.

Of all the big products that Jobs introduced, none was more consequential than the iPhone, which impacted everyone and everything. While there had been other phones, Apple's version was a pioneer that allowed the introduction of a spate of other mobile-oriented digital companies including Airbnb (2008), Uber (2009), and Instagram (2010). The iPhone would also force larger entities like Facebook to drastically shift their business models or shift around it, as Google would in 2008 with the introduction of its Android platform.

I would always try to figure out how Jobs reinvented products over and over again, since they were not derivative, as so many inventions were, and expanded the market rather than contracted it. Thanks to the iPhone, the company would ten times its value under CEO Tim Cook (while also gaining far too much power over the app ecosystem). I cannot underscore how hard it was to conceive of a massive idea like this at that moment in time, especially since Apple was facing an already entrenched market that was dominated by Samsung, Nokia, and others.

In one interview with us, Jobs let loose with what seemed like a hokey bromide that I had heard from far too many in tech, who never seemed to deliver on the promise as much as deliver for themselves. "Let's stop looking backward," Jobs declared. "It's all about what happens tomorrow. Let's go invent tomorrow." Of course, the cynical journalist in me thought such statements were largely meaningless. But when Jobs said it, I actually believed it. Maybe I, too, had slipped into Jobs' reality distortion field, but the more time I spent with him, the more I thought what he said made sense and his intensity was at his core. One of the many things I thought his critics got wrong about Jobs was that he was passionless and cold. My take: As an entrepreneur, Jobs was too passionate, which led him to push hard—and sometimes too hard—on what he believed in. Over time, he and what he represented would prove to be a rarity.

Near the end of his life, Jobs spoke about how people consumed media. "The media industry is kind of screwed since the best technologists are working for people like me and not you," he told me and many others, at a meeting with Rupert Murdoch's executives. He had been invited at the behest of Murdoch, since he and Jobs had become friends of a corporate sort, with Jobs determined to liberalize the old media dragon and, presumably, Murdoch determined to figure out the magic of Apple. There and elsewhere, Jobs noted that tech would become the new gatekeepers of media in the digital age. He had already moved in that direction earlier than anyone in Silicon Valley and he was not stopping. Jobs had sent the warning much earlier at an unforgettable event when he introduced the iPod in 2001 at the Town Hall auditorium at Apple's old headquarters. As he pulled the small and elegant device out of his jeans pocket, he uttered the memorable marketing slogan: *"1,000 songs in your pocket."*

As usual, Jobs was spot on: Media was screwed.

CHAPTER 8

Sillywood

Millions are to be grabbed out here and your only competition is idiots. Don't let this get around.

—HERMAN MANKIEWICZ

What do you get if you cross Hollywood with Silicon Valley?

Sillywood.

Anyway, that's the way the dumb joke went back when people thought there would be a copacetic marriage between the mandarins of digital and the moguls of the entertainment industry. Separated by only 350 miles along the I-5 highway spine of California, these two power centers of the modern age seemed primed for synergy. As it turned out, they would struggle from the start to find common ground as old media took hit after hit—and not the good kind—to its business model. Meanwhile the tentacles of tech spread ever outward. From the music, newspaper, book, and radio industries to the movie and television studios of Burbank, no medium escaped the inevitable march of digitalization. Each got disrupted and sometimes destroyed.

Like Silicon Valley, Hollywood was an industry built on

tech—late-nineteenth- and early-twentieth-century tech. Most historians credit William Kennedy-Laurie Dickson with the design of the first motion picture camera. Sadly, for Dickson, when it came time to fill out the 1891 patent application for the Kinetograph, his boss Thomas Edison decided to put his own name down as the inventor, a classic tech-bro move. Over the next century, movie technology evolved. Sound was added, then color. Video revolutionized TV. Cameras got smaller. Special effects got bigger. Digitalization transformed almost every aspect of the process, including cameras and editing systems and distribution. Most storytellers disdained these changes to the art form, but the smart ones knew that resistance was futile.

A perfect example was an interview I did with George Lucas, one of the most successful moviemakers of all time, largely due to his creation of the *Star Wars* universe at Lucasfilm. Lucas was also deeply tech savvy, the only American ever to receive both the National Medal of Arts *and* the National Medal of Science and Technology. They were deserved. He seeded a graphics group at his company that would be spun off in 1986 as a computer animation studio called Pixar. The big funder and majority shareholder was, of course, Steve Jobs. To say Lucas, who operated his businesses in the Bay Area, was the perfect ambassador for the intersection between these two worlds seemed obvious.

The number of tech nerds who revered him was huge and included fanboy Chad Hurley, the cofounder of YouTube. So, it was Chad and other YouTube executives who waited with me by the door of my annual conference in 2007 in Southern California, late in the evening, for the filmmaker to arrive. When he did, I introduced Hurley to Lucas as the YouTube guy. As much as Hurley's face lit up, Lucas's reaction could not have been less thrilled. "You're ruining storytelling with your service," he told Chad flatly. "What you do is like throwing puppies on a freeway."

Oh. That.

Lucas continued to discuss the merger between technology and storytelling in a wide-ranging interview the next day with Walt and me. "Painting, music, any kind of art form is essentially technological. The most important part is to be able to communicate emotions. That is the key to what we do," Lucas said. "Digital technology is a tool. Whatever you do, it's going to get abused. Sound was abused, color was abused, everything gets abused. But that's just the nature of human nature: When you get a new toy, you want to use it until it breaks, and then you start to calm down."

He was anything but calm about Internet video, and its leading service, YouTube. Cue the dead puppies: "There are two forms of entertaining. Circus is random. And voyeuristic. It's basically what you see on YouTube now. I call it feeding Christians to the lions. The movie term is throwing puppies on a freeway. It's very easy. You sit there and watch and see what happens. You don't have to write anything, you don't have to do anything, you just sort of watch it happen, and it's interesting. Then you get to art. Art is where a person contrives the situation and tells a story, and hopefully that story reveals the truth behind the facts. Storytelling is trying to come up with an idea that is insightful in terms of giving you a different insight into how things work or is amusing."

Lucas was one of the more insightful and prescient players in entertainment—disliking much of what was happening but understanding what was coming and using the new tools to his advantage. Those who would thrive were able to understand what technology could do to aid storytelling, and also what it could not do. What was most important was to not be cowed by the way Silicon Valley depicted what it was doing as akin to magic, with themselves as invincible wizards. That was perfectly articulated in 2011 by one of the Valley's most manipulative thaumaturges, Marc Andreessen, who asserted with both threat and certainty that "software is eating the world." It was an understandable feint to try, especially when he and other techies had become so fantastically wealthy creating tools to make digital content and had begun to control the means of distribution of media, too.

Remember my prediction that everything that could be digitized would be? And so it was and continues to be true in media, perhaps more than any part of the business and social ecosystem impacted by tech over the last twenty-five years. While the sloppy collapse of the Time Warner and AOL merger seemed a respite from the encroachment of the fleeced geeks on the cashmere-clad princes of media, it was only a momentary stumble, a pause of a tsunami of change that would soon resume unabated. Not that the media princes understood that. In late 2003, as the company moved into a glossy eighty-story tower in Manhattan's Columbus Circle, the board of AOL Time Warner decided to remove AOL from the name of the company. The new CEO, Richard Parsons, released a statement: "We believe that our new name better reflects the portfolio of our valuable businesses and ends any confusion between our corporate name and the America Online brand name for our investors, partners and the public."

I like Parsons well enough, and he certainly was a competent media executive. Still, I nicknamed him, "the non-carbonated beverage," for being for the merger until he was against it and then smoothly taking over from the tarnished Gerald Levin in 2002 and promptly pretty much ignoring the tech revolution. In other words, Parsons went down easy and did not cause the troops he commanded any gaseousness. Given what was coming, the company might have been better off with a more frantic leader, who better anticipated the future. Instead, the executives of the industry dearly hoped the Internet revolution had died, especially after the crash of the tech stocks and washout of AOL. They had doubled down on that theory, with the earlier lawsuits waged by the Recording Industry Association of America and the band Metallica against Napster, a peer-to-peer file sharing service that allowed users to download copyrighted music, cofounded by Sean Parker (who would later be a key Facebook investor). Napster was shut down in 2001, to the cheers of the music industry and artists, proclaiming, "So glad that's over!"

Using the courts to push back the inevitable had worked once, so in 2007, Viacom sued Google over copyright violations on YouTube, demanding $1 billion in damages. But Google had tried to lessen the problem by taking down material anytime media companies contacted them, which other tech companies had not done. It was enough to protect them; regardless, I was often on the end of unconvincing explanations by tech-ignorant CEO Philippe Dauman about why Viacom would win the suit, which it did not. Eventually, Viacom settled for nothing. It was laughable and expensive and, really, just stupid.

I often felt that executives like Dauman might as well give up. In tech, the young ate the old, largely because the old were not creative or quick enough to avoid it. Case in point was traditional media's most frightening and crusty of kings, Rupert Murdoch. Uncle Satan, as I call him as much as I can, proved adept at creating popular content from the *New York Post* to Fox News to 20th Century Fox. But when it came to the Internet, he was a stone-cold loser. Murdoch's failed businesses included Delphi Internet Services in 1993 (sold in 1996); the IGuide portal in 1996 (closed in months after partner MCI pulled out); Fox Interactive at the end of the 1990s (closed down by 2001); Photobucket (acquired in 2008 for $300 million and sold for a fraction a year later); The Daily in 2011 (an iPad-only news product which was costly and badly executed); and so many other digital flubs.

The most famous, of course, was Myspace, which Murdoch bought for $580 million in 2005. To be clear, Myspace seemed like the right deal when Murdoch purchased it, as it was growing exponentially and News Corp definitely needed a play in the arena. By August of 2006, Myspace had overtaken Yahoo and had signed up its 100 millionth user. Perhaps most cannily, the company struck an advertising deal with Google, which was competing with Yahoo and Microsoft. This alliance guaranteed Myspace $900 million in advertising over three years. It was a nice cushion, but due to sloppy management and its inability to innovate from a noisy, one-note offering to a service that was easier to use and more of a utility than a party, Myspace soon foundered. Myspace's kiss of death was that it was trendy rather than useful, unlike Facebook. And it lost its status as a daily addiction to Twitter. Soon enough, Snapchat would grab the communications crown in social media. News Corp unloaded Myspace in 2011 for $35 million, with Murdoch noting that we "screwed up in every way possible." Right, he was.

Part of the problem was Murdoch's mindset, which often seemed stuck in the mid-1950s—he was the original ink-stained wretch (emphasis on wretch). He was also, how can I put this delicately, old school when it came to women. When Walt and I launched *AllThingsD* at the *Journal,* for example, Murdoch focused his attention mainly on Walt. When we met in person, Murdoch seemed only to regard me as that mouthy girl who was always tagging along. I desperately wanted to ask him if he knew my name every time we met, since I doubted he did for a long while. Eventually, Murdoch realized that I was good at news scoops and started to pay a little more attention only because I might be useful to him. He even started reaching out to me now and again, hoping I could feed him information he could use to his advantage. While he might have stumbled when it came to tech, Murdoch's lizard brain (emphasis on lizard) did grok that tech was a major danger to his empire.

His longtime personal assistant, Dot Wyndoe, would usually place the calls and always very early in the morning in California. What three-hour time difference? The world ran on Uncle Satan time! His tone on these calls was constant ire and frustration at the growing power of Internet companies and their founders. His recurring question: Which entrepreneur was crazier? He wanted to know all about their proclivities and weirdnesses and personal lives. A tech outsider, he had managed to strike an unlikely relationship with Jobs, whom he admired for creating wealth and power out of nothing, as he perceived he had done.

Moreover, Murdoch had a persistent desire to get in on the action. At the same time, he was a manipulative and destructive powermonger who tirelessly plotted to thwart these tech entrepreneurs by tattling to regulators and strategically yelling in public forums. These tirades were usually delivered by News Corp CEO and top minion Robert Thomson, whom I nicknamed "the naughty vicar" for his nudge-nudge, wink-wink mannerisms and sly wordplay. Thomson negged on the tech world, referring to them as "bot-infested badlands," "the fake, the faux and the fallacious," "mindless myrmidons," and "solipsistic sophistry," even as he struck deals with them.

Murdoch's calls to me got comical at points, as the newsdigger-in-chief tried to extract useful information for deals he was clearly working on. He asked about grabbing Yahoo at one point along with Microsoft (fat chance, I told him) or investing in Vice Media (please don't, I advised; he did it anyway). I never revealed anything that Walt and I had not reported publicly, but that never stopped Murdoch from pressing. His aggression was the most fascinating to me. I saw it for what it really was: existential fear only a hardened survivor could feel in his creaky bones. Murdoch saw what was coming and he wanted to stop it. And if he couldn't stop it, he wanted to steal some of the lucre for himself.

Not every media mogul feared change. Bob Iger of Disney was able to keep calm and carry on amid the growing tech threat aimed directly at the Magic Kingdom's gates. His sanguinity was unusual among his contemporaries. As he once said to me in a 2005 interview, "If someone is going to eat our lunch, it might as well be us." He'd certainly faced worthy adversaries before as he clawed his way up the slippery ladder of power at Disney. I met Iger in the early 2000s and started to visit him more after he was named CEO. Unlike many, the handsome and smooth executive—whom I nicknamed the Cashmere

Prince—befriended techies, including Jobs, who would become Disney's largest shareholder when Disney acquired Pixar in 2006.

Iger's predecessor, Michael Eisner, had grasped the value of Silicon Valley, but never quite managed to capitalize on it, largely due to a toxic combination of arrogance and ignorance. He also liked to yell. Eisner created the Disney Online unit in 1995, headed by Jake Winebaum, who rolled out DisneyStore .com and Family.com, which soon merged with the Seattle-based Starwave's Family Planet and then morphed into Dailyblast .com, a family-focused content subscription site. In 1998, Disney launched a directory called Dig.com (short for Disney Internet Guide), and then acquired a search engine called InfoSeek, which became a site called Go. It wasn't long before Go went.

Still, Eisner's Disney and later Iger's kept trying, acquiring sites and companies including Kaboose, Babble.com, Amazing-Moms, Tapulous, Club Penguin, and even one called Kerpoof. That maker of cartoon avatars and Kerpoof Koins went, as did most of these efforts, *kerpoof*. It got so bad that I could hardly keep track of all the name changes of the online divisions over the years: Disney Online, Disney Interactive, Buena Vista Internet Group, Disney Interactive Studios, Disney Interactive Media Group. During Iger's early tenure, the company continued to ping-pong all over the digital map. Other Iger investments included $400 million in Vice Media, which Disney later wrote down to nothing. He also flirted with buying *BuzzFeed* for $500 million in 2013, but instead initiated a different disastrous purchase of YouTube-focused Maker Studios for $675 million in 2014.

Like clockwork after one of these messes, I would lob in

a call to Iger, who was always cordial and much funnier and pointed than in public. After the initial "good try" speech, I would move to the more obvious: *WTF, Bob?* I made one of these calls in 2010 when Playdom's John Pleasants and former Yahoo executive Jimmy Pitaro were named coheads of the digital unit. I was dubious about the latest move that put two executives in one box—which usually did not turn out well—and in what I considered Disney's most important unit. Iger insisted it would work. It did not.

Still, despite setbacks, Iger kept at it. In a joint interview I later did at a *Vanity Fair* event with him and Andreessen—the software cannibal—Iger never pretended the threat was not there, which made him unique among old media execs. "You have no real ability to ward [disruption] off or to avoid it," Iger said. "Except by embracing it in some form and using it for the good, or your own good. And so, I just really believe that when it comes to changes that technology is bringing in our businesses, or in storytelling, for instance, bring it in and use it to your advantage. It's that simple."

This is why I always liked Iger. He was not an insecure ostrich who hid from the trouble headed his way. And he was patient. It took until 2019, with the rollout of Disney+, for some tech success to come to the Magic Kingdom. Disney+'s breakout hit was *The Mandalorian,* a *Star Wars* spin-off made possible by Iger's 2012 acquisition of Lucasfilm. The pricey plunge into streaming was the right call for the company, which had the intellectual property to fill up its offering and satisfy its customers. Disney+ reached over 160 million subscribers in 2022 (including me since my daughter needs to watch *Frozen* at least eight times a week). Still, the battle to attract new sign-ups and hold on to old ones would get tougher over time and cause Iger and the other older entertainment companies to move faster than they should have. But to not be in the game would have been much worse, and it was the new cost of doing business.

Another longtime Hollywood icon who embraced tech early was Barry Diller. The colorful and often sharp-tongued mogul—for whom I had no nickname, because, *yikes*, he would have killed me—had spent his entire life in the entertainment industry. His résumé included creating the *ABC Movie of the Week*, serving as CEO of Paramount Pictures and 20th Century Fox, and founding Fox Broadcasting. At one point, Diller started investing in teleshopping, first via QVC and then the Home Shopping Network, which morphed into a group of Internet assets under the IAC/InterActiveCorp conglomerate. IAC was an ever-evolving dog's breakfast of digital companies, such as HomeAdvisor, LendingTree, Match Group, Citysearch, Ticketmaster, Vimeo, CollegeHumor, and Tinder. Diller also had control of the travel site Expedia.

Diller and I clicked from the moment we met in 1999 at the old headquarters of Ticketmaster off Sunset Boulevard. (Diller had gotten control of Ticketmaster and merged it with Citysearch.) Immediately, the flinty mogul switched our roles, asking me a rat-a-tat series of questions about the various Internet players up north, from Yahoo's Jerry Yang to those new Google characters. As with Murdoch, he wanted to know his next rivals, so he could beat them or join them. Unlike Murdoch, Diller enjoyed the tumult, seeing opportunity everywhere. Except for keeping the luxury yacht summers and buttery leather loafers he often wore, Diller was moving away from the entertainment world that had spawned him. That was clear in a live interview he gave me at the 2008 *All Things Digital* conference in which he uttered the memorable line: "Hollywood is a community that's so inbred, it's a wonder the children have any teeth."

That quip got him in trouble with his pals back at the Polo Lounge, but he also did not hesitate to smack around the techies either. Diller has been dinged for several high-profile legal fights—including with Liberty Media and also with the founders of Tinder over allegations that he had purposefully undervalued the explosive dating service. The Tinder lawsuit was settled without admission of wrongdoing in 2021. No matter, Diller zeroed in on the lack of innovation in the entertainment industry. And though the hodgepodge nature of IAC always made Diller seem more of a dabbler than a builder, he has always been an acute observer.

"Hollywood is now irrelevant," Diller told me in a 2019 interview. "Netflix has won this game. I mean, short of some existential event, it is Netflix's. No one can get, I believe, to their level of subscribers, which gives them real dominance." And although studios did catch up to some extent, Diller said out loud what Hollywood had refused to acknowledge for a decade.

I got a big taste of this denial when the Sundance Film Festival in Park City, Utah, invited me to moderate a panel on tech in 2009. I'd been attending the event for many years at the behest of its organizers. Every year, I tried to warn them of impending doom like some tech Cassandra. They didn't believe me either. By the end of the aughts, the disruption wasn't abstract and I put together a panel titled "Where Do We Go from Here? Icons of the Digital Age." Those icons included Netflix cofounder Reed Hastings, YouTube cofounder and puppy-murderer Hurley, and Hulu CEO Jason Kilar.

Hulu had been created in 2007 as an unholy marriage of News Corp and NBC Universal. Both owned big studios, and along with a $100 million investment from Providence Equity Partners and a spate of Internet distribution deals, they hoped to get in on the Web action. Hulu's name came from two Mandarin Chinese words for gourd, as in holder of precious things (yes, I know, very twee). Two years later, Disney would join the gang, making Hulu even more unwieldy.

Netflix was founded by Marc Randolph and Hastings as a DVD delivery service that depended on the U.S. postal service. In 2007, they announced a shift to a video on demand service of OPC (other people's content). Netflix would not generate original content until *House of Cards* in 2013. At first, Netflix offered a sweet deal for the studios, creating another lucrative revenue stream. That is, until they realized that they were selling away their seed corn that allowed Netflix to feast and grow huge. Iger likened it to giving a nuclear weapon to a developing country, which was quickly followed by a pig pile of media competitors trying to go digital together. What could go wrong?

YouTube also seemed to come out of nowhere, founded in 2005 by former PayPal employees Hurley, Steve Chen, and Jawed Karim. After cleaning the clock of Google Video, YouTube triggered a bidding war between the search company and Yahoo. The founders finally agreed to selling to Google in 2006 for $1.65 billion. (Some fifteen years later, YouTube generated $28.8 billion in revenue for Alphabet in a single year.)

While under fire from companies like Viacom, the real threat that YouTube presented to Hollywood was alternative new content by a class of creators that were breaking free from the strictures of the system. Not only had YouTube seized the means of distribution, but it was also attracting new audiences in mass. Arguably, the first viral video came in 2006 from Lonelygirl15, a confessional high schooler. Lonelygirl15 presented herself as an authentic troubled teen but, of course, turned out to be an actor with a script and a pair of producers. Fake, yes, but it heralded a new age of content discovery.

YouTube also showed it could goose old media. The Lonely Island's "Lazy Sunday" first aired on *Saturday Night Live*, but then garnered many millions of views on the service until NBC—idiotically in hindsight and even at the time—demanded that it be removed. This move was a flashing sign to me: "We hate our audience."

So, it came as no surprise to me where Sundance put this panel of new media entrepreneurs doing astonishing things. Obviously, in a dank basement room as part of a digital area, far away from the real action and with not a celebrity in sight. It was a clear signal that the audience of film folks did not take this trio seriously. I tried to push back anyway. "I have assembled the future," I declared at the start of the panel to scoffs from the indie film crowd.

The audience liked almost nothing about our discussion. I tried to stress the most pertinent fact: It was the dawn of an age when users would be in charge of the content, both making it and consuming it. Programmers? Replaced by algorithms. Broadcast schedules? Tossed, in favor of anytime, anywhere, and on anything. Theaters? Shrinking, as the Web replaced them as the primary distribution vehicle for content, including Sundance films, which could now be targeted to just the right viewers. Hastings called for an "on-demand revolution," with Hurley adding that "the linear broadcast model of today is going to disappear." Kilar chimed in that even ads would be selected by consumers.

This was gold, as far as I was concerned. Tech was offering a lifeline to a section of the industry that had never been able to find its audience easily and was captive to multiplexes that had zeroed out anything but the noisy blockbusters and franchise tentpoles. Still, the love of films seen in theaters with sticky floors was a pernicious habit that Hollywood could not seem to shake. During a Q&A, several people got up to decry the movie-going experience that would be lost. Yes, yes, yes, we all said, the silver screen is very romantic, but we also thought it was silly to fight innovation that could attract new and better audiences. I pointed out that it was also probably jarring when electric lights glared after centuries of candlelight. But lightbulbs turned out great, right?

But the Sundance crowd seemed to lean back in horror as Hastings, Hurley, and Kilar predicted a range of changes, such as ubiquity of broadband and a new class of creators who would be paid in a different way. The worst reaction came when they talked about the inevitability that movies would probably stream on the Web at the same time as they appeared in theaters, with Kilar noting that the TV screen would essentially become nothing more than a blank monitor fed largely by the Internet. Ironically, even though Kilar was right, slightly more than a decade later, he would get into hot water for doing exactly that. As head of WarnerMedia during the pandemic, Kilar announced that it would release its 2021 film slate on what was termed a day-and-date release. Filmmakers and talent responded angrily.

Well-known director Christopher Nolan, who made *Inception* and *The Dark Knight*, released a statement: "Some of our industry's biggest filmmakers and most important movie stars went to bed the night before thinking they were working for the greatest movie studio and woke up to find out they were working for the worst streaming service." (Save the drama for the movies, Chris!) In a December 2020 interview, I asked Kilar, "For as long as I've known you and certainly when you were the CEO of Hulu, you've been complaining about windowing, which was the old school model where content goes to movie theaters first before other platforms, essentially. I think you've wanted to do this forever. Does that feel good?"

He replied: "It does feel good. And it feels good for a number of reasons. The most important thing is it feels good from a fan perspective, from a customer perspective. But it also feels good through a number of other lenses, which is we're in the middle of a pandemic, and many, many businesses are suffering, and clearly, the exhibition industry is suffering. But what we're doing here is giving fans choice, which they haven't had, and I think that's a really powerful thing. And the other thing we're doing is guaranteeing a steady supply of big-budget great movies to movie theaters in the middle of a pandemic. And we feel really good about that too because the alternative is not to have any movies in exhibition in a movie theater."

But the Nolans of the industry got him. Within months, Kilar had to backtrack from this "feel good" stance. In another interview at my Code conference, held in the heart of the Beverly Hills beast, MSNBC's Stephanie Ruhle asked him about the move. "I will be the first one to say, and the responsibility rests on my shoulders, that, in hindsight, we should have taken the better part of a month to have over 170 conversations—which is the number of participants that are in our 2021 film slate," said

Kilar, being as apologetic as he could muster, though I think it was purely for show. "We tried to do that in a compressed period of time, less than a week, because of course there was going to be leaks, there was going to be everybody opining on whether we should do this or not do this."

Backstage, I listened to Kilar's apology and was crestfallen. That he was pilloried in 2009 and again in 2020 for the same thing said more about the intransigence of Hollywood than it did of him. Kilar, who lost his job when Discovery took over the company soon after, might have made his move prematurely, but the direction he was running in was inevitable. Theaters were not going away, but they were no longer going to be the center of the action for most movies, aside from whatever Tom Cruise and James Cameron served up to great fanfare. That was definitely here to stay, especially for quality films that connected with audiences (like Nolan's *Oppenheimer* in the summer of 2023), but everything else was up for grabs.

It was a sad and long-in-the-tooth song that Hollywood could never seem to stop singing. I was reminded of a famous comment made by Time Warner CEO Jeff Bewkes, who replaced Parsons. When discussing Netflix in 2010, Bewkes claimed streaming was part of an "era of experimentation" that was "coming to a close." But he did not stop there: "It's a little bit like, is the Albanian army going to take over the world? I don't think so." The industry laughed along with Bewkes and his clever slight, even though this prediction would turn out be completely wrong. As it turned out, the Albanians had a lot more firepower than anyone realized.

Like, I said: Sillywood.

CHAPTER 9

The Most Dangerous Man

What do we have to appease the great forces?
And I think in the end this was the question
that destroyed Agamemnon, there on the beach,
the Greek ships at the ready, the sea
invisible beyond the serene harbor, the future
lethal, unstable: he was a fool, thinking
it could be controlled. He should have said
I have nothing, I am at your mercy.

—LOUISE GLÜCK, "THE EMPTY GLASS"

As sweat poured down Mark Zuckerberg's pasty and rounded face, I wondered if he was going to keel over right there at my feet. I had been told by several Facebook executives that this sometimes happened when their CEO became nervous. But I didn't know whether they were kidding or not. "He has panic attacks when he's doing public speaking," one had warned me years before. "He could faint."

I suspected that might have been a ploy to get us to be nicer to Zuckerberg. It didn't work, obviously, as Walt and I grilled the slight young man on the main stage at our annual *All Things Digital* conference in Rancho Palos Verdes, California, in 2010. Zuckerberg was sitting in one of the same iconic red chairs as legendary tech legends like Steve Jobs, who was there again that year, and for the last time. Zuckerberg told me he was eager to sit with Jobs over dinner by the Pacific Ocean, which I found touching and earnest. The *ATD* interview occurred only five years after the founding of Facebook and two years before its public offering. In many ways, Zuckerberg sitting down with Walt and me was his splashy public debut.

But the rivulets of moisture began rolling down his ever-paler face. In retrospect, I suppose such a disaster was inevitable. While we had talked frequently since he founded TheFacebook in his Harvard dorm room in 2004 before bringing it to Palo Alto, Zuckerberg had only done one major public interview with me, and he had not come alone that time. His then COO, Sheryl Sandberg, sat by his side, expertly deflecting tough questions. It was on brand for the smoothly effective executive, coming right after she was hired to be the "adult" in the room, a role that I thought felt more like a hipper older sister. She was, in many ways over the years, Mark's safe space. I had broken the story of Sandberg's escape from the Death Star that Google had developed into, where she had run its profit-spewing AdWords unit. She had clicked with preternaturally awkward Zuckerberg in a meet-cute tech moment at a holiday party and very quickly and presciently agreed to become his second in command, with purview over a vast part of Facebook.

It was an even better move on Zuckerberg's part, as he had struggled to find a copacetic business partner for his hot startup. The stench of persistent operational chaos was growing around the company, even as it had been valued at an unheard of $15 billion after a $240 million investment from Microsoft in 2007. Bill Gates had become a mentor to the young entrepreneur, but it was Sandberg who would prove to be Zuckerberg's most important ally over the next decade. And indeed, the company quintupled in size to 500 million users in their first two years together, as Sandberg tuned up the moneymaking ad engine and Zuckerberg helmed the aggressive product expansion. Facebook's valuation had soared even further, as its revenue grew quickly. But the worrying signs were there—as they had been from its earliest days as a service when internal texts from Zuckerberg revealed his true feelings about users who handed over data so easily. "They 'trust me,' dumb fucks," he wrote. Seems nice.

While Mark later expressed regret over that sentiment, it was an accurate narrative of a hardening culture that prioritized growth over safety. And it was built into the DNA of the company, too. Facebook had already skated around numerous disasters concerning bad use of customer information. Beacon was an advertising software designed to track users' activities, like buying things off-site, and then move that information onto Facebook. Facebook rolled Beacon out as a "commerce alert system," but it felt more like a stalker system. The Federal Trade Commission agreed and dinged the use of the software in 2007. Sean Parker, who advised Mark in the early development of Facebook, later said that the site's goal was simple: "How do we consume as much of your time and conscious attention as possible?" He did not mean this in a positive way.

It added up to Facebook having a reputation of pushing the popular term "growth hacking" to dizzying extremes that made AOL, Yahoo, and even Google seem shy. It was no surprise that by the summer of 2010, Facebook was buffeted with regulatory investigations centered largely on its sloppy and rapacious privacy practices, which the company had continued to cavalierly slough off as it pushed forward. Along with that noise, *The Social Network*, an Aaron Sorkin–penned movie about the founding of Facebook, was about to be released. Advance word was that the movie portrayed Zuckerberg in a less-than-flattering light and suggested that his oily behaviors had seeped into the company.

Seated next to me at a meal just before our interview, Mark was clearly agitated about the upcoming release, including how the movie depicted him as having stolen the idea for the social network from his Harvard classmates, the Winklevoss brothers. (These handsome hustlers, who were twin rowing champions, got paid out by Facebook later and then launched a cryptocurrency exchange, so let us not shed a tear for them.) Facebook had complained self-righteously and loudly to the Hollywood executives in charge about the portrayal, which of course brought even more attention to the film. I advised Zuckerberg to laugh it off and told him to go to the premiere and even hug actor Jesse Eisenberg, who was playing him. "Control the narrative, Mark," I said. "It's coming whether you like it or not. And who cares, because you'll be richer and more famous than any of them in the end."

While he later did laugh it off, including appearing on *Saturday Night Live* with Eisenberg, Zuckerberg was not of that mindset at this time of the conference. "This is what people will think I'm like, because they believe what's on the screen," he said to me, furrowing his unwrinkled brow. Mark had just turned twenty-six and had almost no sense that life was long and that he should be preparing for what would become a marathon of scrutiny. He was unnerved, with his emotional agitation made worse by what seemed like the start of the flu. In truth, Zuckerberg seemed very vulnerable to me, especially since he appeared less angry than perplexed as to why the world was being so unfair to him. After all, he had gifted it the invention of Facebook. This was the first, but far from the last, flash of a persistent victim mentality that would plague him and the company for years to come as fair criticisms mounted.

Victimhood was an ever-present emotion that would flare across the entire tech brotherhood, especially as founders and executives began to get much-needed pushback. This attitude was in full flower for Mark when the Harvard dropout returned to give the university commencement speech in 2017. Starting off with the lofty idea of having purpose as your guide, he then veered quickly onto the grievance highway. "It's good to be idealistic. But be prepared to be misunderstood. Anyone working on a big vision will get called crazy, even if you end up right. Anyone working on a complex problem will get blamed for not fully understanding the challenge, even though it's impossible to know everything up front," he said. "Anyone taking initiative will get criticized for moving too fast, because there's always someone who wants to slow you down."

The seeds of this mentality were already sprouting in 2010 as he questioned why screenwriter Aaron Sorkin was picking on him. I just couldn't understand why he cared about a stupid movie more than the real-world impact he was having. "Be notorious, Mark," I joked before getting up to prepare for our onstage interview.

Unfortunately for him, he did just that. As Walt pressed on the issue of privacy and "instant personalization," Zuckerberg's angst began to physically manifest onstage. Sandberg sat in the front row, her face twisted in a horrified grimace as she began to see what I could see up close. Mark was in full meltdown.

But, like, a *real* melt.

His increasing moistness reminded me of the scene in *Broadcast News* in which Albert Brooks's character, Aaron Altman, becomes a puddle of sweat while pinch-hitting for the weekend news anchor in a vain attempt to be one. Zuckerberg was worse, if possible, and as much as I enjoyed my reputation as a pugnacious interviewer, I didn't want to be known as the one who sunk Silicon Valley's latest wunderkind in a puddle of moist. So, I jumped in and suggested he take off his omnipresent hoodie to cool down. It was me in mom mode, trying to get him out of an obvious jam. Stopping this drippy disaster was not entirely altruistic. I did not want this to end with me having to slap his baby face if he fainted. Mark declined, even as it became clearer to him that he was suffering. "I never take off my hoodie," he said in a limp attempt at a joke.

But moments later, when he realized how bad it was, Mark gave in. "Maybe I should take off the hoodie," he said. As he stripped off his protective layer, revealing metastasizing sweat stains under Mark's armpits and down his back, I tried to make small talk to calm him down.

Kara: It *is* a warm hoodie.

Mark: It's a thick hoodie—a company hoodie. We print our mission on the inside.

Kara: What? What is it? "Making the . . ."

Mark: "Making the world more open and connected."

Kara: Omigod. It's like a secret cult. Look at that: "Making the world open and connected. Stream. Graph. Platform." And this weird symbol in the middle, which is probably for the Illuminati.

Everyone laughed, and the room let out a sigh of relief as Zuckerberg recovered and continued the interview. Later, he would send Walt and me a gracious email about the incident. He even thanked us for the interview, although he certainly did not have to, especially given the painful visuals that quickly rocketed around the tech world. It was a uniquely weak performance by a CEO in a clutch moment. As it turned out, it wouldn't be his worst performance when talking to me.

It was like that from the moment we met, Mark seemed to think of me—and maybe all the press—as an adversary. Case in point: the first thing Mark ever said to me.

"I heard you think I'm an asshole."

This was his opening line—an aggressive move, for sure, as most baby entrepreneurs tried their best to charm me since I worked for an important business publication and what I wrote about them mattered. Despite his opening salvo, Zuckerberg certainly seemed harmless enough and looked more than a little like a newborn something, all fawn-like eyes and wide forehead, like some not particularly interesting anime creature.

But he was wrong. I did not think he was an asshole. I thought he was *probably* an asshole, an opinion based on what many others had told me. Some people I respected who had met Zuckerberg walked away with what could most kindly be described as a *meh* impression of him. Some thought he was a lightweight. Some thought he was extremely arrogant. Most thought he was just another tech bro who was—say it with me now—frequently wrong, but never in doubt. For sure, no one thought he was a game-changer. It was still the very early days of the social network, so he was not yet what he would later become: one of the richest and most powerful people on the planet.

I had been urged to meet Zuckerberg by Facebook's then COO, Owen Van Natta, whom I had known since he was an early Amazon executive. Van Natta was a slick operator who seemed to both be in on the utter nonsense of the tech scene, while also inexplicably raking in the dough all the time from that joke. He had managed to ingratiate himself into Zuckerberg's good graces, and he seemed to be holding fast despite Zuckerberg's history of embracing and then dumping a series of male executives. "You'll love him, he's the best, the best, I *sweeeeear*," cooed Van Natta, trying to affect a Boy Scout demeanor even though his vibe was more used car salesman. "Aren't you sick of those Google guys?"

He made a good point. I was sick of those Google guys, who had taken their search company public in 2004. Brin and Page had since shifted from pointedly *adorkable* to increasingly odd, as everyone indulged their myriad weirdnesses 24/7 now that they were billionaires. Luckily, as was always the case, Silicon Valley was onto the next big thing and Facebook was definitely the startup of the moment. I knew I had to eventually meet Zuckerberg. And so, I found myself strolling down University Avenue in 2006, stopping at Pizza My Heart to get a mushroom slice before heading to Facebook. When I arrived, he was standing in the doorframe of his shabby office blurting out that he'd heard I thought he was an asshole.

And here's the first thing I said to Zuckerberg: "Since I just met you, I don't know if you're an asshole or not yet. But we'll soon find out." What Zuckerberg was wouldn't be clear to me for a long time, and certainly not that day when he asked me to go on a walk with him around Palo Alto. This quaint practice was a bit of a trope that felt lifted from Steve Jobs, who was a big walkabout type in the same area.

Unlike the perpetually intriguing Jobs, Zuckerberg had almost no charm or game and it was painful how socially awkward he was then. He hemmed, he hawed, he looked anywhere but into your eyes. This was not uncommon among the many techies I had covered over the years, including Microsoft founder Bill Gates, who was prone to rocking when you talked to him, a tic he seemed to later overcome. Gates had worked hard to smooth the edges, like many entrepreneurs as they gained wealth and power, getting better clothes, better haircuts, better bodies. Early Zuckerberg had yet to become the muscled MMA fighting, patriotic foil-boarding, bison-killing, performative-tractor-riding-calf-feeding man that he would develop into over the next decade. You can glimpse that young man in a 2007 video camera that I used to carry around to capture the techies in their natural landscape. Mark and one of his earliest VCs, Jim Breyer of Accel Partners, came to say hello while I was at lunch in the Silicon Valley hangout Il Fornaio with my *AllThingsD* staff.

As I wrote at the time: "Graciously and mostly because he had zero choice after I whipped out my annoying tiny white Pure Digital video camera, Zuckerberg gives a quick update in the video below about the recent much-ballyhooed opening of the hot social-networking platform to third-party developers. But when I ask him about the buyout rumors that had swirled around the company for a good long time—the new one has Google sniffing about, by the way—he scoffed, but then got mighty uncomfortable in a hurry." In the awkward video—which the *Wall Street Journal* somehow lost, although the article about it remains—Mark stammered and huffed, as if I had asked him to dance a jig for me. The offers had indeed been coming in fast and furious, starting with a $1 billion one from Yahoo in 2006.

But he seemed intent on working to improve himself continually, a trait I admired. In 2009, for example, at a birthday party at the St. Regis hotel in San Francisco for Sheryl Sandberg, he was clearly working on improving his conversations and his public presentations, which his executives told me was a priority for him. "I think I'm doing better than when we first met," Zuckerberg said in earnest.

"Sure," I said out loud, but in my head, I added, "Marginally." In truth, despite the discomfort, I enjoyed that first meeting a lot, although it ended on a down note. When I left, I was handed one of Zuckerberg's famous business cards that said "I'm CEO . . . bitch"—an obnoxious comment masquerading as a joke. God, I really hated that card. Still, Zuckerberg's first verbal chess move impressed me. He had a quality I actually liked: He did not hide his bottomless ambition as other smoother young entrepreneurs did. Clad in their soft fleece hoodies and comfortable shoes, their sartorial choices reminded me mostly of grown-up toddlers. In fact, I had taken to dubbing them "manboys," which was not nice, I know, but it was true for these people who felt half-formed and opaque to me with no discernible edge or interesting bits. Worst of all, they were different in ways that made no difference. They'd insist that they wanted to "change the world" and "it was all about the journey" and "money was not the goal." Those were all lies, of course, made more problematic by the fact that these men were lying to themselves most of all.

In contrast to the shark babies who tried to feign cuddly, Zuckerberg openly craved power and historical significance from the get-go. For a long time, the bottom of the Facebook home page included the tag: "A Mark Zuckerberg Production." Even more to the point: "His hero is Augustus Caesar, for fuck's sake," said one of his investors to me over dinner one night. While most of the venture capitalists I knew tended to judge their startups by the very lowest of ethical bars, I assumed this investor was relieved that Zuckerberg's childhood hero was not someone more problematic. (Not Stalin, not Hitler, not Mussolini? *Phew!* Let's proceed with Series A!) Zuckerberg had underscored this imperial crush in a 2018 profile in the *New Yorker* after encountering the historical emperor while "studying good and bad and complex figures" from back when he attended Phillips Exeter Academy in high school. That would definitely apply to Augustus, who rose to power in Rome after the assassination of his adoptive father and thwarted dictator, Julius Caesar.

"Basically, through a really harsh approach, he established two hundred years of world peace," Zuckerberg explained to writer Evan Osnos. "What are the trade-offs in that? On the one hand, world peace is a long-term goal that people talk about today. Two hundred years feels unattainable." That was the CliffsNotes version of Pax Romana, with only a glancing acknowledgment of the price of that peace, including subjugation, colonization, and so, so much death. Zuckerberg seemed to grok the downsides, noting the era "didn't come for free." He even admitted that Augustus had to "do certain things" to maintain order. Despite those peculiar caveats, Zuckerberg seemed to land on the side of Augustus Caesar and the belief that an emperor's gotta do what an emperor's gotta do.

Osnos summed up Zuckerberg's attitude perfectly, noting, "Between speech and truth, he chose speech. Between speed and perfection, he chose speed. Between scale and safety, he chose scale." That idea of "mistakes were made" in service to the bigger idea would carry throughout Zuckerberg's career and bleed into Facebook's culture. This approach was distilled in the "Move fast and break things" posters that adorned the company headquarters early on. While this motto was a geek coding reference to software, it was a telling choice. The aim was to "break things" instead of "change things" or "fix things" or "improve things."

In July 2021, Casey Newton of *Platformer* asked Zuckerberg about President Joe Biden's declaration—later softened—that misinformation about vaccines and Covid on Facebook was "killing people." Zuckerberg's response was deeply revealing. "When you think about the integrity of a system like this, it's a little bit like fighting crime in a city. No one expects that you're ever going to fully solve crime in a city. The police department's goal is not to make it so that if there's any crime that happens, that you say that the police department is failing," Zuckerberg said. "That's not reasonable. I think, instead, what we generally expect is that the integrity systems, the police departments, if you will, will do a good job of helping to deter and catch the bad thing when it happens and keep it at a minimum, and keep driving the trend in a positive direction and be in front of other issues too. So, we're going to do that here."

The pertinent fact he left out is that when trouble happened, as it often does, citizens can fire a police chief and elect a different mayor. In contrast, Zuckerberg had permanent job security as ruler-for-life of Facebook. Thanks to Facebook's intentional corporate structure, he controls the voting shares and the board and can never be expunged in any kind of democratic way for bad management. Let me break it down more simply: *Mark. Cannot. Be. Fired. Ever.* Neither can his progeny. He is an absolute emperor. And very much like the analog Augustus Caesar, his dream is to connect the world, no matter the cost. He talked about this over and over in our many conversations through the years, sometimes late at night on the phone: a world bound closer together by his invention, bound by digital ties, where we could all finally be one.

I wish that I had a share of Facebook stock for every time Mark said the word "community" to me, even though he was really talking about filling up his empire with the masses. I would be very rich. Very early in Facebook's life, in fact, I was offered a job by one of Mark's underlings who thought I should come and work on unspecific "editorial" issues. "Do they even care about editorial, about journalism, about anything except letting the algorithm rule?" I asked the executive, arrogantly astride my very high media horse.

"No, but you could buy a Gulfstream someday," he replied. Fair point, but it was lost on me. Coach was fine, and, perhaps someday, first class. And, best of all, I would not have to sit there and nod my head eagerly to a CEO yammering fifteen years later about pivoting Facebook into an all-encompassing virtual reality experience. (The "metaverse" was an idea Zuckerberg shoplifted from *Snow Crash* author Neal Stephenson and others before he rolled out his version of their vision in the summer of

2021.) So, instead of having piles of money to jump in, I get to say: Fuck your metaverse, Mark. Just fuck it.

It's also worth noting that his "fighting crime in a city" analogy came only six months after a mob attacked the Capitol on January 6, 2021. Social media, particularly Facebook, played a role in the ability of then President Donald Trump and his minions to amplify hate and lies and spin them into violence. While it's difficult to pinpoint how much culpability the tech companies have—and all of them have tried to thread the toxic needle here, rather than just reflecting in horror about their roles—there's no question that tensions were heightened by sloppy management of these ubiquitous platforms. (Yes, yes, as techies point out, Rupert Murdoch and Fox News were also to blame. You'll get no argument from me.)

Still, while tech argues—backed by some studies—that correlation does not equal causation, others disagree and are backed by other studies. A few things are absolutely clear: More people across the globe get their news and cues from social media, it has a scary ability to generate anxiety and rage, and it is addictive. Expert after expert I talked to over the years has made the same point—in the new paradigm, engagement equals enragement. This is made worse by the people who run these companies, for whom anticipation of consequences is lacking and whose first instinct is to let it all through the gate, regardless of potential damage of danger. What's the opposite of the Mommy state? Parent-free chaos.

And it is all private, with no accountability. In fact, if you wanted to extend Zuckerberg's quaint city metaphor, you could imagine a digital megalopolis in which a single company controls all the economics like rent (paid for with your data), while providing inadequate water, sewer, police, fire protection, gas, electric, roads—and even the signage sucks. Moreover, some parts of the city operate like "The Purge." And, oh yeah, we paid for it all by funding the creation of the Internet with taxpayer dollars and then with our own data. They owe us. Yet, when the violence actually does harm, the companies respond with nothing more than apologies and persistent insistence that they will "do better." But they will not do better, because they are incapable. In fact, the way the platform was built—the architecture, the DNA, the very bones of it—makes it impossible for them to "do better."

Speaking of fucked, I am sorry to say: We are.

Exhibit A: In 2016, Zuckerberg posted on Facebook, "It's great to be back in Beijing! I kicked off my visit with a run through Tiananmen Square, past the Forbidden City and over to the Temple of Heaven." The photo he shared with the world shows him in a gray T-shirt and black shorts, blowing past a portrait of Mao Zedong in the background. He has a huge grin on his face, and there's no acknowledgment that hundreds, maybe thousands, of student protestors were massacred by Chinese government troops in that same place. Zuckerberg was only five years old at the time of the Tiananmen Square Massacre, but it's hard to believe the topic never came up during his fancy education at Exeter and Harvard. In the photo, Zuckerberg is surrounded by five or six other joggers, presumably from his team. Did none of them know the historical significance of the place? Did someone tell Zuckerberg and he ignored it? Or were they too scared to mention it? When I pressed him about it in a meeting and told him he seemed like a tool of the Chinese government—which had dined out on the photo—he flatly told me no one else had raised this issue with him.

Exhibit B: My next long interview with Mark after the sweaty one took place in mid-2018 when he sat for a *Recode Decode* podcast and he told me that Holocaust deniers might not mean to lie. Say *what*, I thought, even though it was clear he did not understand the dangers of the proliferation of underbaked conspiracy theories, hoaxes, and misinformation on Facebook. We had started out talking about Alex Jones, one of the worst people on the Internet (and in the world), who had pushed mendacious conspiracies about the mass murder of children in the Sandy Hook school shooting. He used Zuckerberg's social network as his vehicle, even as he gamed it by breaking all the rules that the company had laid down.

I wanted to know why Jones had not been tossed off the network, but Mark decided to double down on him in the interview. "Look, as abhorrent as some of this content can be, I do think that it gets down to this principle of giving people a voice," he said. Then, I suppose to try to shake me, he decided to shift the topic to the Holocaust, which is never a good idea if you have a less than strong grasp on history. Also, as I said, it was one of my major areas of study in college. He forged ahead anyway, noting, "I'm Jewish, and there's a set of people who deny that the Holocaust happened."

"Yes, there's a lot," I said, not quite sure where he was going. But rather than jump in and school him, which was my instinct, I decided to keep quiet for once and watch this spin out of control. That did not take long.

"I find that deeply offensive. But at the end of the day, I don't believe that our platform should take that down because I think there are things that different people get wrong. I don't think that they're intentionally getting it wrong, but I think—"

I had to interrupt here since it was an astonishingly stupid thing to say, telling him: "In the case of the Holocaust deniers, they might be." But then I stopped myself and decided to just let it play out, since I needed to understand the depth of his shallow thinking on this important and dangerous topic. Sometimes, it's best to go very quiet in interviews, and this was that time.

And so, I just said: "But, go ahead." And he did, driving himself at full speed, with me watching him crash. "It's hard to impugn intent and to understand the intent," he said, though it is not, at least when it comes to Holocaust deniers. My producer, Eric Johnson, who was taping the podcast interview at Mark's office at 1 Hacker Way—I kid you not—in Menlo Park, could not believe what Zuckerberg had said either and stifled a gasp. Neither Mark nor his staff present seemed to understand that what he'd said would attract attention. Perhaps he felt safe at his office, rather than on my stage; perhaps he thought he was being sincere by using his own religion to make a point; perhaps he had exactly no sense of history and far too much power. Whatever. All I know is that as soon as we could, we ran to the car, hightailed it up to San Francisco on the 101 and posted the interview.

Of course, Zuckerberg's comments blew up like a Roman candle across the world, and he emailed me, trying to clarify what he had said. "I personally find Holocaust denial deeply offensive, and I absolutely didn't intend to defend the intent of people who deny that," he wrote, even though that was exactly what he had done. Still, Mark allowed Holocaust deniers to stay on the platform for two more years, when he decided that the platform should "prohibit any content that denies or distorts the Holocaust."

Two years of damage by these heinous people until the penny finally dropped for Zuckerberg. "I've struggled with the tension between standing for free expression and the harm caused by minimizing or denying the Holocaust," he wrote in a Facebook post. "My own thinking has evolved as I've seen data showing an increase in anti-Semitic violence, as have our wider policies on hate speech."

Evolved? Good lord. In a column later, I would call it the "expensive education of Mark Zuckerberg"—by which I meant society's expense and never his. I never got another interview with him after that, but I hope I do someday. (Third time's a charm, Mark! Call me!) Zuckerberg had equaled Augustus in reshaping the world in own his image, with no need of spear-throwing legions. While Zuckerberg was not evil, not malevolent, not cruel, what he was, and continued to be, was extraordinarily naïve about the forces he had unleashed. Time has since shown that Zuckerberg was woefully unprepared to rein in the power of his digital platform as Facebook's population swelled to 3 billion active users and it became the most important and vast communications, information, advertising, and media behemoth the world had ever seen.

No, Zuckerberg wasn't an asshole. He was worse. He was one of the most carelessly dangerous men in the history of technology who didn't even know it. Unfortunately, he wasn't the worst of them.

CHAPTER 10

The Uber Mensch

I never turned anyone into a pig.
Some people are pigs; I make them
Look like pigs.

—LOUISE GLÜCK, "CIRCE'S POWER"

In early spring 2017, I scored a reservation at Mourad, the latest swanky downtown San Francisco restaurant that catered to newly rich techies. Like most of these new places, Mourad managed to be both classy and louche, with lots of big vases full of big flowers propped on smooth surfaces of expensive stone. Naturally, it had one Michelin star for its "modern interpretation of a cuisine deeply rooted in the past," in this case, Moroccan.

To be fair, it was a very good restaurant, run by Mourad Lahlou, a soulful chef who had also won the Iron Chef America competition in 2009. I arrived early and made my way to the bar. While I don't consume alcohol much, I did enjoy Mourad's candied harissa-spiced pecans and that's where they were. It's also where loudmouth moneybags were always skittering about, and that night one well-known investor buttonholed me at the bar.

"When are you going to stop?" he asked, with a vaguely threatening tone I was not even slightly scared of.

I knew he was referring to *Recode*'s increasingly critical coverage of Uber and its pugnacious CEO Travis Kalanick. Still, I decided to bait the investor, knowing full well that his Tesla Model X, Gulfstream upgrade, third home in an exclusive Montana ski club, and whatever else he needed to feel alive depended on my "stopping."

"Stop? Stop what?" I asked, trying my best to be irritating by playing dumb.

"When are you going to stop attacking Travis?" the investor huffed, sticking a stubby finger in my face. It made him even less scary. Never, I thought, knowing something he didn't. At that moment, *Recode* was prepping a truly horrific story about a top Uber executive who had obtained the medical files of a woman who had been raped during a ride in India. The company had gotten the medical files not at the victim's request, but because it questioned whether she was telling the truth. Apparently, Kalanick didn't interfere with, or even question, this despicable act. Many at the company were distraught over the egregious invasion of privacy, which seemed a bridge far too far in an endless series of crappy bridges crossed at Uber.

Me too. That's why I wasn't going to stop. I was going to hit as hard as I could, through fair reporting of Kalanick's long running and increasingly terrible behavior as a CEO. I decided to tell this investor the truth: "I'll stop when Travis stays down for good." The investor acted surprised, although I suspect he wasn't.

"So that's your job?" he asked with palpable derision. "To speak truth to power?" I smiled, popped a delicious pecan in my mouth, and said nothing, since it was so overly dramatic and I knew I wasn't going to persuade him of anything. When the truth stands between a man and his next $100 million, the truth is always going to be escorted off the premises. More to the point was that this investor, like so many others, had become morally bankrupt, backing ever more cretinous characters like Kalanick. I didn't say it out loud, but in my head I screamed a line that I wanted to say to an increasing number of players in the Internet space: "You're so poor, all you have is your money!"

To be clear, I liked making money and had done really well with our Dow Jones conference deal, pulling in close to $1 million annually myself for one event. It was pretty good for a reporter, I thought, although it paled compared to what those I covered were raking in, paydays that had started to warp far too many. Over the years, with increasing alarm, I watched idealistic young founders aiming to change the world with miraculous digital innovations become sloppy and careless Internet moguls due to ungodly financial windfalls. Even when presented with data that they were doing harm, they shrugged off the consequences of their inventions on the larger world. Worse still, they had started to play the victim. I had dubbed this trend "the grievance industrial complex," which like the military industrial complex would swell to grotesque proportions over time.

Responsibility, which tech titans interpreted as "blame," was not their thing. But in the space of two decades, they made a huge external mess. Sites like Facebook, YouTube, and Twitter spread hate speech and disinformation like toxic waste. Social media has also contributed to escalating rates of depression among young people, who are often addicted to their digital devices, mostly because the creators designed them to do just that.

Which brings us back to Travis Kalanick and his company,

which felt like the appalling apogee of this trend. Uber had ridden a simple "gig worker" idea in 2009 to a $70 billion valuation by 2017, with Kalanick in charge and lionized by those he enriched. He was the adored poster boy of the new Silicon Valley, praised for his hard-charging manner and take-no-prisoners style.

I had spent a lot of time with Kalanick and was alternately repulsed and fascinated with his development as a leader of the wolf pack. While working on a 2014 profile of Kalanick for *Vanity Fair*, I met his lovely parents, who lived in a modest suburban home north of Los Angeles. I tried to figure how he started in this quaint street lined with weekend fishing boats and ended up being on the warpath against . . . everyone. As the magazine's subhead noted: "His enemies include the taxi industry, regulators around the world, his rivals, and even, on occasion, his customers." I kept up the violent metaphors in my lede paragraph: "Every now and then, when he's spoiling for a fight, Travis Kalanick has a face like a fist. At these times, his eyes crinkle, his nostrils flare, and his mouth purses just like a clenched hand readying a punch. Even his Marine-style, salt-and-pepper hair seems to stand on end and bristle, as it were, at whatever the thirty-eight-year-old entrepreneur happens to be facing down."

Kalanick's aggression was palpable, and to say his ascendance made me uncomfortable is an understatement. It made me sick to my stomach. No tech CEO had so explicitly signaled that he couldn't have cared less. That was especially true when he told me in an onstage interview at the 2014 Code conference that he looked forward to the dawn of autonomous driving. His reason wasn't because it would be an amazing technological and societal achievement to remove humans from the driver's seat and save countless lives from accidents. No, he was eager for the shift, because—big shock—it would make him even richer.

And he said so. "The reason Uber could be expensive is because you're not just paying for the car—you're paying for the other dude in the car. When there's no other dude in the car, the cost of taking an Uber anywhere becomes cheaper than owning a vehicle," he glibly explained to the audience. "So, the magic there is, you basically bring the cost below the cost of ownership for everybody, and then car ownership goes away." Oh God, I thought, as the words fell out of his mouth with hardly a pause. Kalanick was actively bragging about using people—or rather "dudes"—as fodder until it was easier and cheaper to replace them with a machine. And it was a day he actually looked forward to.

I suppose I should have appreciated that he was at least telling the truth, something that the lords of Silicon Valley had started to do less frequently. But Kalanick personified the ever-uglier face of tech. And his dehumanizing attitude became business as usual for Uber, extending to drivers, customers, and even employees. This was his modus operandi. Someone leaked to me (and I later published) a 2013 memo that Kalanick sent about a company party at Miami's Shore Club, marking the rollout of Uber's fiftieth global city. The memo was titled "URGENT, URGENT—READ THIS NOW OR ELSE!!!!!" and in case that didn't work, he told his staff, "You better read this [memo] or I'll kick your ass." Mature, right? It got worse. The memo listed a series of "don'ts," including vomiting (or risk a $200 "puke charge"), drug use, and throwing beer kegs off buildings. These sounded more like house rules for a particularly bad college frat than for a global company.

Worse still, Kalanick then outlined how proper fornication between employees should be conducted, writing: "Do not have sex with another employee UNLESS a) you have asked that person for that privilege and they have responded with an emphatic 'YES! I will have sex with you' AND b) the two (or more) of you do not work in the same chain of command. Yes, that means that Travis will be celibate on this trip. #CEOLife #FML." (FML means "Fuck my life.") The memo was stunning to read, given it was a public document that emphasized an increasingly pervasive culture of sexism at the company run by a leader who made constant jokes about partying and having sex and, mostly, fucking the man—even though he was, in fact, the man.

Kalanick's toxic masculinity vibe continued, even as the valuation of the profit-free startup accelerated. That is, until February of 2017, when Uber employee Susan Fowler blew the whistle on her way out the door, blasting the lid off the company with a blog post titled "Reflecting on One Very, Very Strange Year at Uber." Fowler chronicled a deeply chaotic workplace that tolerated sexual harassment of women and maintained insane levels of political infighting. Obviously frustrated, Fowler wrote at the end: "And when I think about the things I've recounted in the paragraphs above, I feel a lot of sadness, but I can't help but laugh at how ridiculous everything was. Such a strange experience. Such a strange year."

I admired Fowler for what she'd done and was more than a little frustrated with Uber myself. At *Recode*, we'd been reporting on the company's antics for years, and the reaction ranged from a shrug to a demand in a bar that we stop. We were seen as out of line for pointing out the execrable pile of misdeeds committed by Uber's leaders while they kept getting rewarded. But it was bigger than just Uber. More and more, the white male homogeneity in tech was creating problems that the people at the top could not perceive or even understand. Who makes products and what characteristics they have matters a great deal as to how products turn out—especially when those products become damaging.

A truism began to form in my brain about the lack of women and people of color in the leadership ranks of tech: The innovators and executives ignored issues of safety not because they were necessarily awful, but because they had never felt unsafe a day in their lives. Their personal experience informed the development of unfettered platforms. And, in turn, this inability to understand the consequences of their inventions began to curdle the sunny optimism of tech that had illuminated the sector. Silicon Valley had perfected the image of itself as a meritocracy and touted that as one of its greatest strengths—that anyone could become a billionaire. In fact, tech has always been a *mirror*tocracy, full of people who liked their own reflection so much that they only saw value in those that looked the same. They keep copying themselves, choosing slight variations on the same avatar template. Financial success was proof of their talents, which was like the old cliché of starting on third base and thinking you hit a home run.

Heterogeneity in nature makes for stronger species, but tech was pushing forward one of the most homogenous structures possible, in which true differences would never inform better decisions. I tried to make this point early on. In a 2007 *AllThingsD* story titled "The Men and (No) Women Facebook of Facebook Management," I posted photos of the top management at the company, all of whom were, you guessed it, men.

The reaction from the company was, not surprisingly, negative and they called it unfair. My response was that I had simply replicated Facebook's management page, so perhaps their anger was misplaced. The call was coming from inside the house, I told them. A year later, Zuckerberg hired tech marketing executive Sheryl Sandberg from Google. I joked then that I guessed she counted for four women since she was such a star.

Three years later, I followed my Facebook poking with a story titled "The Men and No Women of Web 2.0's Boards," to further make the point that these boards of directors were dominated by men. Since tech boards average nine members, this seemed intentionally egregious. Then three years later, when the diversity needle had barely moved, I thought, fuck it, and moved directly into repeating penis jokes about Twitter's board, which did not have a single woman. My lede pointed out that the company had no women, but "two Peters and a Dick"—Peter Chernin, Peter Fenton, and Dick Costolo—as its directors.

Dick Costolo, who was Twitter CEO at the time, called me after the story appeared and said it made him laugh, a compliment since he had done stand-up and improv before becoming a tech executive. He did point out that Twitter was seeking to add women and people of color to broaden its board composition for a service that had long been surprisingly diverse in its audience. I published my piece in September of 2013, and in early December, Twitter finally added its first woman director, Marjorie Scardino, the former CEO of the Pearson PLC.

Getting to inclusivity was a painfully slow process, always hindered by the excuse that there was a "pipeline problem" and that the always male leaders needed to maintain "standards" of quality. The problem I had was that (a) the tech leaders themselves installed that pipeline; and (b) the word "standards" was never uttered when it came to those all-male operations that were spewing losses and hurtling toward ignominy. Instead, the leaders of tech were always looking for an excuse for failure, a helping hand, and an "Attaboy!" attitude for the next endeavor they wanted to try.

It felt like these men had the benefit of an if-at-first-you-don't-succeed rule, while women got only one shot, if that. And if women complained about the unfairness of the situation or any mistreatment at work, they were ejected from the game. This became startlingly clear in the gender discrimination and retaliation lawsuit waged by Ellen Pao against the famed venture firm Kleiner Perkins. Pao busted into the boys' club with a formidable résumé that even the tech bros couldn't deny. After nabbing multiple degrees from Princeton and Harvard and stints at a series of jazzy startups, Pao joined Kleiner, whose greatest hits include Sun Microsystems, Google, Amazon, and Genentech. In 2005, she was appointed chief of staff to its star partner, John Doerr.

But her tenure got more complicated as Pao tried to climb the ladder at Kleiner. She was named a junior investing partner, but never promoted to senior partner. When she was fired, she accused the firm of gender discrimination, which the firm denied and which led to her 2012 lawsuit and culminated in a 2015 trial. The *Recode* staff covered the trial extensively, offering wall-to-wall coverage, along with a series of scoops and features on top of that. One thing I was particularly proud of was that our relentless courtroom reporting shoved the topic into the mainstream and garnered an enormous amount of much-needed attention. Revelations included that women staffers on equal or higher levels than some men were asked to take notes in meetings. Women were also excluded from all-male ski trips and dinners where work was definitely discussed.

Of course, Kleiner's high-priced team of lawyers always had an explanation for women being treated as lesser employees. I attended the trial several times, and it was pretty clear that Pao was outmatched legally. She ended up having to defend herself as they artfully painted her as a disgruntled employee out for revenge. She lost her case, but the trial still had impact. No matter how clever those lawyers were, the accusations against Kleiner resonated for women at all levels of tech companies. They started calling me or stopping me at events with stories that sounded as if they were channeling Pao. At one gathering, a top woman executive told me a harrowing story of sexual harassment she had endured on her rise to the top—full of objectifying language from men and everything from cloddish attempts to have sex at off-sites to outright groping—as well as innumerable smaller slights. She never reported any of these incidents out of fear she'd be branded "a complainer" and "not a team player."

The overall reaction from men to the lawsuit and our coverage was more curious to me. Even those I knew to be decent bosses were shocked that such things took place. Most said they had never noticed the rampant sexism and ensuing discrimination before. One venture capitalist even told me that he had started calling on his two women partners after he realized only men spoke in meetings. "Wow, they had some great ideas," he said with incredulity that triggered my incredulity. "I can't believe that I let that go on."

"You're an idiot," I told him. He looked at me pained by what I thought was an obvious assessment of his dumbfoolery. I quickly apologized and decided to take his newfound efforts at inclusion as a win, however minuscule (and it was minuscule). Still, his attitude crystallized my belief that the worst men operated with impunity, while the best were utterly clueless. In the years ahead, we published story after story about these issues across the spectrum of companies and venture firms. Sadly, there was little change in numbers of women in top positions at companies or on capitalization tables—which basically explain who owns what—in comparison to men. Yet the Pao trial was a moment of importance, however futile it seemed, because as we noted in *Recode* at the time, only four percent of top VCs were women, with zero in key roles. Throughout the sector, women were mainly concentrated in supporting roles, such as HR and PR, and if they behaved anything like Kalanick, they were typically dinged for aggression rather than celebrated like him.

It was an impossible situation, as Pao wrote a year later in her book *Reset: My Fight for Inclusion and Lasting Change*. "Is it possible that I am really too ambitious while being too quiet while being too aggressive while being unlikable. . . . If you talk, you talk too much. If you don't talk, you're too quiet. You don't own the room. If you want to protect your work, you're not a team player. Your elbows are too sharp." Pao would have even less luck in her next job at Reddit, the online comment network where she was ousted as interim chief executive only a few months after she lost the Kleiner Perkins trial. During her Reddit tenure, Pao was attacked relentlessly for trying to remove revenge porn and all other manner of racist and misogynistic hate speech (the classics!). In that "controversy," she was subject to a truly heinous series of attacks on her personally by Reddit users, which veered into violent threats. What started out as small became global and huge, as do most attacks on the Internet against women, which quickly become a swarm of hate.

After Pao left, some Reddit insiders told me she went too far too fast and with not enough finesse at the free-speech absolutist site, which caused internal tensions. "She was too caustic," said one person to me, a quality that it seemed to me was perfect for those seeking to clean up the hateful discussion groups. Still, when the next Reddit CEO, cofounder Steve Huffman, made a lot of the same moves, he was feted for his strength in facing down malevolent trolls. I will say that Huffman can be very affable, and he certainly deserved the praise. But so did Pao for taking those first steps.

So, Pao surprised me when she came across as hopeful rather than bitter in an interview I did with her at Code in 2017. She outlined a series of ideas to make tech more equitable and said she saw that the younger entrepreneurs were more willing to face tough issues rather than deny them. "I think that next generation is much more aware. I'm hoping that people telling their stories makes them even more aware, so that they are looking for the right companies to join . . . who are not taking the old admissions-committee model of cultural fit and 'Do I want to be on a plane with you for twenty-four hours in a row?' as their guides," she said.

People in the audience were surprised by how not caustic Pao was in person, where she was able to speak freely and not be hamstrung by legal issues of a courtroom. She had been urged to be non-emotional by her lawyers and later said that had been a mistake, since she ended up being characterized by opposing counsel as inscrutable, a ridiculous trope often applied to Asians. "She's actually very likable and reasonable," one male

VC commented about Pao to me right after the session. "Not at all like I imagined." What could I answer at that point? I could not keep calling people I covered "idiots," so I just shrugged and said, "I guess you need a better imagination." He laughed, I laughed, and I just let it go, hoping these small wins would add up over time.

They did not. If anything, the Pao trial shedding light on the issue and prompting similar tales made it clear that the exclusion of women was not an oversight but deliberate. You could blame the culture for a lot of this, but some individual men had a very deep problem when it came to women and nobody was telling them to stop. One of the suggestions to solve the problem came from Sheryl Sandberg, which focused on "leaning in" to your life, and famously suggesting to women "don't leave before you leave." While some thought that put too much onus on women, her campaign to get more women in positions of power actually started with a pair of speeches that signaled her own frustration with the culture and how it expected women to behave and how it punished women when they didn't conform. Her goal was to surface these biases in order to help women understand the playing field and be able to spot the landmines, which sometimes included their own behavior.

In a best-selling book she later wrote, Sandberg told a lot of stories about women to whom she offered jobs and how they worried about taking the job because they could become pregnant. She told them: "Take the job anyway and then get pregnant." I had first met Sandberg when she was a top Google executive and got the scoop of her jump to Facebook. At the search giant, she had been responsible for online sales of its ad and publishing products, gaining experience that Facebook sorely needed. It was a good pick by Zuckerberg, and while the pairing would later become problematic as they both lost sight of the impact of Facebook on a broader range of issues—more on that coming up—there is no question that Sandberg was a key beacon of hope for women in tech.

To help, Sandberg threw "Women of Silicon Valley" dinners at her home, bringing in top speakers, from Oprah Winfrey to Microsoft's Steve Ballmer, for off-the-record conversations and a whole lot of networking. She often urged me to ask the toughest question I could think of, in order to get the sessions going. Then if a speaker became flustered, she'd break into an "oh-that's-Kara-what-can-I-do" shrug. Although our relationship degenerated once I started to criticize loudly and pointedly what Facebook was turning into, I liked Sandberg a great deal for getting in the room and trying to focus on women. Even I realized she should not have to bear the sole responsibility to change persistent misogyny, and I think the pressure of being such a symbol was destined to be too much.

While she did not show the pressure a lot—Sandberg was the very smoothest of executives with not a hair or word out of place—she was unusually frank when I called her in 2011 to tell her that Meg Whitman had just been named the CEO of Hewlett-Packard. "Now you've moved down the stack to become the second most powerful woman in Silicon Valley," I kidded her.

"I'd like to be the sixth," she responded with a sigh. "Or the fiftieth—wouldn't that be great?" Both of us knew that would never happen. I was also exhausted by sexism and the debate about what to do about it, and yet the stories kept coming. In 2017, I reported a scoop that Uber's SVP of engineering had not disclosed to the company that he had left Google in a dispute over a sexual harassment allegation, which he denied to me. And who did the due diligence for Uber, post-Fowler blowing the whistle? The company's leadership? The board of directors? Nope. Me.

The take-no-responsibility attitude stubbornly persisted. Tech leaders had promised to "change the world," but when it came to societal shortcomings like basic sexism, they simply reinvented the wheel. I found it dispiriting to watch the same problems that plagued older industries prosper in this allegedly brave new world. I'd been to this sexist rodeo before when I worked for John McLaughlin and saw how his casual sexual harassment ruined the lives of his targets. Worse still was that any amount of criticism from me and other reporters was seen as either sour grapes or outright hostility. The mirrortocracy sure hated anyone holding up a mirror to them. This dynamic was only going to get worse as the tech sector's mistakes bled into the world in ways no one—including myself—had anticipated.

One good thing, Kalanick resigned under pressure in 2017 after the investors who once indulged his behavior turned on him. (That said, he walked away with billions, after he sold his shares and later founded a ghost kitchen startup for delivery-only restaurants that thrived during the pandemic.) He was replaced by the quantumly more professional and experienced Dara Khosrowshahi, a news story I happily broke (and, in fact, it was how he found out he had been hired). At a press gathering soon after at a cool whiskey joint, he lifted a glass and said to us: "Thanks for the job. I *think*." In addition, twenty Uber employees were fired after an internal investigation, with some facing even more dire legal action.

It was about then I "stopped," and I wondered if the cretinous Uber investor at the bar was happy. But I still felt like sexism was never going away—I could see it everywhere, sometimes comically. Standing outside a holiday party for one of Uber's earliest and most loyal investors at his fabulous mansion, I was dumbfounded to see an actual reindeer in the driveway greeting guests on the way in. The investor had rented the huge creature as a prop, a decoration, and, I suppose, as an example of his growing wealth, much as he had put his pricey cars on display at previous events. The reindeer was visibly wilting and looked decidedly uncomfortable in the far too warm climate, so I asked the minder if the animal was going to be okay.

"It's not an ideal situation, but she'll be fine," the minder responded. Of course, it was a female reindeer. Unable to do anything but stare, all I could think was that she was anything but fine.

CHAPTER II

Staying Vertical

Let go, live your life, the grave has no sunny corners.

—CHARLES WRIGHT, "HIGH COUNTRY CANTICLE"

Until the day Steve Jobs died, he kept surprising me. That included backstage at *ATD* in May of 2005, when he quizzed me about the cross-adoptions of my sons. Until then, every one of our conversations had been about tech and work. But Jobs had been adopted himself, which was clearly a formative experience in his life.

So that day, Jobs decided to get personal, and he asked if I knew who the biological father of my boys was. I explained that the donor selected was a "no-donor" who did not want to be contacted by the kids even when they turned eighteen. Without prompting, Jobs then recounted a story that was not well known until after his death about how he had eventually met his birth parents and how he was sorely disappointed and thought it was a mistake since his adopted parents were the ones who made him who he was. His only joy, he said, was finally meeting his biological sister, novelist Mona Simpson, whom his birth parents had raised after putting him up for adoption. He and Simpson went on to have a rich relationship. "The people who love you are the only ones that count," he said to me. Then, tearing up, he added, "Don't waste your time on anyone else." And then, wonder of wonders, he gave me a hug.

Yes, I got a hug from a tearful Steve Jobs, and it was as awkward as you might imagine.

While the emotionality was a surprise, his feelings were not. Jobs had just gotten a reprieve from a rare type of pancreatic cancer, for which the surgery to remove the tumor had miraculously worked. He would talk eloquently about the insight he'd gained from the experience in a speech he gave at Stanford University a month later. The speech had a key line: "Remembering that I'll be dead soon is the most important tool I've ever encountered to help me make the big choices in life. Because almost everything—all external expectations, all pride, all fear of embarrassment or failure—these things just fall away in the face of death, leaving only what is truly important. Remembering that you are going to die is the best way I know to avoid the trap of thinking you have something to lose. You are already naked. There is no reason not to follow your heart."

Of all the things I learned from Jobs' life, this was the most important. Onstage after our private talk, I asked him, since his illness had been life-threatening before he had recovered, "Health wise—how are you?"

"I'm vertical," was Jobs' reply, a terse answer that was also as truthful as it gets. And he was, until he wasn't. When his cancer returned, he got a liver transplant in 2009, and took a six-month medical leave from work. He returned to work and received an enormous amount of criticism about his ability to do the job and about his secrecy around the illness. I declined to pile on because it was increasingly clear he was dying and that he thought of the critics as crepehangers. My take is that after having cheated death once, he never thought his condition was fatal. Some part of him thought he was going to live forever.

And even though he was also rail-thin when Walt and I interviewed him in mid-2010, Jobs was certainly lively and bristling with ideas for future plans. But things got worse by early 2011 and he had stepped down as CEO of Apple by August. Jobs picked his longtime operations genius Tim Cook to take over, the least flashy choice he could make among his longtime executive group. At an event, I once asked Jobs why he sucked up all the oxygen in the room, and he insisted that Apple had a deep bench. "You're not Willy Wonka, right?" I joked, implying all the other Apple employees were basically Oompa-Loompas. He only smirked at me at the thought. But it certainly felt like there would be no one like him again.

I was sitting in a chair in my bedroom looking out at my view of San Francisco, as the October fog drifted over Mount Sutro and spilled down Twin Peaks toward my home in the Castro, when Walt called to tell me the news. Jobs died on October 5, 2011, in Palo Alto, not straying too far from where he had spent the bulk of his life. It felt unreal, but Walt and I quickly launched into full-scale reporting mode, planning out what to do, from the news story itself to a what-next for Apple to a history of Jobs to an essay only Walt could write, given he was the journalist who had been the closest to Jobs over each of their entire careers.

Immediately, we contacted top News Corp executives, including Rupert Murdoch, and requested that all the video and audio of Jobs' appearances at our *AllThingsD* conferences be made free for anyone to listen to forever (on Apple iTunes, of course). The company owned all our intellectual property, so we were nervous it might gate some of the most substantial interviews of tech's most important visionary in his prime years. To sell them on the idea, we described it as a "gift to humanity." To our surprise, they complied. Apple helped us get the material up quickly before Murdoch or his many unctuous minions could change their minds.

At the time, I appeared on a *WSJ* online show and was asked about the reaction to the death in Silicon Valley. "People are letting it sink in and talking about him and what an icon he is," I commented. When the show's lead reporter suggested that the news would knock Apple off its pedestal, I pushed back. "Steve Jobs' DNA is in Apple and that's not something that's going to be gone even though he is. He's such an iconic figure in Silicon Valley that you can't follow him."

The reporter kept insisting that the death of Jobs would lead to the death of Apple. "Kara, surely Apple's tablet market share is at its peak now?" he asked.

"I don't tend to make predictions like that, because I don't know," I replied (the "you dumbass" was implied). "They have an amazing staff at Apple. They continue to dominate the thinking around [the tablet]. The real focus is this guy changed everything and there's nobody at his level playing this game."

Over ten years after his death, Jobs' unicorn status has held. Bezos has come the closest, I suppose, reinventing commerce, seeing the importance of the cloud and innovating logistics. While Tim Cook has proven himself a worthy successor, ballooning Apple to the most valuable and most profitable company in the world, he never was a symbolic replacement for his boss. Because, even with all his faults and quirks, Jobs' myriad achievements represented the best that tech had to offer the world, with some key values—privacy, quality, and design—that were enduring.

As the crush of news accelerated that week, one story stood out for me. Written by Mona Simpson, Jobs' sister, it offered an account of her brother's last moments: "Steve's final words, hours earlier, were monosyllables, repeated three times. Before embarking, he'd looked at his sister Patty, then for a long time at his children, then at his life's partner, Laurene, and then over their shoulders past them. Steve's final words were: OH WOW. OH WOW." I had to marvel at that and did many times that week. The consummate performer and tech's greatest showman had even died with the kind of style that befitted him. It was, as far as goodbyes went, just-one-more-perfect-thing. Like Apple products, Jobs' last utterances were both minimal and wondrous.

His death triggered my usual ruminations on mortality, which was always a major part of my psyche since my father had died so young. I read and then re-read and then listened to Jobs' 2005 Stanford commencement speech, and it began to feel like he was speaking directly to me. "You've got to find what you love," Jobs told the graduating class. "And that is as true for your work as it is for your lovers. Your work is going to fill a large part of your life, and the only way to be truly satisfied is to do what you believe is great work. And the only way to do great work is to love what you do. If you haven't found it yet, keep looking. Don't settle."

And settling is what I had started to feel was happening at *All Things Digital*. Walt and I were still operating awkwardly inside

Dow Jones, where we'd been given stability but not the opportunity to grow, as well as complete operating autonomy and editorial independence by contract. Others in the company resented the freedom we had. Typical of a newsroom, they crapped all over us trying new things while they stayed in line for whatever advantage they thought standing still gave them. Walt and I were also becoming increasingly repulsed by Murdoch and his neverending toxic antics. His U.S. assets like Fox News were discomforting enough, but he was also under investigation in Britain for a phone hacking scandal. Particularly heinous: at Murdoch's *News of the World,* journalists—and I use that term loosely—had hacked into the voice messages on the phone of a thirteen-year-old girl who had disappeared and was later found dead.

The gross invasion of privacy was on brand for Uncle Satan, and we wanted to distance ourselves from it, even though Walt and I had tried to make it work. We spent vast amounts of time meeting with various weasels—and Rupert weasels were a particularly noxious breed—bringing them ideas of how to expand. Our conference was always a reliable moneymaker, but it was too small and we needed reasonable investments to move into new and potentially more lucrative areas.

While we offered a good plan, all the Dow Jones executives could seem to do was point out how well we were paid. "But that new revenue would never have existed without our ideas and ambition," I told one who seemed particularly riveted to the big checks that Walt and I got. "We invented it and we should get paid for it." I had clearly been infected by some of the entrepreneurial spirit of the people I had been covering, and I was becoming increasingly grumpy at the *Journal,* which I had started to think of as a velvet coffin. The idea of being trapped in a box was a metaphor that resonated with me. I had fully soaked up another trait of Silicon Valley: the need for next.

I had done well by walking away many times before when I did not feel great about my career situation. And, once again, I had begun to hear the far-off warning bells that Nora Ephron wrote about so insightfully in *Heartburn*, her veiled novel recounting the breakup of her marriage with Carl Bernstein. Ephron wrote: "And then the dreams break into a million tiny pieces. The dream dies. Which leaves you with a choice: you can settle for reality, or you can go off, like a fool, and dream another dream." I had gotten to know the writer and director when Ephron called me out of the blue to talk tech. A closet geek, she wanted to understand how the shift to online was going to impact media. Ephron had been an early contributor to the *Huffington Post* and was a shareholder, too. In fact, when I broke the news in March of 2011 that AOL had bought the *Huffington Post* for $315 million, Ephron was the first call I got late that night.

"Am I rich?" she asked in a deadpan voice. All kidding aside, more than most, Ephron understood how power changed, whether in a marriage or in technology. Rather than decry it, she decided to jump right in, even if it was to kvetch as she did in an epic essay, "The Six Stages of Email."

My favorite stages were the last two:

Stage Five: Accommodation

Yes. No. Can't. No way. Maybe. Doubtful. Sorry. So sorry. Thanks. No thanks. Out of town. OOT. Try me in a month. Try me in the fall. Try me in a year. NoraE@aol.com can now be reached at NoraE81082@gmail.com.

Stage Six: Death

Call me.

I wish I could. Ephron died less than a year later, in 2012, of pneumonia from acute myeloid leukemia. Very few knew she was dealing with this illness since she told only her family and remained upbeat and charming to the end. I loved Nora and everything she represented, including the ability to transform over and over.

As the idea of dreaming another dream and not settling lingered in my head, I was soon confronted by my own mortality, too. Only a week after Jobs died, I was on a thirteen-hour flight to Hong Kong for our first foray into the international market with an *AllThingsD* conference in Asia. Walt and I had traveled to Korea and Japan to scout locations, before landing on Hong Kong as the city that worked best as a nexus in the region. Asia was becoming a critical innovator in tech, especially China, which is why we picked it, with hopes to expand over time to other key tech hubs such as Israel and Brazil.

But we were loath to make more great content and products for Dow Jones. In post-event surveys, *D* attendees ranked Walt's and my rapport, our interviews, and even the food higher than our affiliation with the *Wall Street Journal*. This penny was beginning to drop with a lot of media figures, as it became clearer that you could build a powerful personal brand—and business— without a big media name behind you. Walt was a pioneer in this shift as he established trust with his readers directly. At *AllThingsD*, our team of more energetic reporters started breaking scoop after scoop, and companies, especially startups, paid increasing attention to our spirited and often cheeky tone that also delivered quality information.

Very cheeky, in fact. One favorite of mine was a comical illustration that our earliest staffer, John Paczkowski, made of Eric Schmidt in a big red ball gag that we used every time the Google CEO made a verbal gaffe, which he did often enough to put the visual into active rotation. We called Yahoo, as it descended in value, the "Yangtanic" after its cofounder. We ran one story with only the words "Apple" and "Twitter" to show how focusing on click-bait virality over real news was a problem. We published serious investigations, funny videos, and bracing essays. It was an "anything goes" attitude which felt fresh and current and, at least to our readers, interesting. The *AllThingsD* site was never boring and the conference was on fire.

And now we were going global. I already traveled a lot for my job, and the week before *AsiaD* was particularly busy. I had flown to New York for a Women in Tech event for *Glamour* magazine, then stopped in Chicago to meet the Groupon people to figure out the disaster that was developing at that once-promising e-commerce company. Then, I flew back to San Francisco and quickly jumped on a flight to Hong Kong. It was a lot, and because News Corp was cheap, we were not able to put all our staff in business class. So, in order not to be a complete jackass, I flew in economy with the rest of the team. I thought I was being a great boss by giving up my business class seat. My window seat in economy was made smaller with two very hefty men next to me, and I was basically stuck there for the thirteen-hour flight. I tried to move around a little bit, but I gave up quickly. I also avoided drinking a lot of water. For anyone who's had a baby post-thirty-five-years-old, you know what I'm talking about. You really can't drink a lot without having to go to the bathroom a lot, and so I abstained.

Instead, I sat and drew up a plan for what a Newco that we owned and ran would look like and how we could make it into a business that could sustain itself with a mix of advertising, sponsorship, and ticket revenue. Did I mention that it was a very tight seat? And that I did not get up? (You must believe those stories about walking around and drinking on airplanes. I used to scoff at them.)

By the time we landed and I got to the Grand Hyatt hotel in Hong Kong where *AsiaD* was taking place, I was equally exhausted and excited. I immediately went to scope out the ballroom awash in the bright red bunting that was the signature color of the site and our signature Steelcase interview chairs. After looking over the stage and having dinner with Walt, I went to my room and crawled into bed. I woke up at 5 a.m. the next morning with a massive headache and a deadline for a story on Yahoo. It had become one of my morning rituals to write about disasters at Yahoo. That day, I was reporting on the CTO's departure and problems with the nutty Yahoo board.

When writing, I often talk to myself, and that morning, I said, "What a circus act that company is." It came out *"nauwmatthungInlevah."* That was curious, I thought. Why was I speaking so strangely? I tried saying something else and it, too, came out like I was speaking a foreign language. I went to the bathroom and started singing the Oscar Mayer "my bologna has a first name" jingle in front of the mirror. I don't know why that popped into my head as the thing I should test my speech with, but it was. It sounded like even more gibberish than the actual song. Next, I tried to eat a strawberry, but it fell out of my mouth and one single finger tingled like it was asleep. Since I could not speak well enough to call down to the front desk, I texted Walt. I also checked in with my brother, Jeff, who is an anesthesiologist in San Francisco and described my symptoms in another text. I was not particularly alarmed as I suffered from persistent migraines and thought it was a combination of that, jet lag, and a crappy seat on a plane.

Neither Walt nor my brother responded immediately. For the first time in many years, Walt was sleeping late and Jeff was likely in the middle of a surgery. As I was waiting for them to respond, I decided to get dressed and go upstairs for breakfast. I was feeling much better, and when I spoke to the hostess, my words made sense although my mouth felt like it was full of Novocain. I was enjoying the local congee in the restaurant, which had a stunning view of the harbor, when Jeff called me back. "It sounds like you are having a stroke," he said urgently.

A stroke? I wasn't that old. "You're the worst doctor ever," I said to him. But Jeff was adamant. He told me to get to a hospital immediately and have an MRI. I went with one of the conference staff in a cab to a hospital recommended by the hotel, even though I thought it was a waste of time. After taking the test, I felt fine and ready to get back to interviewing people like Yahoo CEO Jerry Yang and former Vice President Al Gore. I was merrily texting and reading news when a doctor in a mask came up to me and said: "You had a stroke and we're going to hospitalize you immediately since it looks like you are still having one right now."

I couldn't speak. My only thought was about my two sons, the youngest of whom was about the age I was when my father died. It was only then that I started to cry, both for them and also for my five-year-old self. For that one moment again and not because of the stroke, I was completely rendered mute, which I think a lot of people in Silicon Valley would have enjoyed except for the circumstances. Fortunately, as it turned out, I had the Four Seasons of strokes. I had the Prada of strokes. I had the Manolo Blahnik of strokes. In short, it was a very easy experience considering it was a stroke, except for the stroke part. With medication, the clot dissipated quickly, and I made a video from bed for the site to show everyone I was recovering. I also showed off the lovely view from my hospital room overlooking a racetrack.

That's where I was for five days. I couldn't attend *AsiaD*, but some of *AsiaD* came to me. Gore stopped by my hospital room and so did Yang, who brought me a single perfect plum, which was one of the sweetest gestures I can recall, especially since I had given him such a hard time in print. One nurse was surprised by the stream of visitors. She asked me who I was that famous people were coming to see me. I said I was very important and I couldn't explain why. Then, I put on my sunglasses and rested on my pillow like the star I wasn't.

During my stay, doctors discovered that I had a hole in my heart, which apparently is common—20 percent of people are born with a small or large hole in their heart (which is something more than one of my exes had told me). Since the news was out about my stroke, friends and colleagues started to check in. One key call was from Anne Wojcicki, who had cofounded the genetic testing startup 23andMe. A year earlier, I had taken one of those spitting tests to generate genetic information. It was a jokey demo for our conference where my genetic results were compared to Murdoch's to see if we were linked. Thankfully, we were not.

I never read my full results, but Anne had, with my permission. She informed me that I had a mutation in my blood called factor V Leiden, that made it even clottier and increased a patient's chance of developing abnormal blood clots, most commonly in the legs or lungs. She urged me to share that information with my doctors. Between the sticky blood and the hole in my heart, I had two hidden genetic elements that when combined with a long sedentary flight had created a perfect storm for a stroke. My brother flew to Hong Kong to spring me out of the hospital, which wanted to keep me for another month. Jeff and I bought first-class tickets back to San Francisco (on Murdoch's dime). The prognosis was that eventually I would need surgery to repair the hole in my heart and I should take it easy.

But rest was a state I quickly found tiresome. The never-ending inspirational emails about how I should "slow down" and "stop and smell the roses" didn't help. If anything, they agitated me. The lesson I learned from my stroke is that I didn't want to slow down and that I enjoyed what I do and that I did not want to smell any flowers. The experience got me thinking about what is normal and how it's different for everyone. As Jobs discussed in his Stanford speech, I was confronted by a series of questions: How much time should you spend on your personal life? How much time do you spend on your professional life?

One conclusion I came to was that I really enjoyed my professional life. This became clear after someone sent me a note asking me, "When you are on your deathbed, are you going to remember any time you're at work?" And I answered them, yes, I've had some fantastic times at work. I've had some very important times at work. I have a passion for my work. I really love interviewing people. I love doing stories. I love telling stories. And, most of all, I would regret it if I didn't do it. I thought a lot about Jobs, and it occurred to me that his most productive years were after he was initially diagnosed with cancer. In that period, he created the iPhone and the iPad and was working on reinventing television when he died. And I realized that was why I was so obsessed with his speech. Like Jobs, I truly believe that you should push yourself in areas where you are passionate, and if you don't feel passion toward something, get out of it.

Jobs never talked about not doing. He never said relax. He never said slow down. He pushed himself very hard until the very end. Walt told me that Jobs was still planning and plotting up to the last weeks of his life. This is something I admire, even if many disagree. The stroke crystallized that I wanted to be one of those people who did not die before they had lived. I also thought a lot about my late grandmother Sue, who was a fantastic woman and a stay-at-home wife for most of her life. And stay-at-home was quite literal. Sue wasn't a traveler. She liked to sit in her small living room in Old Forge, Pennsylvania, and watch the Weather Channel, the soaps, and Penn State football games. She had a housecoat and loved cooking.

And I loved her, perhaps more than anyone, since she had been a constant and loving presence after my father died and she tried her best to replace all that I had lost. I called her several times a week to talk about everything and nothing. She'd often say, "You work too hard, come visit me." She was an Italian woman and she liked to make me feel guilty. I tried as hard as I could to drive up from D.C. frequently to see her. Still, much of the time I'd have to say that I couldn't visit because I was too busy with work. Her standard reply would always make me laugh: "The graveyards are full of busy people, honey."

My grandmother was one of the most important people in my life, but she took the opposite meaning from this saying than I do. Yes, the graveyards are full of people who did amazing things, and in the end, that's where we all end up. But since death was a certainty, it meant that I did not have any time to waste. Walt, who'd had his own brush with death from having open-heart surgery, did not want to waste any time either.

And with two permanently broken hearts, we began to plan our next escape in earnest.

CHAPTER 12

Good Bones

Any decent realtor,
walking you through a real shithole, chirps on
about good bones: This place could be beautiful,
right? You could make this place beautiful.

—MAGGIE SMITH, "GOOD BONES"

Our scheme could not happen soon enough. Walt's and my relationship with the *Journal* and parent company Dow Jones was badly frayed. Even though our events were adding millions of dollars in revenue to the bottom line, I'm pretty sure they thought we were assholes. We certainly thought they were.

Still, we tried to save the marriage. In 2011, we sat down with then News Corp digital media CEO Jon Miller, whom I knew well from his stint running AOL. The three of us discussed expanding the *All Things Digital* brand to other areas like sports (*All Things Sports*), finance (*All Things Money*), and more. Each vertical would have its own events and offerings, fueled by both advertising and subscriptions. It was an ambitious concept, and we doubted Dow Jones had the flexibility or the energy to execute it. Sure enough, once again, bureaucracy trumped innovation. Like most new ideas at old media companies, our plan died when Miller exited and Walt and I had to deal with another new and even stupider and slow-moving executive.

The next suit was at least colorful and filled by a chest-thumping dandy named Lex Fenwick. At least his name sounded fun. He was not. Walt and I sent over a proposal requesting $1.6 million in funding that would be used to hire three new salespeople, two video producers, and some app developers. This seemed like the bare basics necessary to run a digital media operation. Fenwick never responded to our plan. Instead, we ended up having one truly odd meeting with him where Fenwick lectured us on digital issues, which he knew little about, while an army of very busy-looking women assistants scuttled in and out. Guess what? We got no actual support and zero new investment.

The *Journal* newsroom was even less friendly with the print side, stubbornly refusing to attribute scoops to *AllThingsD*. It is considered proper journalistic practice to acknowledge when a story is broken by someone else. On our site, we always linked to whatever news organization had prevailed on any great story, as a small nod of respect. Plus, linking to a scoop can goose traffic. That's why it was so strange that our own colleagues would rarely give us attribution and nitpicked our wins.

For example, *AllThingsD* broke the story that new Yahoo CEO Marissa Mayer had secured a $1.1 billion acquisition of blogging platform Tumblr. It was a major scoop at the time with lots of details. Yahoo quickly followed with an official announcement that included the "promise not to screw it up." They did. Eventually, Tumblr passed from Yahoo to Verizon and, in 2019, was purchased by Matt Mullenweg, the founder of Automattic's

WordPress, for $3 million. Still, back when Tumblr was worth over a billion, we reported it first. A day or so later, a similar story appeared in the *Journal* that built on our reporting but did not acknowledge our work. I complained to the *Journal*'s top editor, Gerry Baker, whose response dripped with condescension, which seemed to be his favored style. "It's unfortunate that we at DJ and *ATD* don't seem to do as effective a job at collaboration as we clearly should," Baker emailed back, ignoring his own responsibility in creating that "unfortunate" situation.

After so much attitude from him and with me post-stroke, I was just not having it. I wrote back: "What is clear is that your reporters were very late to a major story, so please excuse me for being irritated here by the complete lack of respect for our efforts at *ATD* and the persistent need to minimize our work in order to justify not extending us the courtesy even the *New York Times* did."

Was it petty? Yes. And what a waste of my wild and precious life dealing with newsroom politics and the fatuous executive popinjays who ruled the roost. Worse, even though Walt and I were proving daily with a very small staff that we could compete in the big leagues, instead of giving us more funding, the *Journal* announced they were beefing up their own staff to—wait for it—compete with us. I was incredulous since we were right there, doing great work and bringing much-needed digital heat to the company.

By the end of the summer of 2013, our latest contract was nearing an end, so Walt and I decided to hit the road and talk to a range of possible new investors. We quickly made a list of A, B, and C prospects. We also decided to keep venture capitalists off the list, largely because we knew they would eventually fuck us.

Our preference was to have two investors—one big media company and one media fund.

The A listers all wanted to meet with us and we came away with these quick assessments: the *New York Times* (super nice folks, super arrogant, super old school); Hearst (interesting range of assets, odd corporate culture, unclear who actually made the decisions); the *Atlantic* (owner David Bradley was a spiffy gentleman, but we did not relish being tied to another rich dude who would control our fate); Bloomberg (the terminal was the only god there and we were but a shiny trinket for them to play with); Condé Nast (a snakier snake pit than Dow Jones, with a very weird proposal about "shadow" shares, Walt and I would be separated, he to *Popular Science* and me to *Wired*).

Hearst was intrigued by a great but crazy idea to remake the *San Francisco Chronicle* into a digital media and event company. I pitched the motto "Finally, the *new* news organization that San Francisco deserves," which was definitely obnoxious. When Walt and I weighed all the variables, it became apparent that NBC News was offering the best deal and partnership. We liked the idea of linking with a national broadcast outlet, and both of us had previous contributor relationships that would be extended to our staff in new ways. We also thought these partners could help us with events, advertising, and marketing. As the second investor, we picked former Yahoo CEO Terry Semel, who had started a media-focused investment fund after he left Yahoo. Semel offered strong ties to Hollywood after his long career there. But mostly, we chose him because he was a truly lovely and generous man.

Our escape seemed imminent with one catch: By contract Dow Jones had a right of first refusal on investing in whatever we wanted to make next. That meant we were required to meet with News Corp CEO Robert Thomson (the return of "the naughty vicar"!). Thomson's jaunty nature did not disappoint as he fired off an email on September 7, 2013, with the subject line "AllThingsDecision." His long and mellifluous note read as if he wanted us to stay:

> I realize there has been some chatter about the future, though we haven't yet received an extraordinarily lucrative offer from a Mexican magnate or a Mumbai mogul or a profligate PE for—part of me was hoping that you and News would benefit from such exceedingly excessive generosity as you did the rounds of potential partners/acquirers. Anyway, I have no problem whatsoever with the structure you suggest and would ask you to ponder the global potential of a separate company that is able to leverage the network of News and DJ, having its own distinctive commercial and editorial team in places from Seoul to Rio, and Bogota to Berlin, being able to share offices and intelligence, thus keeping costs to a minimum and elevating access to a maximum. It's worth considering the length and breadth of your collective ambition.

Thomson seemed ready to play ball, but would he follow through? Six months earlier, he'd sent us a similar email which claimed a decision was imminent about *ATD*. We didn't appreciate the snarky comment about us making the "rounds of potential partners/acquirers." We felt we needed to make it clear that our intention was to build a new company without News Corp. So, Walt replied:

"While we enjoyed your alliteration, we are not out there trying to sell the *ATD* brand or assets, because you own them. And that would be wrong." Walt also reached out to our banker, Quincy Smith, noting, "All we really want from them is the assets in return for a reasonable sum or small minority stake." Mostly, we wanted to move on from a soured relationship with Dow Jones. Still, they had that right of first refusal so, a week later, we met with Thomson, Baker, and some other execs. To signal our lack of interest, we pushed them off until late in the day, which is the dating equivalent of "I'll meet you for coffee." We proposed a valuation of close to $20 million, which was not completely ridiculous considering content companies like *BuzzFeed* and *Vice* were soaring, but still completely made up and decidedly kooky. With our deal with NBC almost complete, we could not imagine Dow Jones executives saying yes. In fact, throwing in that we had to own 51 percent and have complete control, we wanted them to say no.

And they did. In another clever email to us on September 17 that Thomson titled "High Noon," he requested an additional call with him and Baker. "As long as we are Gary Cooper," I replied. As expected, they put forward a proposal in which Dow Jones would get majority control without guaranteeing a fixed investment. This was a nonstarter and we declined. The call was actually quite cordial, with Thomson praising Walt and me for being pioneers in digital journalism. He also said he'd consider selling us the *ATD* brand and its archives. We did not believe him for a second. In fact, we later tried to buy the *All-ThingsD* URL and feed, offering Dow Jones a sum of just under $1 million, which was generous. They countered that Murdoch wanted more like $10 million, which was laughable.

"I could buy Fuckyourupert.com for $10," I told the News Corp minion, who chortled quietly. They clearly weren't going to let any of it go, even if they were not going to use the assets. The best I could do was extract a promise from the CTO that he would preserve the archives of *AllThingsD*. Guess what again? That promise was broken, too, later on. A system upgrade has since made it impossible to find much of our content, including historic videos, like one I did with Peter Thiel and another in which I waylaid Mark Zuckerberg at a restaurant. Apparently, the Internet was *not* written in indelible ink.

But at the time our most pressing concern was to obtain a promise from Thomson that he had no intention of disrupting the lives of our staff, all of whom wanted to come with us. We had no noncompetes, so we weren't worried about any vindictive legal action or any retribution from walking away from the Death Star. But News Corp was rapacious and so we fretted. Walt and I contacted our lawyer and informed him that we were done with the *Journal* and to close the deal with NBC News and Semel. We'd escaped! Still, one top News Corp official warned me that Murdoch would definitely try to mess with us, which I thought was silly since we were so small in size and revenue. "Yeah, you left and he's a son of a bitch," said the executive. "They'll fuck with you."

It happened immediately. Walt and I were on separate planes to Grand Rapids, Michigan, to visit the headquarters of Steelcase, makers of our red chairs and a longtime partner and sponsor of *ATD* events. Over the years, Steelcase had provided all kinds of expensive furniture gratis that saved Dow Jones millions of dollars in costs. Midair, we each received a draft of the news release about our departure. The statement implied that Dow Jones had declined to renew our contract and read as if the company had fired Walt. (I was under contract and not an employee any longer.) I was incensed that they would treat Walt, who'd been such a key financial and editorial contributor over decades, so shabbily.

In separate emails, we communicated that we were furious. In response, Gerry Baker stubbornly stuck to the script that Dow Jones had broken up with us, a tale someone at the company was also peddling to the *Journal*'s reporter for an exclusive news story. This would not stand. I told the PR person on the phone that somehow the alliterative emails from Thomson praising us might end up in the hands of, say, a *New York Times* reporter. When asked how that would happen, I replied: "The *Times* has *amazing* reporters." Meanwhile, Walt talked to the *Journal* reporter to make sure she understood our side (i.e., the truth), although we doubted she had a lot of autonomy on this particular story.

We also pinged Thomson, who thankfully took a less obstreperous tone. The final joint statement read a lot like a celebrity breakup, in which everyone parts amicably. "For years, Dow Jones/The Wall Street Journal has enjoyed working with Walt Mossberg and Kara Swisher . . . however, after discussions, both parties have decided not to renew the agreement," said Baker.

If you're thinking, "Well, at least they did the classy thing in the end. . . ." No, they did not. In a final fuck-you, Baker added that the *Journal* tech coverage and conference would be expanding with twenty additional editorial staff. I imagine the cost worked out to a lot more than the $1.6 million that we had asked for and been denied. Baker's obvious kick on the way out pissed me off even more when he wrote directly to say that he admired our work and hoped we'd see each other in the future. *As if.* Murdoch himself mumbled a similar sentiment to me at a noisy *Vanity Fair* Oscar party months later, as if such behavior was just business and not personal. I only had one reply to him.

"Is never good for you?" I said with a smile. "Because it works for me." I doubted that Murdoch could make out what I'd said through the din since he was straining to hear and cupped his hand at his ear. So, I just waved at him and moved on to ogle the real celebrities.

I really did want to move on. As I noted in a memo to our staff: "I am eager to get back to the news and also building things and giving everyone new challenges and ways to do great journalism we do so well already. With added resources, we can do so much more, and we will. While I know how trying all this coverage can be (and how wrong so much of it has been) and it's untoward how our current partners have chosen to behave, we need to keep our heads down and try our best to ignore it until we can unveil our next iteration. And that WILL be something to talk about."

By the end of November of 2013, a $10 million investment from NBC and Semel's Windsor Media had been deposited in the bank account of our new company, Shut Up and Listen LLC. Our new partners owned a minority stake, while Walt and I controlled 51 percent of the company. On the last day of the year, Walt and I put up our final *AllThingsD* post. We referenced my first post on the site in April 2007 as we wrote: "In taking a page from the tech industry we cover—it's once again time to refresh, reimagine, remake and reinvent. (You'll see what *that* means soon enough.)"

Two days later, Walt and I rented a large hotel suite in San

Francisco and invited the *ATD* staff to dinner as we waited to push the button. Just after midnight on January 2, 2014, our new venture went live. *Recode* was born, a name we came up with after wrestling with a naming company; we named the conference simply, Code. We were off with a renewed purpose and a fitting startup mentality. No longer part of a mothership, we decided to push as hard as we could to distinguish ourselves by taking immediate aim at the growing power of companies like Uber and, especially, Facebook.

Why? It was clear that social polarization was happening due to tech, which is why I soon took to calling the social networking giant "antisocial media." The violations of privacy had been obvious at Facebook from the early days and continued on. These breaches were always met with an after-the-fact apology by Zuckerberg or Sandberg. The "we're so sorry" became a joke to some of the reporters who covered the company. Each month brought another instance of Facebook grabbing information from users without their permission, some regulator investigating it and perhaps levying a small fine. Rinse and repeat.

The most perfect example of this was a consent decree that the company signed in 2011 that required users to be notified when their data was being shared by Facebook with third parties. After the scandal erupted in 2018 over whether political consulting firm Cambridge Analytica had been able to access data of 87 million Facebook users without their permission, the Federal Trade Commission got a $5 billion settlement from the company over violating the first agreement. Even though it was a landmark figure in the U.S., I called the fine a "parking ticket," since it's hard to imagine that Facebook's executives saw the payment as anything other than a cost of doing business. They paid the ticket and continued with an ad-based business model that relies on getting and keeping the attention of users, and the ability to gather and mine data was critical.

In an interview with me just after the settlement was announced, Zuckerberg again broke out into the old "we're so sorry" routine. "You know, frankly, I just got that wrong," he told me. "I was maybe too idealistic on the side of data portability, that it would create more good experiences. And it created some, but I think what the clear feedback was from our community was that people value privacy a lot more. And they would rather have their data locked down and be sure that nothing bad will ever happen to it than be able to easily take it and have social experiences in other places." He kept talking, barreling on until, I suppose, I might see the light and agree with him.

I did not agree with him, and so, he marched on. "I think we remain idealistic, but I think also understand what our responsibility is to protect people now. And I think the reality is that in the past we had not had a good enough appreciation of some of this stuff. And some of it was that we were a smaller company, so some of the issues and some of these bad actors just targeted us less, because we were smaller. But we certainly weren't in a target of nation states trying to influence elections back when we only had 100 million people in the community."

Blah. Blah. Blah. And I might add: *Blah.* Of course, idealism and openness, as well as the more specific idea of data portability, did not have to conflict with privacy, even though it was crafty on Zuckerberg's part to make it seem that way. But what stood out most for me was that he was zeroing in on a bigger issue, which I was becoming significantly more concerned with—the danger of these platforms using data to become the most powerful tool in history for propaganda and manipulation by malevolent people.

Social media sites were built and monetized on engagement, and nothing, as I pointed out often, fueled engagement like enragement. Zuckerberg kept yammering about "creating community," while forgetting that nothing pulls a community together faster than hating on another community. Zuckerberg once called me late at night in early 2017, to get feedback on an essay he wrote with the riveting title "About Community Standards." In one of its first sentences, he asked: "Today I want to focus on the most important question of all: Are we building the world we all want?" Zuckerberg mused on this subject for six thousand words, finally arriving at the conclusion: "There are many of us who stand for bringing people together and connecting the world. I hope we have the focus to take the long view and build the new social infrastructure to create the world we want for generations to come."

I dubbed the essay, "The Mark Manifesto," and while I thought it was in desperate need of a copy editor, I appreciated his incessant need to virtue signal for a better experience, even when it never seemed to happen. Yet, I was also astonished at his inability to anticipate just how badly things on his platform could go. I told Zuckerberg that I did not share his hopefulness of creating a constructive community. In fact, I was certain that Facebook was moving toward becoming a mecca for those intent on destruction.

In our interview in 2018, Zuckerberg remained painfully simplistic, as if all he really needed to know about free speech that he learned from CliffsNotes. "Freedom of speech and hate speech and offensive content. Where is the line, right?" he said.

"And the reality is that different people are drawn to different places, we serve people in a lot of countries around the world, a lot of different opinions on that." You can still make choices, I told a man who did not want to make choices, other than the choice of capitalism over community.

What Zuckerberg wanted most was to wash his hands of it. "You know, what I would really like to do is find a way to get our policies set in the way that reflects the values of the community, so I'm not the one making those decisions. Right?" he said. "I feel fundamentally uncomfortable sitting here in California at an office, making content policy decisions for people around the world. But things like, where is the line on hate speech? I mean, who chose me to be the person that [decided]."

Well, Mark, *you* did. And what he was saying in 2018 was disingenuous since the hands-off attitude was already deeply entrenched at Facebook. That much was clear in 2016, when a memo titled "The Ugly Truth" was leaked to *BuzzFeed* just days after the 2018 FTC settlement announcement. Written by Facebook vice president Andrew Bosworth, one of Zuckerberg's tight circle of advisers, the memo addressed the thorny issue explicitly: "Maybe it costs a life by exposing someone to bullies. Maybe someone dies in a terrorist attack coordinated on our tools. And still, we connect people. The ugly truth is that we believe in connecting people so deeply that anything that allows us to connect more people more often is *de facto* good."

Reaction to the memo was very fast and very furious. Zuckerberg said Bosworth got it wrong and clarified that "We've never believed the ends justify the means." He added: "We recognize that connecting people isn't enough by itself. We also need to work to bring people closer together. We changed our whole mission and company focus to reflect this last year." Bosworth himself backed away from his own memo, deleting it once it was leaked and insisting he only posed this terrible scenario and immoral conclusion to start a debate internally. His how-dare-you-question-me defense was painful to witness. "If we have to live in fear that even our bad ideas will be exposed then we won't explore them or understand them as such," he wrote in his 2018 memo about his 2016 memo. "We run a much greater risk of stumbling on them later."

But stumble Facebook had and stumble they would continue to do. Many began to question what role the company played in the 2016 presidential election and whether the Russian government manipulated Facebook's platform to help elect Donald Trump. While I do not believe it was the only venue for the malevolent players of that country, initially Facebook tried to act as if it had no part. When he was asked in 2016 about possible Russian interference via spreading misinformation, Zuckerberg's original reaction was to pooh-pooh the very notion. "The idea that fake news on Facebook—of which, you know, it's a very small amount of the content—influenced the election in any way, I think, is a pretty crazy idea," he said in an interview with David Kirkpatrick at the Techonomy conference. "Voters make decisions based on their lived experience."

While Zuckerberg was right that many underestimated the appeal of Trump, to then pole-vault that into an argument that it was crazy to ascribe any impact from Facebook seemed disingenuous verging on ignorant. The kneejerk dismissal of the assertion as "crazy" made me wonder if the company had tried to gauge the extent of the problem at all. As famed management guru Peter Drucker said: "If you can't measure it, you can't manage it."

In fact, Russian attempts to interfere and impact the election on Facebook were ongoing and persistent, which was no surprise since it was the biggest platform. Facebook engineers had already detected suspicious Russian activity months before that. Years later, the Justice Department would act against more than a dozen Russians and three companies "for executing a scheme to subvert the 2016 election and support Donald J. Trump's presidential campaign," according to the *New York Times*. "While the indictment does not accuse Facebook of any wrongdoing, it provided the first comprehensive account from the authorities of how critical the company's platforms had been to the Russian campaign to disrupt the 2016 election," the *Times* noted. "Facebook and Instagram were mentioned 41 times, while other technology that the Russians used was featured far less."

When I first heard the disturbing "crazy" quote from Zuckerberg, I dialed up Sandberg, who was politically savvy. Sandberg had spent time in D.C., including working at the Treasury Department as Larry Summers's chief of staff. It seemed like she would understand my concerns about possible foreign influence and the need to investigate before speaking. I was trying to catch a flight to John F. Kennedy Airport, so when we connected on the phone, I was unable to take notes. Still, I remember clearly that I unloaded on her about Zuckerberg making statements about important issues that might be inaccurate. There was no way, I said, without a proper and deep investigation, for anyone at Facebook to know the extent of the potential manipulation by those seeking to misinform for political gains. I added, if this turned out to be true, even in part, who would take responsibility for allowing it to happen? As someone deeply concerned about propaganda and its impact on our democracy, I was intense, especially when I added, "This is going to end very badly for Facebook."

Sandberg, for her part, listened and then said in her silky-smoothest of voices some version of "Calm down, Kara. We're handling it." Well, they didn't handle the propaganda. Not from the Russians. Not in Iran. And not in Sri Lanka, where a Buddhist mob attacked Muslims over false information spread on Facebook, prompting a government official to tell the *New York Times* in the most perfect of metaphors: "The germs are ours, but Facebook is the wind." More like a hurricane. There have been deeply reported and detailed stories about the misinformation that flooded Facebook and the platform's weak efforts to stop it, full of examples from across the world.

The *New Yorker's* Evan Osnos put it best in a piece about the reckoning coming for Big Tech, most especially Facebook, writing, "Zuckerberg and Sandberg have attributed their mistakes to excessive optimism, a blindness to the darker applications of their service. But that explanation ignores their fixation on growth, and their unwillingness to heed warnings." *Bingo.* Whether it was used to boost fears of Hillary Clinton or spread anti-vax nonsense, Facebook was a platform designed to create crisis and rage as the rubles rolled in. It was a system-wide problem and company execs continued to act as if it was easily fixable. If that were true, why didn't they ever fix it? The truth is moderating the flood of information they facilitated was an impossible task.

What was particularly galling was that Facebook executives repeatedly made the argument that not many people were impacted, like it was a minor leak in its social network basement, and they might have mopped up the dampness while missing the large mold infestation. And when the mold flared up again, they would shift to saying their job was to just create tools and that they had no responsibility for what happened when people used those tools as weapons. Zuckerberg never seemed to deviate from this attitude, including in 2018 when I asked him if anyone at Facebook should have been fired for the Cambridge Analytica mess.

"Well, I think it's a big issue. But look, I designed the platform, so if someone's going to get fired for this, it should be me," Zuckerberg said with a "mistakes happen" verbal shrug.

I naturally followed up. "But to be clear, you're not going to fire yourself right now? Is that right?" I was not trolling him—I wanted to know what level of responsibility he felt for the unintended consequences of his creation.

It seemed to me that he wasn't sure whether to laugh or cry. "Not on this podcast right now. Do you really want me to fire myself right now? Just for the news?" he said. "I think we should do what's going to be right for the community." And what was right in his estimation, at least, was more Mark Zuckerberg since Facebook was born as and always would be a Mark Zuckerberg production. The rest of us would continue to pay the price for his education.

Into this mess and void, naturally, moved a master manipulator and chaos creator like Trump, whom Facebook and Zuckerberg would inevitably cozy up to, until he went too far on January 6, 2021. Trump—the greatest troll in social media, as I dubbed him—understood intuitively that much of his success would depend on connecting with his base, whether it was in person or, at scale, via social media. Which is why Trump—with a big assist from Facebook investor and board member Peter Thiel—summoned all the tech leaders, including Sandberg, to that gilded room at Trump Tower. He had needed and used the help of Silicon Valley to spread his propaganda. And now that Trump had squeaked out a win in three pivotal states, they needed him.

So, I didn't even bother to dial up Sandberg either before or after that meeting, because she seemed long past listening and what was the point? I did call one person, though, whom I thought could make a difference.

Hello, Elon. It's me.

I got my love of sunglasses from my dad, who would only live a few years after this photo was taken.
Kara Swisher

Don't judge me for my Izod and tan—it was college in the 1980s. *Kara Swisher*

My older sons, Louie and Alex, are tall.
Megan Smith

My son and daughter Sol and Clara are not (but will be). *Amanda Katz*

This monkey Elon Musk carried into one of our meetings would have made a better Twitter CEO. *Kara Swisher*

I still don't know why Elon Musk wore a kerchief for this interview and I wish I had asked. *Asa Mathat*

Despite our differences, Elon Musk is always a bracing interview. *Asa Mathat*

Elon Musk did not always believe my heart was seething with hate. *Kara Swisher*

Mark Zuckerberg didn't just kill democracy—he also killed an actual bison. *Kara Swisher*

The infamous Illuminati hoodie.
Kara Swisher

Right after we took this friendly selfie, Mark Zuckerberg told me Holocaust deniers did not mean to lie. *Kara Swisher*

The *schvitz* heard round the tech world. *Asa Mathat*

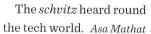

Barry Diller

Kara Swisher

Brian Chesky

Kara Swisher

Dave Goldberg

Kara Swisher

Dick Costolo

Kara Swisher

Jack Dorsey

Kara Swisher

Jerry Yang

Kara Swisher

Kevin Systrom

Kara Swisher

Kim Kardashian

Kara Swisher

Mark Cuban

Kara Swisher

Malala Yousafzai

Kara Swisher

Megan Rapinoe

Kara Swisher

Peter Thiel

Kara Swisher

Sergey Brin

Kara Swisher

Tony Hsieh

Kara Swisher

Tristan Harris

Kara Swisher

Yoel Roth

Matt Winkelmeyer / Getty Images for Vox Media

Andy Jassy

Asa Mathat

Barack Obama

Vjeran Pavic for Vox Media

Bill Gates

Asa Mathat

Bob Iger

Asa Mathat

Carly Fiorina

Asa Mathat

Gavin Newsom

Photo © 2023 by Rick Smolan/Against All Odds Production

Hillary Clinton

Photo © 2023 by Rick Smolan/Against All Odds Production

James Cameron

Asa Mathat

Reed Hastings,
Jason Kilar, and
Chad Hurley

*Chad Hurst/
Getty Images*

Jony Ive, Laurene Powell Jobs, Tim Cook

Asa Mathat

Larry Ellison

Asa Mathat

Reid Hoffman and Marc Andreessen

Asa Mathat

Rupert Murdoch

Photo © 2023 by Rick Smolan/Against All Odds Production

Sheryl Sandberg

Asa Mathat

Satya Nadella

Asa Mathat

Steve Jobs

Asa Mathat

Bill Gates and Steve Jobs

Asa Mathat

Sundar Pichai

Photo © 2023 by Rick Smolan/Against All Odds Production

Susan Wojcicki

Asa Mathat

Travis Kalanick

Asa Mathat

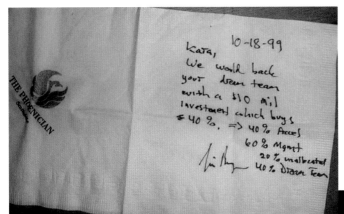

This $10 million napkin was my chance at being rich and I blew it.

Kara Swisher

Our first foray into conference still looks fabulous, especially with our giant stipple drawing heads.

Asa Mathat

We called our first blog foray at *All Things Digital* "tech-tastic," but it looks kind of bad in hindsight.

Screenshot

I had obviously had it with these Internet leaders on January 6, 2021.

Screenshot

Let me say in no uncertain terms @jack @vijaya @kayvz: If you do not suspend Donald Trump's Twitter account for the next day at least, this mob attack on Congress is also on you. Sorry, but he has incited violence for days, using your tools in large part and you need to act now.

Kara Swisher
twitter.com

CHAPTER 13

I, Asshole

Houston, we've had a problem.

—JIM LOVELL

The world's richest man and most famous living tech entrepreneur had to be fucking kidding. But Elon Musk was not joking when he emailed me on October 17, 2022, with the subject line: "You're an asshole."

Just a week earlier, Musk had been friendly toward me, as was typical. In fact, he'd asked me for my thoughts about Twitter, the beleaguered service he was forced to buy after pretending that an ironclad contract was not made of iron. And despite engaging in the business equivalent of a toddler tantrum after agreeing to overpay for the company without contingencies, Musk had won the prize. Well, to be more accurate, the booby prize. While hugely popular and addictive to politicians, the media, and promiscuous id-brains like Musk, Twitter had long been the little tech engine that couldn't.

What was so weird about Musk labeling me "an asshole" was that—unlike many critics—I had taken a fair wait-and-see attitude about his purchase of Twitter. I had covered many deals that had some element of bullshit introduced in the midst of the battle, such as Microsoft's failed attempt to buy Yahoo, and this seemed no different. Musk filed a lawsuit in Delaware's Court of Chancery to challenge the deal he'd agreed to, but just before his deposition, he balked. In the end, Musk had to fork over $44 billion for Twitter and no amount of rage tweeting was going to change that.

So, it's true: I welcomed Musk's takeover. I'd covered Twitter since it debuted in 2006, and for most of its history it had been a woefully underperforming business. A lot of the blame for this falls on the bony shoulders of cofounder Jack Dorsey. At the time of Musk's offer, Dorsey was a part-time CEO whose attention was divided by his work at the innovative payments company Square (later called Block). A genuine visionary, Dorsey had started to foist his personal habits on his employees, like opening a company meeting with a community meditation. He also decided that he was so smart he could run two companies at once. Narrator: He could not run two companies at once.

While heads nodded publicly about how amazing he was to pull it off, privately most people decried his tone-deaf arrogance to me. I agreed. Typically, one or both businesses suffered, and only tech CEOs of a certain type considered themselves so important as to be irreplaceable. But, as my grandmother correctly noted, the graveyards are full of once-busy people.

And whistling past the cemetery is where Twitter always seemed to be, barely making it as a business, with its stock mainly hovering around its IPO offering. Still, it had created a splash well beyond its small size. Despite a tiny $5 billion in annual revenue, Twitter's influence was often compared to Meta's, which pulled in $116 billion in 2022. Twitter dominated the zeitgeist, populated by a coterie of celebrities, politicians, and media heavyweights all vying to be the dunk master of the platform. That title, eventually, went hands down to @realDonaldTrump, who used Twitter as a megaphone to become the world's biggest troll.

But the real story of Twitter was not in the noisy heat it generated, but in colder and harder math. The premise of Twitter was dead simple: A registered user logs in via the Internet or a mobile phone and answers the question "What are you doing?" in 140 characters or fewer. It was immediately clear when I signed on in 2007 that its lightweight design and newsy bent would soon make it the buzziest product in Silicon Valley. It was also the glitchiest. Its revenue, user growth, and most important of all, stock price all remained in the doldrums. The basic product remained stuck, too. Early Twitter looked an awful lot like current Twitter, where doubling the number of allowed characters counted as innovation. These drags combined with a persistent drama among its founders meant the company never realized its potential. Actually, it was a minor miracle that the bird stayed aloft. While Twitter had received acquisition interest over the years, negotiations always ended in tears once potential buyers realized the company was a hot mess from both a tech and product perspective.

Maybe this was inevitable since Twitter stumbled into being in the wake of failure. Dorsey and his cofounders, Ev Williams and Biz Stone, had originally staked their claim in an early podcast-focused startup called Odeo. When that did not catch on with users, the team saw promise in a microblogging communications company based on software that Dorsey invented. They found one of the more perfect names for the startup:

Twitter, after a bird. Twitter was always good copy thanks to its bickering founders, who traded the CEO job back and forth. I once called the company "the most emotionally driven in tech," and covering it often felt like watching a soap opera, but with less attractive characters. When I wandered into company headquarters in San Francisco a year after it debuted publicly, I had a lot of questions. From that first visit, it became clear that Twitter was a goat rodeo.

In late 2008, I broke a story about how the then-private Facebook had offered to buy Twitter for $500 million in stock and some cash, trying to grab some buzz and solidify its dominance in the status update space. In an interview at the time, Zuckerberg called Twitter an "elegant model" and said that he was "really impressed by what they've done." After Twitter repelled his offer, Zuckerberg adopted a more correct—and honest—take. In "Hatching Twitter," journalist Nick Bilton quotes Zuckerberg telling close friends, "[Twitter is] such a mess, it's as if they drove a clown car into a gold mine and fell in."

That was funny. But there was still a feeling among Twitter's investors and executives that the startup could increase its revenues up from zero to something that matched its cultural relevance. As one executive told me at the time: "It's more about timing. There is a strong feeling that there is still an opportunity—even with the economic downturn—to blow this thing out." That opportunity never materialized, despite the best efforts of Dick Costolo, another well-regarded entrepreneur who was brought in to professionalize the founder-moshpit approach. Earlier in his career, Costolo had cofounded ad software FeedBurner, which Google had acquired. He remained at Google for two years before jumping to Twitter as COO in 2009. A year later, Williams took paternity leave and Costolo was named temporary CEO. Costolo remained at the helm, taking the company public in 2013. Twitter shares went out at $26, then leaped to over $50 and closed at about $45, giving the company a market value of about $25 billion.

And that is where the valuation pretty much parked, even after Dorsey had taken over from Costolo and its shares bumped along the bottom in May of 2016 to $14.01. Shares rose to a high of $77.63 in March of 2021, which was what had prompted the higher price from Musk. But the business was a bust overall, as the service got worse. Even Costolo was becoming frustrated with trolling, noting in a 2015 internal memo that he was "frankly ashamed" at the company's response. "We suck at dealing with abuse and trolls on the platform and we've sucked at it for years," he wrote.

It got worse, and what had really begun to occupy my attention was the Trump factor on Twitter. I watched in real time as his crass and cruel comments began to warp politics. He tweeted openly racist and antisemitic sentiments, causing his supporters to retweet him in solidarity and his detractors to retweet him in anger. Either way, his lies and name-calling were spread. Trump had gamed the platform malevolently, much as Alex Jones had done on Facebook. This continued throughout his presidency. As Trump's activity ramped up and verged into coded speech promoting violence, I wrote a *New York Times* column in October 2021 titled "Trump Is Too Dangerous for Twitter." I called on the platform to ban him, predicting what could happen if it did not:

It so happens that in recent weeks, including at a fancy-pants Washington dinner party this past weekend, I have been testing my companions with a hypothetical scenario. My premise has been to ask what Twitter management should do if Mr. Trump loses the 2020 election and tweets inaccurately the next day that there had been widespread fraud and, moreover, that people should rise up in armed insurrection to keep him in office.

Most people I have posed this question to have had the same response: Throw Mr. Trump off Twitter for inciting violence. A few have said he should be only temporarily suspended to quell any unrest. Very few said he should be allowed to continue to use the service without repercussions if he was no longer the president. One high-level government official asked me what I would do. My answer: I would never have let it get this bad to begin with.

On January 6, 2021, the scenario that I had concocted—which Twitter executives in 2019 told me was preposterous and irresponsible to write—became a reality. As I watched the images of the chaos unfold on Capitol Hill from my D.C. home less than a mile away, I returned to Twitter, of course, to make a plea.

"Let me say in no uncertain terms," I wrote, directly tagging Dorsey, chief counsel Vijaya Gadde, and head of product Kayvon Beykpour, "if you do not suspend Donald Trump's Twitter account for the next day at least, this mob attack on Congress is also on you. Sorry, but he has incited violence for days, using your tools in large part and you need to act now. This is about public safety and the safety of those trapped in Congress now.

He has no part in calming down the mob he incited—this will be up to the police and the National Guard."

Twitter management dithered for a day, plunged into crisis over suddenly becoming a handmaiden to sedition. Trump took advantage of that dithering and continued to tweet like the madman he is. In the one that finally sunk him, Trump tweeted: "The 75,000,000 great American Patriots who voted for me, AMERICA FIRST, and MAKE AMERICA GREAT AGAIN, will have a GIANT VOICE long into the future. They will not be disrespected or treated unfairly in any way, shape, or form!!!" A second tweet affirmed that he did not plan to attend the inauguration of President-Elect Joe Biden, which many saw as a signal to his followers that he did not intend to go along with "the peaceful transition of power," a key concept in a democracy.

That was Trump's last tweet for years, after Twitter finally decided to act. On January 8, the company announced, "After close review of recent Tweets from the @realDonaldTrump account and the context around them—specifically how they are being received and interpreted on and off Twitter—we have permanently suspended the account due to the risk of further incitement of violence." As CEO, Dorsey was responsible for the call to ban Trump, even though he tried to distance himself from the decision. Years later, Dorsey explained that he thought it was the right call at the moment. "We faced an extraordinary and untenable circumstance, forcing us to focus all of our actions on public safety. Offline harm as a result of online speech is demonstrably real, and what drives our policy and enforcement above all," Dorsey said. He could've stopped there but he didn't. "That said," Dorsey continued, "having to ban an account has real and significant ramifications. While there are clear and obvious exceptions, I feel a ban is a failure of ours ultimately to promote healthy conversation."

Facebook moved fast and presumably broke things and by 8:30 p.m. on January 6, the platform announced Trump had committed "two policy violations" and his page would be locked for twenty-four hours. That bought Zuckerberg time to call his higher-ups and let them know that he had decided to suspend Trump's account. Zuckerberg explained that "the risks of allowing the President to continue to use our service during this period are simply too great. Therefore, we are extending the block we have placed on his Facebook and Instagram accounts indefinitely and for at least the next two weeks until the peaceful transition of power is complete." When these platforms lowered the boom, it felt like a relief. Still, it was troubling that only a handful of people made the decision to pull the plug on the still-official president of the United States. We had, in essence, privatized our public discourse and were now allowing billionaires to implement the rules of the road.

At the time, in an unpopular take, Musk indicated that he would never have done such a thing, even insisting Trump's removal was "morally wrong." Musk would soon start to insert the word "moral" into a lot of his discourse. I agreed that there were issues of free speech at play and they can get thorny (see the ACLU defending a neo-Nazi group's right to march through Skokie, Illinois, in the late 1970s). But from then on, certainty about the idea of what free speech meant started to animate Musk's feed a lot. He was even more irked over Twitter's suspension of Babylon Bee, the right-leaning parody news site. Occasionally funny and mostly achingly juvenile, Babylon Bee had gotten suspended by Twitter management for linking to a trans-phobic joke news story about awarding the title "Man of the Year" to U.S. assistant secretary for health Rachel Levine after *USA Today* named her to its "Women of the Year" list.

It was a tasteless and stupid joke, but Twitter's twelve-hour suspension of the Bee account was stupider, including demanding that the Bee take down the offending tweet. Twitter wading into the humor arena was not a good idea and actually gave the low-brow dudes of the Bee the high ground. "Twitter could, of course, delete the tweet themselves. But they won't. It's not enough for them to just wipe it out. They want us to bend the knee and admit that we engaged in hateful conduct," wrote Seth Dillon, the Babylon Bee CEO, like the moral grandee that he decidedly is not. "I can promise you that's not happening. Truth is not hate speech. If the cost of telling the truth is the loss of our Twitter account, then so be it. We won't compromise the truth just to keep our account."

Truth? More like a puerile stunt from a mostly unfunny comedy site, which still deserved more leeway to serve the needs of its dopey fans. The childishness is probably what attracted Musk and his increasingly self-righteous leanings to the "cause." Within three days of the Bee suspension, Musk put up a Twitter poll asking his followers: "Free speech is essential to a functioning democracy. Do you believe Twitter rigorously adheres to this principle?" Musk later mused: "Is a new platform needed?"

By then, Musk had already been buying up Twitter shares, and within a month he was offering a staggering $44 billion in an all-cash deal. "I think it's very important for there to be an inclusive arena for free speech," he said in an interview days after the bid. He promised to make its technology more transparent, rid it of spammy bots, and that he would be "authenticating all humans." He also said he wanted his worst critics to stay on the platform and have at him, because "that is what free speech means."

Musk's lofty rhetoric struck me as vintage tech billionaire blah-blah talk, but as an active user for both personal and professional reasons, I had long hoped some company or person would turn Twitter around. If I had to come up with names of those who could do it, that short list would have included companies like Microsoft and risk-takers like Musk. He was a fan of the product and had both the vision and the skills to transform the platform into something that was more useful and easier to use. I had compiled a long list of what Twitter could have been: the world's instant news ticker, a real-time collaboration engine, the digital equivalent of Stone Soup, and a place for delightful entertainment. But it never seemed to get there in any of these ways, even as other offerings, like TikTok and Instagram, supplanted and surpassed it.

Still, I had hopes that Musk, girded by his don't-give-a-fuck persona, endless wealth, and deep interest in transforming the media, could be the owner to help Twitter realize its potential. Looking back now, I was obviously and completely wrong. And, even at the time, I became increasingly tweaked by the variety of odd antics Musk employed to try and slip out of the deal, all of which cast him as the aggrieved party rather than the aggressor. At first, I ignored it, as strange and silly behavior had always been a small part of Musk's personality. Over the years I'd known him, I'd seen him range from puckish to juvenile to deeply obnoxious. In 2019, I brought A. G. Sulzberger, the publisher of the

New York Times, to meet Musk at his Tesla offices in Silicon Valley for a presumably serious discussion. Instead, Musk arrived cradling a small stuffed monkey cradling a small bottle of Bombay Sapphire gin. Musk said the monkey was named "Harambe," after the gorilla that was shot and killed after he grabbed and dragged a three-year-old boy who had slipped into the enclosure at the Cincinnati Zoo. He set Harambe on the table and left him there for the entire meeting, even addressing the stuffed animal now and then. Musk seemed to think this was hysterical. Sulzberger, the polar opposite of Musk, did not seem to notice.

I felt a lot of Musk's behavior involved letting off steam from the high-pressure high-wire act of his business and personal life. But as he got more and more famous, his pique—and paranoia—got more pronounced. He was always deep into whatever dank meme was floating around the Internet and would express sadness, irritation, or delight, emoting readily and maybe too dramatically. He loved to behave as if he were much younger than he was. Over time, his harmless fun became less harmless and less fun.

The signs were certainly there. In 2017, Walt Mossberg was retiring from journalism, so his colleagues at *Recode* thought it would be amusing if some of the people Walt had interviewed over the past forty-seven years had the chance to turn the tables on him. Everyone I approached about recording a question for Walt said yes, including Sheryl Sandberg, Mark Cuban, and Tim Cook. I called Musk with the same simple request, noting that he could record it quickly on his phone and ask Walt anything.

The reply came as a shock. "Is this the same Walt that attacked me on Twitter?" he responded. While Musk sometimes reacted in ways that seemed unusually tetchy, I was flabbergasted. In the nicest way possible, I pushed back. "I have no idea! I am sure you took it the wrong way, as per usual. It's the same Walt that did two amazing interviews with you though. Be the bigger man. Good lord. I meant everyone on Twitter takes things the wrong way. It's a hellish medium for healthy communication. Look, sorry for asking. I had no idea you were so upset by Walt's tweet. Sorry it hurt you." I was even more confused once I looked at Walt's supposedly offensive tweet. It kicked off with Walt stating that he absolutely loved Tesla.

Walt went on to accurately note that given its stock price, the company was worth more than a whole bunch of car companies with more massive revenues combined. He was clearly making a comment about the stock market and not even about Tesla's prospects, even though most reasonable people thought the innovative car maker was overvalued—including some guy named Elon Musk who had repeatedly called the stock overvalued. It's not like Walt had brought up valid questions about Tesla's treatment of factory workers, lax safety measures, or allegations of misleading marketing. At the 2016 Code conference, Musk sat onstage with Walt and me and asserted that the Tesla Model X "can drive autonomously with greater safety than a person right now." Three years later, video of this assertion was cited in a lawsuit brought by the family of Walter Huang, an Apple employee, who died when his Model X crashed into a highway barrier. In response, Tesla's lawyers questioned the validity of the Code video, implying that it could be a deep fake. Was that really Musk at Code? Who knows?

I know. He was. The lawyer's ploy backfired when Huang's lawyers said the easiest way to get to the truth would be for Musk to authenticate the video himself. The judge agreed and called for Musk to be deposed. The point is there were plenty of attacks Walt could have made, but all he said was that Tesla was trading on future hopes and dreams rather than real fundamentals. Musk's overreaction indicated that he had the thinnest of skins.

Thinner, apparently. He responded to my defense of Walt: "'As per usual.' Kara, don't ever email me again." So, I did not, as it was so ridiculously juvenile, like arguing with an overly sensitive seventh grader. Actually, my two older sons were never that bratty when they were in seventh grade.

It was also biting the hand that fed him. The same year that Musk cut me off, Tesla filed an annual report with the SEC that noted: "To date, for vehicle sales, media coverage and word of mouth have been the primary drivers of our sales leads and have helped us achieve sales without traditional advertising and at relatively low marketing costs."

Whatever, I thought, another mogul bites the bust. But, about a year later, Musk texted me about a range of topics. When I asked him if he was still pissed, *as per usual*, he seemed to have no idea what I was talking about. Had he recovered from the pain of the non-attack? Forgotten his misguided tantrum? Never actually been angry but texted me in some 3 a.m. stupor? Who knows? Who cares. In the interim, Musk's odd antics had continued, mostly on the hair-trigger Twitter platform. In 2018, Musk called a British caver a "pedo" after he declined Musk's offer of a tiny submarine during the rescue of Thai schoolboys. This prompted a defamation lawsuit. Musk defended himself in part by telling the court that the phrase "pedo guy" was common in South Africa. The jury sided with Musk.

That same year, Musk posted his infamous "Am considering

taking Tesla private at $420. Funding secured" tweet. Many assumed it was a weed joke, but the SEC wasn't laughing. Neither was I. In order for a 420 joke to be funny at this point in human history, the audience must all be high.

Regulators launched an investigation into whether Musk's tweet misled shareholders. An eventual settlement resulted in financial penalties and corporate governance reforms at Tesla—including Musk's removal as chairman. Investors also brought a lawsuit, claiming that they'd been defrauded. At that trial, Musk claimed the 420 reference was actually a mathematical coincidence and not a weed joke. Sure, dude. Ultimately, the jury found Musk was not liable for investors' losses, which prompted Musk to declare, "Thank goodness, the wisdom of the people has prevailed!"

These two victories likely emboldened Musk to see himself as untouchable when it came to his childish outbursts. Sadly, this kind of touchy behavior from Internet folk was not unusual. Sean Parker once sent me a series of late-night rants when I simply retweeted two different takes on his $4.5 million *Lord of the Rings*-style woodland wedding. VC Ron Conway fired off a how-dare-you email, taking me and Walt to task for making helpless and hapless Mark Zuckerberg sweat onstage. Still, as a journalist, I preferred to have Musk speaking to me than not, so I sloughed off his door-slamming antics as late-night, what-the-fuck itchy fingers and we continued to interact just fine. There was still a minor run-in over Musk's claims in 2020 that Covid was overblown (he was wrong), and he threatened to walk out of one remote interview over the topic.

"Kara, I do not want to get into a debate about Covid," he suddenly said after claiming he had declined vaccination for himself and his many children. "If you want to end the podcast now, we can do it." Of course, he did not end that interview. A year later, Musk was sitting knee-to-knee with me at the 2021 Code conference in Los Angeles. He was wearing a black bandana, like a Western bad guy, and cracking endless jokes about the penis shape of Jeff Bezos's rockets. Musk also talked about cryptocurrency (which he claimed was his "safe word"), his efforts to implant computer intelligence in human brains via his Neuralink company, and the progress of his impressive Starlink satellite communications network, which would soon play a key role in the Russian invasion of Ukraine. It was a good interview and the audience loved it. Musk did, too, and thanked me for a good time.

When the Twitter deal closed in October 2022, I emailed Musk requesting an interview, as I noted, once the clouds of dust he had kicked up during the Twitter acquisition effort had settled. "Haha true, so much dust!" Musk wrote back in the tone of the old Elon. "I'd appreciate hearing your thoughts regarding how to improve Twitter at some point." I assumed he was reaching out to many power users and longtime observers of the social media platform. I quickly responded: "Happy to publicly when we TALK! I have lots. Here are two: Put the focus on Twitter and not Elon—you are *obvi* interesting, but you need to make Twitter interesting/entertaining/useful beyond a rage machine of the left and right (see TikTok, the actual product). Get a great CEO and no need to kick the previous folks on the way out."

Musk wrote back. "[I] certainly do not try to put the focus on myself and, as you know, very rarely give interview." I let his obvious delusion slide.

"People need to be riveted to Twitter on a daily basis and in a much more enjoyable way," I responded. "And, in fact, in the interviews, you actually typically communicate a lot more vision and reasoning that is lost on Twitter." I had become concerned about Musk's tweeting, which had grown more manic with fewer stupid jokes and more obnoxious insults. Too often, he punched down, and he seemed to have no idea how awful his legions of followers behaved—especially to women—when he activated them. I guess if my choice was between RTing white supremacists or RTing bad boob jokes, I'd opt for the latter. Still, I thought (again incorrectly) that Musk wanted what he said he wanted: a service that was a happy place to spend your time and not a toxic waste pit. Who the fuck wanted to spend $44 billion on a toilet? Or a sink, which he carried into Twitter HQ on his first day, so he could post a pic with the caption, "Let that sink in."

One of my solutions for a better platform was to elevate the conversation using Twitter Spaces, a feature that had launched in late 2020 to chase a hot audio chatroom startup. Clubhouse had surged in the pandemic, but soon became a place where VCs gathered to insult the media. Did I really want to patronize a place where tech bros verbally trolled me and my profession? Thanks, but no thanks! Media organizations had been vital to Twitter, and news is at the core of the site's utility. Despite persistent glitches, Twitter Spaces showed promise, and I started holding live interviews covering the news of the day with big names dropping in. As our audience grew, a big advertiser became interested in sponsoring my hour-long weekly spaces. I wrote to Musk about our proof-of-concept: "We do it in conjunction with the podcast and then put it on that feed too (there are sound issues on Twitter's side we are working on). We love the audience there and they love it too since they get to have really significant convos on the fly as we are perfecting it as media. It's a small but important step into making Twitter a true daily habit and costs squat. Anyway, that should be iterated around the service."

I added my last pieces of advice for him: "Be entertaining (TikTok), useful (Facebook, but increasingly less so) and must-have (you can't get it anywhere else). Otherwise, it is just a noisy place where idiots rule—that's fine if you want to make a hot mess, but it's not a business. Also make it private or even a public trust. You'd attract better class of board." Mostly, I wanted to secure an interview with Musk (as per usual). "Here's an idea," I wrote him. "Why don't we make it actually useful and forward looking and have a real discussion about what Twitter could and should be from your perspective (owner) and mine (someone who has watched Twitter since it was Odeo) and let the debate ensue. Obvi, we can talk about the deal etc., but what Twitter could and should be is of great interest to a lot of folks. A lot of people, including those suspicious of your intent, would really like to hear it laid out, even if early."

"Suspicious of your intent" was my polite way of saying that I was concerned about his increasingly unhinged shrillness— something he would later accuse me of being, which brings us back to Musk calling me "an asshole." What triggered this put-down was a post of mine that linked to a *Washington Post* article about Musk's Starlink satellite communications system being used for critical communications in Ukraine. The article noted, "A second senior U.S. defense official speaking on the condition of anonymity to be candid, said that there is no system comparable to Starlink and that the cost is likely to run into the hundreds of millions of dollars over the next year. This person had sharp words for Musk saying he 'dangles hope over the heads of millions, then sticks the DoD with the bill for a system no one asked for but now so many depend on.'" The kicker concluded, "'Elon's gonna Elon,' the official said."

Along with the link, I wrote, "Elon's gonna Elon kinda says it all." My tweet was posted at 10:09 a.m., and by 10:22 Elon's brother Kimbal had replied: "No good deed . . ." I assumed he was referring to Musk providing Starlink gratis to Ukraine, offering crucial help at a critical time. It was a real gift to the country and he deserved kudos for his generosity.

Then Musk called me an asshole for—well, I don't know what. I wrote Musk back two days later, because I did not see the "You're an asshole" email until then. I mean, who emails? I spent some time crafting what I considered a fair and thoughtful response saying that perhaps we had disagreed over the years, but "asshole" seemed like a massive overreaction, especially since he had misunderstood the tweet completely.

"I don't AGREE with this quote," I wrote. "In fact, if you actually listen to any of my podcasts (I assume you do not) or see the bulk of my tweets, I said you should be paid, that defense contractors get paid and so should SpaceX and why shouldn't you ask for that since the Starlink services are not a charity, that it's the government's fault for not doing its job and I pushed back hard at those who compared you to a heroin dealer, which was ridiculous. If that makes me an asshole, so be it."

I wasn't done. "BTW, Elon is going to Elon overall and that's not an insult IMHO. Kara is also going to Kara. In addition, when everyone's losing their minds over you doing international relations polls, I have consistently said that you should be able to say whatever you want and that you do not have the power that actual officials have, so that you can tweet as you please, even if I disagree with you on the substance. But that is healthy political debate, and we need more of it. I get strafed for that by many, but I actually believe it. I did call you Madame Secretary, but that was a joke, and it is funny. It is also a compliment since Téa Leoni is a good-looking lady. BTW, at some point, when people are fair to you—who agree and also disagree and always respectfully, which I do—it's a compliment. Steve Jobs never got pissed at me for disagreeing, often publicly, with him since it was an ongoing and, as it turned out sadly, lifetime discussion. We never stopped debating up to months before he died. I am extending that kind of respect to you. But like your bro replied, no good deed goes unpunished . . . I typically get strafed for simply being fair to you, by both your obsessed fans and your obsessed detractors, but did not expect you to be so rigid in your polarity."

I ended it: "Signed, Asshole!"

He never responded.

As it turned out, Musk was projecting once again, and within two weeks, he'd cross a Rubicon. At the end of October 2022, a QAnon conspiracist broke into the San Francisco home of former House speaker Nancy Pelosi and violently attacked her husband Paul Pelosi with a hammer. This shocking and politically motivated act was met with alarm and horror by decent people and prompted Hillary Clinton to tweet, "The Republican Party and its mouthpieces now regularly spread hate and deranged conspiracy theories. It is shocking, but not surprising, that violence is the result. As citizens, we must hold them accountable for their words and the actions that follow." Musk decided to respond to Clinton's tweet. And what did the new Twitter owner say to his 112 million followers and Clinton's 30 million? He tweeted "There is a tiny possibility there might be more to this story than meets the eye" and then linked to an article on a much-derided web site that spun a cruel fringe lie that the hammer attack on Pelosi was some kind of gay sex incident.

It was grotesque. Musk took the homophobic and misinformed tweet down hours later, but it had already spread widely. When I later texted someone close to Musk to express my disgust, that person insisted that the tweet was in error and that Musk had apologized to Pelosi. When I asked Paul Pelosi if that had happened, Paul said that he had never heard from Musk. Of course not, because the brakes were off the Tesla and Musk was guiding the site to parts unknown, all in the name of a schoolyard bully's version of free speech. And it seemed like the more damage he unleashed, the less he cared. On top of that, many in tech defended his behavior as aberrant but excusable, because as Marc Benioff told me: "He could land a rocket ship on a surfboard."

Over the years, Silicon Valley had become full of smart people working on stupid things like online laundry services and food delivery apps and weird hook-up software—so much so that I had taken to describing the world they were creating as "assisted living for millennials." In contrast, Musk had been taking on big ideas like electric cars and solar energy and space travel and, yes, reusable rockets to get us there. Musk's space dreams were perhaps the most intriguing, especially when he made charming jokes about it like "I've said I want to die on Mars, just not on impact." In a 2018 interview with him, I said: "That's kind of the way it should go, right? This is how Elon Musk must die. He must die landing on Mars."

Musk laughed at this and agreed, pointing to the ideas of his friend Jonathan Nolan, who wrote *Memento* and co-created *Westworld*. "[Nolan] has this, like, modification of Occam's razor where he said he thinks 'the most ironic outcome is the most likely.' And then I think that there's some truth to that," said Musk, who also noted that Nolan added the "most entertaining outcome" to the movie. "I mean hopefully me dying on impact on Mars is not the most entertaining outcome."

Such ideas delighted the crowd. It was inspiring and exactly what had originally sparked my own interest in covering him. At the time, many thought Musk might become the natural inheritor of the visionary mantle that Steve Jobs had left. "We are similar in some ways, but very different in others," Musk had once messaged me, when I brought up the comparison. "I certainly don't see myself as the next Steve Jobs. There will never be another." Musk called that right. Because, as much as he was sometimes accused of being an asshole, too, Steve Jobs would have abhorred Musk 2023.

Me? I've since abandoned any hope of redemption, as idiocy has piled on top of idiocy, none of which has made Twitter a better business or a better product. Now, it was one long cry for help from a clearly troubled man, who had potential to spare. Musk's initial flaws have taken over, and he's just curdled into the worst aspects of his personality. While I did not always agree with Tesla Elon or SpaceX Elon, it was Twitter Elon who was doing real damage and very little good. In fact, Twitter Elon was the real asshole. It was a sad revelation that took me too long to come to. I admired the way Musk moved toward big ideas that solved big problems. What was not to like about solar panels and space rockets and electric cars and all manner of true gee-whiz notions?

A lot as it turned out. If Mark Zuckerberg is the most damaging man in tech to me, Musk was the most disappointing. Back in October 2015, when Musk and I were still communicating on a friendly basis, we had an email exchange where I wrote, "The real question is why does everything you say attract so much attention?"

His response: "I would like to fade from public view as much as duty to my companies will allow."

If only. Instead, as the months went by, Musk displayed an increasingly troubling proclivity to descend into adult toddler mode—and a very badly raised toddler at that—by posting a series of controversial tweets including the promotion of clearly antisemitic sentiments on the platform in late 2023. That quickly resulted in big marketers fleeing the platform, which was hemorrhaging ad dollars. Things reached an unhinged height when Musk told advertisers at a live interview in November with *New York Times*'s Andrew Ross Sorkin—whom he inexplicably referred to as "Jonathan"—to "go fuck yourself." He also specifically attacked Disney's Iger, as the incredulous crowd seemed stunned by his childish antics. "I hope they stop. Don't advertise," Musk said. "If somebody is going to try to blackmail me with advertising, blackmail me with money, go fuck yourself. Go fuck yourself. Is that clear? I hope it is." One thing was clear for sure: Musk had almost completely lost the narrative, and it was made worse by toadies and enablers who egged him on. Warping a technique of Jobs, Musk had created a "reality distortion field," except his was a dank and dark mindfuck of a place.

There is no doubt that Musk is a brilliant entrepreneur, perhaps the most of this age, but he has also become a lost cause to me, and I am not sure what he could do to turn that around at this point. He reminds me of that Hunter S. Thompson quote about the U.S.: "The mind of America is seized by a fatal dry rot—and it's only a question of time before all that the mind controls will run amuck in a frenzy of stupid, impotent fear." With Musk, it feels like it is only a question of time before we enter the Howard Hughes—another brilliant rich man who curdled badly—chapter of his story.

And, as heinous as Musk has become, that outcome is one of the saddest developments in my long love story with tech.

CHAPTER 14

The Mensches

If love is the answer, could you rephrase the question?

—LILY TOMLIN

I must confess: I'm an *optimistic* pessimist. But don't tell anyone. In other words, I expect the worst, but hope for the best. More often than not, leaving Musk out of this as he screws up the chart badly, I am happily surprised by people's better natures.

In that spirit, I created a metric, the "Prick to Productivity Ratio" (P2P), that's neither scientific nor is it particularly fair. But it's allowed me to quantify my judgments of the powerful people I've covered over the years. It gives flawed people—and we are all flawed in some way—a little break. In short, I would consider what I thought were someone's accomplishments, including innovative products, visionary ideas, management skills, cool inventions, ability to pivot, and general flexibility. Then, I'd match these achievements against my highly subjective assessment of their characters, based on my own interactions. And if you're wondering who appointed me judge and jury: I did.

A good P2P has a higher second number than a first, or someone's character outweighs their innovation. Steve Jobs could undoubtedly be a prick—cutting to colleagues, sometimes disingenuous about what he was up to, and a really obnoxious parker of his car, with a proclivity to occupy handicapped spots. But his productivity was so high and so impactful that I gave him a lot of slack. Jobs gets an 8 for being a prick and a 10 for accomplishments. Final P2P ratio: 8/10.

For much of his career, Musk's productiveness gave him a wide berth. As the years went on, he would slowly, and then all at once with the purchase of Twitter, shift into the toxic creature we now have to deal with on a daily basis. Loudly sexist, puerile, transphobic, homophobic, conspiracy drenched, and tweeter of unfunny memes, Musk utterly broke my ratio by turning up the prick to 11. To 12. To infinity and beyond. P2P ratio: ∞/WTF.

Bill Gates was once considered a Darth Vader–like character for his aggressive business behaviors. This approach caught up with him when the U.S. government sued Microsoft for anticompetitive practices. After an antitrust ruling, Gates stepped down as CEO and focused his efforts on his charitable foundation. His enormous and admirable efforts in philanthropy have helped turn that narrative around. Mostly. Gates's reputation has been recently tarnished by his far-too-many meetings with sex trafficker and rapist Jeffrey Epstein (a very bad and inexplicable lapse in judgment) and a weird series of conspiracy theories aimed at him during Covid (undeserved since Bill Gates is NOT injecting a chip in you via a vaccine, people). Still, I've developed a grudging respect for his forward-thinking efforts on malaria, childhood blindness, climate change, and more. He's evolved, as they say. FinalP2P ratio: 7/10.

I could go on like this for a while, but it was largely to amuse myself and also to try to grasp the insane amount of wealth these digital pioneers have amassed in a very short time. Save for Saudi Aramco and LVMH, tech companies are the most valuable on Earth in all of history. I don't think this will change in the foreseeable future. As I type this, Apple, the world's most valuable public company, passed a market cap of $3 trillion. Microsoft is closing in on that valuation, too. And, except for luxury czar Bernard Arnault of LVMH and Warren Buffett of Berkshire Hathaway, the top ten richest people (all white men) come from tech.

There is no question that kind of wealth does inevitably warp tech titans as they navigate their frictionless world that allows them to go from private plane to armored car to a home office on an island. And while these overbred poodles couldn't be luckier on this planet at this moment in time, they're swept up in the constant doom cycle of their own design, painting themselves too often as victims. They seem to wonder why we humans of lesser value can't understand their genius. They expect an eternal hall pass for egregious acts and blame demons for their transgressions. They are enabled by all manner of hangers-on. Most of whom are paid for their obsequiousness. What they ignore is that no one takes away someone's genius just because they make mistakes, and that their inability to hear about problems is a problem. These tech moguls are so rarely disagreed with that they now interpret valid questions as attacks.

I have spent my career being hard on powerful people. I have done so because I think it is respectful to do so and because I believe that with great power comes great responsibility. That line and sentiment go far back in history, although they're often only attributed to Spider-Man, especially by techies for whom history classes were too often an elective. It's a shame when people with enormous influence and wealth don't rise to the challenge. And it's inspiring that some do. Over the decades, I have met many good people who are not bent, not arrogant, not so distractingly narcissistic that it zeroes out so much more. I actually like and admire a huge swath of those whom I have covered, even if it might seem hard to accept this far into the book that that's the case. But there are some truly thoughtful people in tech and I have highlighted a few already, including Terry Semel, Dick Costolo, Steve Case, Susan Wojcicki, Steve Jobs, Jim Barksdale, Tim Cook, Reed Hastings, and Jerry Yang, as well as some I have not, like Dr. Lisa Su of AMD, Craig Newmark, and Meg Whitman.

Many more have contributed to both tech and humanity in positive ways, and while this is not an exhaustive list, it's an indicator that there is hope for the future as we are entering the next and perhaps most important phase of tech development. As tech digs into generative artificial intelligence, significant health breakthroughs, autonomous vehicles, and innovative energy solutions to the climate crisis, it is not alarmist to say that these issues present an existential challenge to humanity and serious, contemplative people are required to lead the charge. So, here are some good techies who give me hope and also some whom I miss.

Let me start with a pair of good Marks—specifically Mark Cuban and Marc Benioff. Both are prominent entrepreneurs who started off with a lot more bloviating than was necessary, but who have morphed into reflective and complex thinkers. Both are examples of tech leaders who tried to learn from their mistakes rather than wear them as badges of honor.

Cuban, of course, is now a highly likable sports team owner and reality TV star of *Shark Tank*. I met him in the 1990s when he ran Broadcast.com, an Internet radio startup. The company was founded as AudioNet by Cameron Christopher Jaeb, but Cuban and his partner Todd Wagner got control and expanded it beyond sports. They took it public in 1998 at a $1 billion valuation and rode the Web 1.0 boom to a $5.7 billion sale to Yahoo at the peak in 1999. That same year, the canny Cuban then sold his Yahoo stock for $1 billion and tapped out a winner early. He spent the next years mostly as an investor in a variety of arenas, including movie theaters, crypto, media and privacy, and more, becoming someone who at least tried to weigh the good and the bad of tech. He has never been irritated by disagreement with me, despite many disagreements. His latest foray, Cost Plus Drug Company, into lowering the price of generic prescription drugs has been laudable.

I also like Cuban and call him a lot to get his take, which always surprises me and makes me delve more deeply into issues. When I called him about Senator Elizabeth Warren's billionaire tax proposal, I expected him to rail against it. Instead, he laid out a much more cogent case about the negative consequences of excessive taxation on entrepreneurs and its downstream impact on innovation. While he did not change my mind—rich people, in general, need to pay more taxes—I appreciated that Cuban wasn't starting from a black or white position. Cuban is more colorful than neutral, which is always better.

Benioff has had a similar evolution. He started his career as a hard-charging acolyte of Larry Ellison, under whom he spent thirteen years moving up the greasy ladder at Oracle. With Ellison's help, Benioff founded Salesforce and somehow made customer relationship management software, called CRM, interesting. While we've argued over everything, like Salesforce's controversial work for U.S. Customs and Border Protection, he has always been open to debate and done it with some humor.

"Do you have a catalog of all the things I've done wrong?" he once joked during an interview. Yes, I replied. But I also have a catalog of the things he did right, such as comparing Facebook to a "cigarette company," when no other tech leader would say the obvious about the social media network's behavior. Along with Cuban, Benioff does not lazily blame the media for tech's woes, but places responsibility where it belongs, on the industry itself. While he still likes to hear himself talk, I like a lot of what he says.

The same is true for two more soft-spoken CEOs: Alphabet's Sundar Pichai and Microsoft's Satya Nadella, both of whom rose through the ranks in tech after emigrating from India. Pichai was a product manager on the Chrome browser when we first met, and I've cheered his ascension, especially since he was surrounded by many more obnoxious competitors. When he got the top job in 2015, it was both a surprise and a relief. Pichai has been more cautious than some inside prefer, especially around commercializing AI efforts. Google was quite early to pioneer AI, but slow to productize, a breach that Nadella at Microsoft quickly moved into with his investments in OpenAI and its ChatGPT. I met Nadella as a top exec at Microsoft's online services unit, but he quickly left that quagmire to push through their important investments in cloud, the principal reason he beat out all his rivals. He's since proven to be the Tim Cook of Microsoft, pushing forward both innovation and growth and cutting extraneous businesses that slowed the company down.

He and Pichai both share the trait of acting their age in the best of ways.

While these four are all over fifty, and Cuban, the most youthful in spirit of the group, is now sixty-five, three younger CEOs have surprised me with their emerging maturity: Snap Inc. CEO and cofounder Evan Spiegel, Airbnb CEO and cofounder Brian Chesky, and former Instagram CEO and cofounder Kevin Systrom. Yes, they are all white men, I know, but this is the world of tech. Even so, I'll take it because all three act like real people and are not cosplaying deeply insecure icons. As you have realized by now, I respect change and development into better leadership.

In Spiegel's case, his early frat-boy persona was on full display at a lunch we had in Santa Monica. He was angry at the media for covering some tasteless emails he sent about women during his years at Stanford. I had not written one word about these emails because someone being an idiot in college is not news to me. Still, Spiegel aimed his irritation at me, lumping me in with the media blob. I pushed back telling him to own the dumb emails. Lunch ended with a lot of rancor, but he and I continued to talk. I admired his love of product and design and even dubbed him "Facebook's chief product officer" after that company's persistent shoplifting of Snapchat features. More important was Spiegel's increasing ability to see his mistakes as his own. He made persistent, though not always successful, efforts to bring more women into powerful roles at Snap. And he responded without defensiveness about things like an AI bot that went haywire when introduced.

The same was true with the even more soulful Brian Chesky, who built a wonderful product. I met him and his many cofounders in a San Francisco coffee shop when Airbnb was a very small startup. Chesky talked solely about what he was making and not at all about the money. This immediately struck me as unusual. I could say a lot about the mistakes that Chesky made along the way, including not focusing on safety of users soon enough, but he always tried to correct them and never hid behind excuses. He also understood the dangers of wealth and how it insulated people from criticism. In an interview with me, he laid it out: "I came here in 2015, and around that time, we were like a really big adolescent . . . and one day, it feels like everything you do doesn't matter because the company is too big, and you have to start to run the company fairly differently." Chesky also spoke without embarrassment about his loneliness and the warping impact of money on relationships, which was not a surprise since he has a warm and supportive family.

Instagram's Kevin Systrom, though, remains my favorite in the product department, maintaining a flawless design sense that reminds me of Jobs in his focus on elegant simplicity. First called Burbn, I got the photo-sharing social network the moment I used it in 2010 and hightailed to meet him and his half-dozen employees. The company quickly attracted a lot of funding and, like clockwork, received acquisition offers from both Twitter and Facebook. In that fight, Zuckerberg won out with a $1 billion in cash and stock offer (just before Facebook's IPO) and a promise to let Instagram continue to run independently. It was a big win early on, but I told Systrom at the time that it was too little for his wonderful creation, since it would help the creatively bereft Facebook more and that Zuckerberg would never let him shine or run the place. Systrom had no other choice—it was so much money and the risks of staying independent were great. In fact, a year later, Facebook waged war against Snapchat after Spiegel turned down a $3 billion offer. Much later, after he left Facebook in exasperation, Systrom agreed and told me in an interview that the app had "lost its soul," adding, "my biggest regret, I think, at Instagram is how commercial it got."

There aren't many billionaires railing against capitalism, so points to Systrom. Still, despite all the platitudes about changing the world, money has to be at the center of the ecosystem. In that vein, my reporting often led me to the venture capitalists who grease the wheels with their piles of money. In truth, they are good copy, full of information, and, unlike lawyers, can't stop talking and putting themselves at the center of the action. Most VCs are interchangeable and add almost nothing to the process.

There are a few notable exceptions, such as Aileen Lee, former Kleiner VC and cofounder of Cowboy Ventures, who coined the term "unicorn" for billion-dollar-valued startups in 2013. Lee has always been thoughtful and empathetic to the need for the VC world to get more women on the cap table. Lee was preceded by Mary Meeker, the legendary Wall Street analyst whom I met early on at Morgan Stanley, where she authored the seminal *Internet Trends Report*, which served as the industry bible. While Meeker got zinged for being too much of a cheerleader after the dotcom bust of 2000, when she backed some real losers (eToys!), she was one of the first to understand the importance of the Internet and was directionally correct about the value that was being created. She moved to Kleiner in 2010 and spun out to form her own firm, Bond Capital, in 2018.

Reid Hoffman is both a quirky entrepreneur (PayPal, LinkedIn) and a sharp investor (Facebook, Airbnb, OpenAI) who has somehow managed to hold onto his soul. When I hear about a new company or idea, he's often my first call. Few know the world of tech better, and unlike most VCs, Hoffman is not constantly and exhaustingly selling his own book. He doesn't try to prove that he's the smartest person in the room—even if he's often the smartest person in the room. Unfailingly kind, Hoffman is a progressive unicorn in a sea of libertarian-light. Very few in tech have a well-thought-out or complex political ideology, but Hoffman does and backs it up with leadership in donations, effort, and time. When I heard a Silicon Valley billionaire had paid E. Jean Carroll's legal bills in her victorious sexual assault case against former President Donald Trump, I knew it had to be Hoffman. "Supporting women fighting for progress and justice in philanthropy, politics, and business has been a longstanding priority of mine, as is supporting America against the threat of Trump—a stance that I've not only made public, but also have prioritized over recent years," he wrote. "I believe that the courts themselves, using facts and laws, should decide innocence and guilt. Trump has had many days in court; America and its citizens should have their say as well. And so, I have been proud to help level the playing field in the courts for those whom Trump and his allies have attacked and bullied." Talk about a Silicon Valley unicorn.

I have spent an increasing amount of time talking to government officials and legislators in recent years, since no significant U.S. laws have been passed to rein in tech . . . ever. In fact, the much-discussed Section 230 gives the sector an unusual amount of protection. Still, most regulators and politicians are utterly missing in action. Europe has done a much better job in large part thanks to the scourge of Silicon Valley, Margrethe Vestager, the Danish politician who headed the European

Commission for Competition. Vestager is currently an executive vice president of the Commission for a Europe Fit for the Digital Age. She has brought investigations, fines, and lawsuits against companies like Google, Apple, Amazon, and Facebook. The EU has adopted stringent—if sometimes overreaching—laws that protect users' privacy and target hate speech and misinformation. While sometimes accused of being anti-American in her pursuits, Vestager is a defender of all consumers while so many government leaders in the U.S. have become willing servants of tech.

In the U.S., Lina Khan, chair of the Federal Trade Commission, penned a groundbreaking essay on competition titled "Amazon's Antitrust Paradox," and has tried to press some cases very late in the game. And while much of Congress has been either consistently brain dead on the subject (sorry to the late Senator Orrin Hatch!) or idiotically noisy (not at all sorry to describe Senator Josh Hawley as persistently useless), I have covered many legislators who try their best to make a difference. This group includes Mark Warner, Amy Klobuchar, and Michael Bennet in the Senate and David Cicilline and Ken Buck in the House. Senator Klobuchar has been the most determined to pass antitrust and other pieces of critical legislation, all of which has been stymied by tech lobbyists and weak-willed leadership.

These government crusaders have been aided by a group of academics and tech employees, who have gone out on a variety of limbs to spotlight critical issues. Joy Buolamwini, a computer scientist at the MIT Media Lab, created the Algorithmic Justice League to bring attention to facial surveillance and algorithmic bias. Alex Stamos, former Yahoo and Facebook chief security officer and current director of the Stanford Internet Observatory, has persistently pushed back on the slowness of platforms to recognize malevolent foreign digital incursions. Timnit Gebru, former co-lead of Google's Ethical Artificial Intelligence team, has backed many critical issues including the dangers of very large language models to both take over all thinking and also vomit up endless misinformation. A product manager on Facebook's civic integrity team, Frances Haugen became Silicon Valley's most famous whistleblower after releasing a spate of internal documents that showed potential damage to society caused by the social platform. Yoel Roth, the former head of Twitter's trust and safety department, was subject to an inaccurate accusation by Musk that forced him to leave his home after death threats, as well as a series of nothing-burger allegations about content moderation. He has inexplicably remained calm and thoughtful.

I wish I had the room to write a lot more about people who take the responsibility of rolling out tech products seriously. When they make errors, they admit them, and when they see abuse, they report it. It shouldn't be hard to do, but it has become increasingly so, as the stakes are rising with ever greater alacrity. Like me, these spotlighters all love tech, but hate some of the things that have been done with it in the pursuit of profits and power, which is, really, just greed.

This is not to say the goal is some grand holding of hands. I'm just looking for a few good guardrails to make everyone safer. I am, at heart, a capitalist and obviously love creating businesses. I have done so over and over again, taking risks that most journalists have not and moving into new areas without a fear of change. I love change, largely because I am more aware than most of the limited amount of time we have to be here. Life's ephemerality requires a commitment to not waste those hours, a fact that I was reminded of by my stroke and later heart procedure to correct the issue. Which is to say, none of us has infinite time, no matter how rich, how privileged, or how protected.

That was sadly true for the late Zappos founder and CEO Tony Hsieh, whom I think about a lot these days. Tony turned out to be a cautionary tale of what happens when too much creativity and entrepreneurship mixes with drug and alcohol abuse. Wild success gave Tony an unlimited ability to indulge without any pushback from enabling and self-interested sycophants. When the isolation of the pandemic was thrown into the mix, one has to wonder how it could have ended any other way.

I met the quirky entrepreneur at his headquarters in Las Vegas when he started the groundbreaking e-commerce shoe company. But in his mind, Tony wasn't just selling footwear; he was selling "happiness." He even wrote a book called *Delivering Happiness: A Path to Profits, Passion, and Purpose*. "Our goal at Zappos is for our employees to think of their work not as a job or career," he wrote, "but as a calling." Tony was entranced with the idea of what I thought of as "forced joy." Still, his precepts became his company's guiding principles. The office was draped in silly decorations, rife with childish contests, and of course, there were piles of sweets. I assumed he was going for Willy Wonka in the delight department. Tony also believed in showing real emotion in the workplace and was constantly coming in for a big—and decidedly platonic—hug. Not surprisingly, it was all lost on me and I often jokingly threatened to break his arms if he tried any type of embrace.

"I just know there is a softie in there," he teased. There was not. In fact, in 2010 I wrote: "While in Vancouver, I tried to avoid the happiness-fueled stalking by Tony Hsieh, the CEO of online retailer Zappos. To no avail." The previous year, Tony had sold Zappos to Amazon for $1.2 billion. Becoming a billionaire meant he could turn his visions of a better world into reality. Or so he hoped. I thought Tony's theories were largely nonsense before he took them a step further, trying to transform the company with new management theories, and then part of downtown Vegas into a utopian startup city. At least Tony put his money where his heart was, pouring $350 million into the effort to create what he called "Holacracy."

But Tony was right when he applied his happiness principles to provide top-level customer service, which was a rarity on the Web. "We use the word 'wow' a lot," he once told me onstage at the Code Commerce Series. "The idea of free returns was a big *wow*. Then when we encouraged customers to call our 1-800 number, that was a big *wow*. As everyone moves more toward being more high-tech, we're actually moving more toward humanizing. When we get that right, we have a customer for life."

In all my dealings with him, Tony came across as a very sweet man plagued by a lot of pain that he tried desperately to assuage with tools that grew less and less healthy. One coping mechanism was his belief that we were all living in a simulation—essentially a video game being played by beings far beyond our knowledge or capabilities. This was not an uncommon debate among techies, but Tony seemed to actually believe it. When he brought it up onstage at an event in Vegas, I laughed it off. But backstage, he grabbed my hand, looked into my eyes, and said without a trace of his usual cheeriness: "I'm serious. This is not real. We are not real."

It was a deeply sad moment for me. With all that money and talent, he just could not cope. On later visits to Vegas, Tony seemed more frantic than ever. At an annual Code conference poker party (he was an ace player), he seemed emptier and more inebriated on whatever—weed, ketamine, whip-its, the Fernet-Branca liqueur that he always seemed to have with him. I tried not to judge, since a lot of tech folks were now deeply into psychedelics and would often offer them to me. Tony, thankfully, did not. The last time I saw him at Code, Tony did not even attempt to hug me, and for someone who was on vacation permanently, he looked exhausted. As Covid separated people in 2020, he was wandering the country again and seemed to keep around only the people who said yes more than no and were on his payroll. I could pretend I was surprised when I heard Tony had died of smoke inhalation in a freak fire in a shed where investigators said he had lit candles and fiddled with a propane lighter. A report noted that a friend said Tony always lit candles because they "reminded him of a simpler time."

But it was never really simple with Tony, who created a marvelous company from nothing and ran it well for a long time until he dropped out, too bored and too rich and not happy at all. "It is possible that carelessness or even an intentional act by Hsieh could have started this fire," the report said. We'll never know which it was. Either way, it's tragic and I'm sad that Tony is no longer here even if, according to him, we were never real.

But the Silicon Valley death that hit me the hardest—and was very much a surprise—was someone with whom I clicked with as more than a subject, even though I covered his more famous friends and his spouse regularly. That was Dave Goldberg, longtime entrepreneur in online music and more, investor, adviser, and the husband of Sheryl Sandberg. His death diminished us all.

Why? I trusted Dave—nicknamed Goldie—to tell me the truth whenever I called him, and I cannot say that about a lot of people I cover. It was hard not to feel affection for someone who was such a mensch. In a eulogy about him, I noted: "That is exactly the word you would use to describe Dave—a Yiddish term that means a person of integrity and honor, a stand-up guy, someone to admire and emulate, a rock of humanity."

Of course, Dave was the only one I would pick on a reporting lark I went on to grab a Weihenstephaner Vitus at Redwood City's Gourmet Haus Staudt, where a drunk Apple engineer left the iPhone 4 prototype after he was hoisting too many German beers. He was excited to play the reporter and took notes and asked questions of the patrons there, like he was Woodward and Bernstein combined, even though I only was doing a simple and silly stunt story. We ended up sitting at one of the huge wood tables and just laughing at the absurdity of all of it for hours. "You have the best job," he said to me. I did.

The week before Dave died, we had traded several phone calls, wanting to kibitz about his business (he was then CEO of an online polling company called SurveyMonkey) and discuss plans for a dinner he wanted to throw at my upcoming conference. So, when news of his sudden death from an undiagnosed heart condition—which was initially and incorrectly blamed on a fall on a treadmill that caused a head injury and blood loss—my first reaction, as I wrote in a piece about him, was *no*.

It was for a myriad of reasons, including for his important role as a spouse and sounding board to Sandberg—who lost both a beloved partner and a critical adviser at what would turn out to be an important time—and as a father to their two children. I described one moment I spent with him that I can see perfectly even now: "I have a vivid picture of Dave sitting in his kitchen working with both on homework before one of Sheryl's events for women of Silicon Valley. Let it be said, I am not the most patient of homework-helpers for my two sons; in contrast, Dave was calm and helpful to them and yet not even slightly pushy as so many parents in the pressure-cooker world of Silicon Valley can be. I recall thinking at the time that I really needed to get a grip on my own attitude and schedule, because here was a very busy man who never seemed busy and that manifested so clearly with his kids."

It changed my own parenting for the better. Dave also played an important role in the ecosystem of Silicon Valley writ large, as I noted: "Because Dave was exactly the kind of leader that we need more of here and the kind of quiet conscience critical to transforming the community and its people into the better version of ourselves. We so often fail in doing the right thing and that is why icons of admirable behavior, like Dave, are so important, but—sadly—so lacking. He was truthful without being snarky and hopeful without being deluded. For anyone involved in the evolution of the Web and its many characters, this is rare. Humility is not something common in this world, as you might imagine. Even when he aced other players in poker, a game dear to his heart, he was nice about it. 'Watch Dave,' one player once told me as he played nearby. 'He wins without bluster and bluffing, but he always wins.'"

When he was gone, just like that, we all lost. As Elon Musk morphed into everything that had gone wrong with Silicon Valley, as casual cruelty piled on top of casual cruelty, Dave was his antithesis. A good man who leaned into the future without ignoring the past and wanting to take the rest of us with him. To say I thought of Dave a lot after his death cannot describe the impact he had on me, and it definitely spurred me to change my life once again.

CHAPTER 15

Pivoting

Do I contradict myself?
Very well then I contradict myself,
(I am large, I contain multitudes.)

—WALT WHITMAN, "SONG OF MYSELF"

I should have been a spy. Or even an admiral. Instead—since the skills required are quite similar, including charm, curiosity, tactical and strategic thinking—I became a journalist. Still, I balked at that label and jokingly agreed with the observation that my chosen profession was "the last refuge of the vaguely talented." Over the years, I came to prefer "working reporter," which felt less smarmy.

My upward trajectory was propelled by timing and talent and maybe a small bit of luck. But if I had to choose two reasons for my success, I'd go with: I worked harder than anyone else, and I was good at scenario building, which is a fancy way of saying I'm a good guesser.

Covering Silicon Valley, I woke up every day eager to break news. Unlike an investigative reporter, a working (or beat) reporter's job is to know what's happening, ideally as it happens.

Once I tracked down an exclusive, I'd confirm the facts, reconfirm the facts, add context and background, write the story as quickly as I could, and hit upload. I never tired of the endless news roundelay, even if over time the pace of media quickened to cyber speed and the value of being first diminished.

For a large part of my career, my ability to get inside the brain of companies was an important asset. If I had to choose my favorite scoop of my many scoop children, I'd probably go with one I referenced earlier in which I reported, before he was told of the news by his mentor Barry Diller, that Dara Khosrowshahi would be named Uber CEO. He told the executive that if I said it was so, it was so. That was kind, but the truth is, I seldom made reporting mistakes. My second favorite scoop might be breaking a series of stories about then Yahoo CEO Scott Thompson lying about his academic credits on his résumé. "Calling Encyclopedia Brown to Solve the Case of the Computer Science Degree That Wasn't!" was the subhead I wrote as editor for my own story at *AllThingsD*.

When it comes to scoops, you'd be surprised who's leaking—a secret most journalists will never tell. That's because it's nearly everyone. My sources ranged from student interns and low-level workers all the way to, most of all, CEOs. Sometimes outsiders like waiters and drivers and others who worked in these worlds weighed in. At Yahoo, people joked that I camped out in the heating ducts. While I can neither confirm nor deny this, one time cofounder Jerry Yang was in a board meeting and someone texted me about a decision that had just been made. I immediately texted Jerry for confirmation. His response was approximately "That literally just happened in the boardroom. Who is leaking to you?"

My reply? "Look to the left, look to the right. It's the whole room."

It was a glib response, but, in many ways, I had a competitive edge in my ability to convince people to talk. CEOs had corporate rules that governed what they could discuss and when they could discuss it. Fortunately, I did not have to abide by the same restrictions and could usually find someone who wanted to open up and, at least, tell me their side of the story. Over time, I cultivated a group of trusted sources whom I could call and ask, "What's going on?" I learned to count on certain sources to be honest and tell me, "Oh, yeah, this is a mess," or "What they're saying is this . . . and here's what they're actually doing."

Of course, I remained hyperaware of who was leaking to me and why, because there was always the possibility of manipulation. Once when I was working on a scoop about TV news star Katie Couric decamping to Yahoo, an executive at ABC tried to get me to run a blind quote, calling her an "anchor monster." He clearly thought it was in his company's best interest to insult her and that I would willingly run it. "Would you say that on the record?" I asked. He would not. I declined to use it.

Good reporting requires fairness. I was obsessive about giving the other side a chance to respond. I'd contact the CEO and outline what information I had, saying, "Here's what I plan to report. If I'm off base, please let me know. But I don't think I am." I also tried to offer a professional amount of time to react, although not too much time, so PR people once alerted could not burn me by slipping the scoop to a friendlier outlet. This kind of behavior was irritating but easily subverted. Other techniques to thwart me were not, like one executive who was so annoyed by my scoops that the company started putting out slightly altered internal memos to try and trap the leaker. Naturally, someone leaked the plan to me. From then on, I would make very minor, inconsequential changes to memos before publishing—not in the content but just to mess with the dopey plot.

Employees continued to slip me company documents, to the point where Facebook's Sheryl Sandberg once observed: "It is a constant joke in the Valley when people write memos for them to say, 'I hope Kara never sees this.'"

But I always saw everything. Sue Decker, who was president at Yahoo, once asked me the simple question: "Why do people leak? Are they just disgruntled?"

Since I liked Decker, I decided to level with her. "It's easy to say they're disgruntled or sneaky," I replied. "But they leak because they feel like you're not listening to them and that you do listen to me. And, therefore, employees believe the best way to effect change that needs to happen is to leak. To me."

"I should listen better," she joked, "and put you out of business." She never did, and Decker has since left the day-to-day grind and I am still at it.

Another great source of intel came from contacting employees who had quit or been fired. I often thought of myself as Silicon Valley's HR department, conducting exit interviews right as people were ready to spill. It was time-consuming, but the effort paid off over and over. Remember: People always like to tell their side of the story.

I also always tried to be straightforward with subjects about the intent of my questioning. In the 1990s, a lot of journalists adopted a "seduce and betray" interview style where they would flatter (and in some cases, even flirt with) a subject, to create a safe and friendly rapport in the hopes that the interviewee would let down their guard. Later, the reporter would betray that trust in print. That was never my style. I don't think most people I wrote about were ever surprised by my work.

Sometimes I wasn't even surprised. One of my favorite things to do is reverse engineer a story. I'm really good at piecing various snippets of information together (thanks, cruel stepfather!) and would devise scenarios in classic CIA tradecraft. For example, in 2013, I received a tip that Yahoo was buying *something* for a billion dollars. That was all the info the person gave me, but I could work with it. My first thought was: What would [then CEO] Marissa Mayer want to buy? She wants a splash—she's a splashy lady. What would make for a sexy acquisition?

Next, I made a list of companies that would fit that description and tried to price which companies could be valued in that ballpark. Some splashes were too big, some were too small, but Tumblr seemed just right, bloated to a billion-dollar price thanks to Facebook's interest. Following this logic, I reached out to VCs, who are often happy to talk, and just bluffed: "Hey, I heard you're selling Tumblr to Yahoo for a billion dollars."

The first few VCs just lied to me outright, as it turned out, and told me I was off base. "Oh, I must've gotten it wrong," I'd reply and hang up, no harm done.

On about the fifth VC, my question triggered the desired response: "Oh, my God, how did you know about that?" Eager to spill a boatload of details, this VC was proud to fill me in. I then reached out to Yahoo to comment, which they declined to do. Nonetheless, I confirmed the details of the deal within the company. Three days later, Mayer confirmed all my reporting, announcing on Twitter, "First ever acquisition announced by animated gif :) @Yahoo is acquiring @Tumblr #keepcalmand carryon."

Sometimes, I used rumors as a jumping off point for complex analysis. In 2016, I reported that Disney was looking at acquiring Twitter, which was true. But that scoop began with my theory that Disney needed a social media platform beyond its acquisition of Club Penguin in a deal valued at $700 million (I also predicted, simply based on my historical knowledge of the company, that Disney would not follow through on the purchase because of Twitter's toxicity).

Years later, Bob Iger confirmed my instinct onstage at the last Code conference, in 2022: "Frankly, it would have been a phenomenal solution, distribution wise. Then, after we sold the whole concept to the Disney board and the Twitter board and were really ready to execute a negotiation . . . I went home and thought I'm not looking at this as carefully as I need to look at it. Yes, it's a great solution from a distribution perspective, but it would come with so many other challenges and complexities. . . . You have to look, of course, at all the hate speech and potential to do as much harm as good. We're in the business of manufacturing fun at Disney. . . . As a CEO of a company, I thought it would be irresponsible."

Thinking like these CEOs was a big part of my job and it helped to spend time with them in person. Most people in tech did not like meeting face-to-face and that was *before* the pandemic. Still, there is no substitute for hanging out with no purpose other than to get to know someone and watch how they react to various prompts. (Pro tip: I always asked contacts for a cell phone number when things were good, so I had it when things went sour.) Although I never considered myself a friend of the moguls, when they'd invite me to parties, I'd jump at the chance to go even when I wanted to be home with my kids. It was a target-rich opportunity to observe: Who's friendly with each other? Who doesn't like each other? Who's whispering in a corner together?

Initially, the parties started off pretty normal, like when the cake at one of Google cofounder Sergey Brin's birthday parties came from Safeway and remained in the plastic holder. "Could he not afford better?" I said to Brin's mother, who was standing nearby. She didn't joke back. In fact, it struck me that she looked pretty glum. Why so sad, I asked, on such a happy occasion? Soon, she was complaining to me that she and her husband—a NASA researcher and a mathematics professor who emigrated with their family from the former Soviet Union—thought their son should have pursued a PhD, even as Google was poised for an IPO that would make him a billionaire. This moment over a shitty piece of sheet cake gave me great insight into Brin's psyche and also what motivated him. (Another pro tip: Always meet the parents, who are typically revelatory.)

Of course, the biggest leaks came from the worst-run companies. Yahoo CEO Carol Bartz hated that I got so many scoops and once threatened to fire an employee who she thought had fed me information. That employee wasn't my source, so I called the head of PR to set the record straight. "I never do this," I explained, "but that is not the person who's leaking to me. And if you fire them, I'm going to write a story about how you unfairly fired someone. And, by the way, why is your CEO spending her time on this and not fixing Yahoo?"

Bartz should've taken my advice about focusing on the

business, and maybe I wouldn't have had to report a short time later that she was about to be fired. Bartz didn't like that scoop either, and phoned me. "I'm not being fired," she insisted.

"The board is meeting right now," I replied. "You should be happy that I gave you a heads-up." A few hours later, she posted an announcement: "To all: I am very sad to tell you that I've just been fired over the phone by Yahoo's Chairman of the Board."

Some executives' troublesome professional choices were exacerbated by issues in their personal lives. While I clocked these behaviors, I rarely reported on them directly. Unless the extracurricular activities impacted the business, I kept my focus on what execs did at work because I was not their mama. Still, even if I did not use the piles of information I collected, they often provided useful insight. They also reminded me of a deep truth that I never wanted to forget: that despite some evidence to the contrary, every tech mogul is also a human being.

This was the point Dave Goldberg made perfectly while talking to Benjamin Wallace for a 2014 profile of me for *New York* magazine. Goldberg explained, "[Kara] knows way more than she ever writes, because she doesn't have it really carefully confirmed, or because she doesn't want to write something that's going to be personally painful to someone but isn't relevant from a business standpoint."

Wallace followed this with the example of how someone leaked to me that Marissa Mayer had overslept and arrived at a dinner in Europe with advertisers two hours late. Although Mayer had a reputation for keeping people waiting, I declined to run with the item unless it was in the context of a larger piece on her well-documented struggles with advertisers. Maybe she was jet-lagged. Maybe her alarm did not go off. Who knows?

Other journalists made hay out of it, but my observation was that plenty of male executives were late to meetings with no repercussions or stories chastising them. As with Katie Couric, I refused to carry water for Mayer's enemies.

In fact, how people lived their lives was up to them, and I truly didn't care whom they loved, what they smoked, and how they dressed. I got into an argument with TV host Bill Maher when he started attacking Mark Zuckerberg on *Real Time* for what I thought were the wrong reasons.

"I mean Mark Zuckerberg, I'm sorry, but that is a real nerd. He looks awful. His clothes are terrible," Maher opined, trying— I guess—to be funny by mocking someone's appearance. "He's awkward. I mean Bill Gates looks like Cary Grant next to this guy. He's on the spectrum of dweebiness that I don't think . . ."

Leaving aside that no one would mistake Maher for Cary Grant either, I interrupted: "Hey now, Bill. You shouldn't insult his looks. You can insult his entire service and the way it's ruined democracy, but please don't insult his looks."

There was one big exception to my "personal lives should mostly stay personal" rule. But I didn't find that story—it found me. One beautiful August evening in Provincetown, I was headed to a drag show, when I got a call from 23andMe CEO Anne Wojcicki. Anne explained that she was calling on behalf of her and her husband, Sergey Brin, to let me know that after six years of marriage, they were separating and likely divorcing. I hope I've made it clear how much I love a good scoop, but Anne's news just made me sad for the couple and their two young children.

Still, this breakup had clear business implications given the complex stock ownership of Google, so I assigned the story to the company beat reporter, *AllThingsD* reporter Liz Gannes, and also continued to do some reporting myself. As I dug around, more problematic details soon emerged. I'd recently been to an event where I chatted with Hugo Barra, a charming exec who headed Google's Android team. Barra told me about his girlfriend, Google Glass marketing manager Amanda Rosenberg. They were clearly a social couple since Walt had recently been at a dinner party with them. Now, incredibly, I was hearing that Rosenberg and Brin had started an office affair and that Barra would soon quit his job and head to a competitor, Chinese phone giant Xiaomi.

Gannes posted both these stories in quick succession, which created an immediate sensation on our site. The copy focused on the financial angle, noting that Brin and Wojcicki had a prenuptial agreement that protected control of Google's powerful special founders' shares. We also noted additional business complications, including Brin's investment in his soon-to-be-former wife's medical tech company, and that Anne's sister, Susan, was SVP of advertising and commerce at Google at the time. Barra's departure and the ensuing impact were also covered. Later, *Vanity Fair* would publish a juicy story about the Brin/Rosenberg affair that doubtlessly got a lot of clicks, and I certainly read the entire thing. But it wasn't the kind of story that I wanted *AllThingsD* to publish.

Over the years, it's become harder to ignore the personal issues of tech moguls, given their increasing proclivity to bring their whole selves not just to work, but to social media. Is there any opinion of Elon Musk's, however ignorant, toxic, funny, or just weird, that we are not privy to, given his addiction to tweeting at all hours?

Jeff Bezos, too, became more of a celebrity, perhaps most famously when he failed to keep his awkwardly endearing sexts to his now fiancée, Lauren Sánchez, private. After a tabloid published the intimate messages, I used this cautionary tale to discuss how none of us are safe from the prying eyes of social media. In a 2019 *New York Times* column, I pointed out how the United States lacks any truly toothy privacy law, adding that "we don't even pretend that we think privacy is something to be protected." Five years later, I am still waiting.

These personality quirks used to be hidden. We are now besieged by a clapback culture where the self-aggrandizing seek to trash anyone for almost anything. And, most of all, many of the people whom I interviewed now just broadcast themselves in loud ways without my help. Some are funny and wonderful (Mark Cuban and Aaron Levie of Box, for example), some are jazz-handsing their way to further wealth (VC Chamath Palihapitiya with SPACs), and some have just descended into a noisy and persistent grievance mode over the years for reasons unknown (Marc Andreessen and so, so many others).

The trash-talkers are the most annoying to me, aiming all kinds of barbs at journalists, the government, the "woke" culture, the state of California, and particularly San Francisco, where most of them made their fortunes. They position themselves as populist truth-tellers to their legions of stans. I don't know about you, but it's funny to see the world's richest men urging people to stick it to the man, when they are the man. They are, as often as not, inaccurate and couldn't care less.

Still, it helps to understand how they perceive the world, even when so much of what they project is performative and often born from a deep insecurity and loneliness, with hidden histories of pain channeled into ambition. To my mind, drive is not always fueled by pain. That greatness comes from inner demons is the simplistic trope often used by those seeking to explain their bad behavior and casual cruelties. It is all part of an increasing fetishization of innovators and what I like to call "entrepreneurial porn." More quiet kindness would get them just as far.

But let them spew angry nonsense, because everyone sees their antics publicly as I have endured them privately. And since getting to the truth is not their goal (moneymaking usually is, with petty score-settling ranking second), we must hold them to account for these rants and outbursts, as they are quick to hold journalism to account. Were their comments accurate? Is what they're doing a distraction or a real concern about an issue? Are they transparent about their agenda? What is their motivation?

Unlike these clowns, I have found that most journalists try their best to do their best. Over the years, I've hired dozens of reporters and tried to impress upon them that working for a digital media company requires both quality and urgency. My mantra is: *You can't be wrong. You can't be wrong. You can't be wrong.* And: *You can't be lazy. You can't be lazy. You can't be lazy.* We owe the companies and people we cover our best work. And when we make mistakes, they're also owed a correction.

What irks me the most is when tech folks react to criticism by accusing reporters of just being in it for the clicks. It's laughable, especially since journalism overall has become a pretty bad business. At one point, I even had a crazy notion that some decent VCs who recognized the value of good journalism could offer support. At the 1999 Agenda conference in Arizona, a group of top tech reporters imagined creating a "Dream Team" of tech journalism, and I got VC Jim Breyer of Accel to make an offer on the back of a cocktail napkin at the Phoenician hotel. It read: "We would back your Dream Team with a $10 million investment which buys 40% → 40% Accel, 60% management (20% unallocated, 40% Dream Team)." *I was rich!* Or, at least, *napkin rich!*

The Dream Team stayed a dream. The VCs probably realized that almost no one goes into journalism for the money, although later billionaires like Laurene Powell Jobs (the *Atlantic*), Jeff Bezos (the *Washington Post*), and Marc Benioff (*Time*) provided much-needed funding for what would be small but influential businesses.

Most of the web sites with an advertising business that I've run banged along at break, while the conferences and podcasts have been far more profitable and carry the freight. In my experience, success is possible if you create a small, profitable business where the financial interests of the partners align, revenue is shared, and the content is valuable to either advertisers or subscribers.

And that is just what Walt and I believed we needed to do soon after we left the *Journal*. Despite the $10 million cushion we had, I watched the prices of content companies suddenly soar. *BuzzFeed, Business Insider,* and Vox Media all moved into the multibillion valuation club with shares and cash to entice staff and make all kinds of deals that could kill us easily. Stuck among the super yachts, *Recode* was bobbing along in our little media dinghy. "We're going to need a bigger boat," I said to Walt.

He sighed, since setting up the company and making a business out of it had been exhausting. Still, it was clear that if the economy contracted, we were fucked since we were neither nimble enough nor too big to fail. Our investors and board were, thankfully, in sync with this evaluation, and I relied on their expertise, especially from Joanne Bradford, who had worked at Microsoft and Yahoo and, at the time, held a top job at the *San Francisco Chronicle*.

We cooked up a variety of creative schemes, including a plan to take over the *Chronicle* and turbocharge it into a digital entity. Another thought was to merge into NBC, which was a *Recode* investor. We also discussed merging with *Politico*, which had just launched a magazine and was eager to move into events. But over dinner at San Francisco's Zuni Café, *Politico*'s owner Robert Allbritton and its cofounder Jim VandeHei squabbled so much that even the restaurant's famous roast chicken was not the usual treat. Later, VandeHei asked me for my thoughts about the meeting. I told him that he and Allbritton were headed for a media divorce and I had no interest in that. Two years later, their marriage crumbled.

After a lot of mulling, my preference was to sell to Vox Media, which had an excellent Verge tech site that focused more on gadgets than companies. Flush with cash and ethical standards, Vox's biggest selling point was its leader Jim Bankoff, whom I had met when he ran AOL's content business. We stayed in touch over the years as he built Vox and it was clear that Bankoff, Walt, and I were in sync. Bradford concurred and I trusted her take. We announced the sale of *Recode* to Vox at the next Code conference, in May of 2015. Even with the ups and downs of the media business, it has been the most excellent boat ride ever since.

The Vox deal and Bankoff's willingness to let me try new ideas allowed me to see myself as a one-person media entity. As tech's influence had grown, so had mine. While the word "brand" makes you feel like a jar of peanut butter, I was making something with my name on it and could get my voice out there in ways that had been more difficult before what with all the gatekeepers.

And that is how the *Recode Decode* podcast launched in July of 2015, after this simple pitch to Bankoff: "Tech is full of people who deserve a grilling year-round." I also pointed out that three interviews a week meant 150 shows he could sell to advertisers. In all its incarnations, like my events, the podcast has been solidly profitable from the start.

Recode Decode also allowed me to continue my conversations with Silicon Valley's elite while showcasing new voices. In 2017, I attended a tech event in Germany called DLD (Digital-Life-Design) and watched as Scott Galloway, an NYU Stern Business School professor of brand strategy and digital marketing, delivered a wacko presentation that included him donning a wig and lip-syncing to George Michael's "Freedom! '90" for way too long. While Scott's casual arrogance was familiar to me, his insights were fresh and new. I invited him to join me on *Recode Decode* and he said yes.

On the podcast, Scott spoke quickly, almost as quickly as I did. He introduced himself as an entrepreneur who had spent two years in the fixed-income department at Morgan Stanley, which he called soul-crushing—an "awful place for awful people." Then, he added, "I realized I couldn't be successful in a big firm." Sound familiar? After getting an MBA, Scott cofounded an Internet retail company called Red Envelope. He hinted that the company had issues, so I pressed him for specifics. Before three minutes had passed in our first conversation, Scott said, "Oh gosh, getting to the dirty laundry early."

"Yes, please," I said. Without flinching, he said he thought the Red Envelope board had ruined the company and I loved his honest take. Later, I asked him to give his assessment of different tech businesses and found his insights to be astute, especially in this exchange.

Scott: I think Facebook and Google both face the same issue, and that is they want to sell advertising against content and then say, "But we don't have the responsibilities of a traditional media company."

Kara: That's right, they've abrogated the responsibility.

Scott: It's total BS.

Kara: Thank you for saying that.

Scott: What if I were McDonald's and 80 percent of the beef I was serving before the election day was fake beef, and people ended up getting encephalitis and making bad decisions?

Kara: Right. You'd get sued out of existence.

Scott: I said, "Wait, wait, wait. Hold on, I'm not a fast-food restaurant. I'm a fast-food platform, so I can't be responsible for the beef I serve."

Kara: I adore you right now for saying that.

Listeners noticed our chemistry, too, and the show scored higher in numbers than even my many interviews with Elon Musk. So Scott and I kept talking, and we haven't stopped since. "I want to make a podcast with a crazy professor," I told Bankoff. And with just that—no focus groups, no decks, no spreadsheets—our *Pivot* podcast launched in 2018. Since then,

Scott has made approximately fifteen thousand penis jokes, and I have laughed at precisely two. We were immediately profitable and increasingly so over the years, and we laugh every time a media reporter—most of whom have never run a media business—writes a thumbsucker about how podcasting does not make money. Narrator: Podcasting makes money.

My key realization was that I could be a reporter and also an entrepreneur—a "reportrepreneur," if you will. I have long maintained that journalists who aren't business minded will be subject to the vicissitudes of a market that is shrinking by the second and will not offer the control they need. That is why I embraced the risk-taking part of tech. Now, I get to make a healthy living and, more importantly, I do what I want when I want to do it. Like Scott, I am a bad employee, so I stopped being one long ago.

And what I get to do in this trade is what I love best: asking questions. One of the best examples of live interviewing I've ever seen was Spalding Gray's show *Interviewing the Audience*, which I saw five times at the Kennedy Center in the 1990s. You could actually see it countless times because each show, Gray pulled three audience members onstage to talk. With a little probing, he drew out their stories, which were often both unexpected *and* universal. The takeaway from the show—and Gray's overall point—was that everyone is interesting if you ask the right questions. This has always been my approach to interviewing.

While I have no particular secret, I approach every interview with these three goals: (1) to make it a conversation, (2) to not be afraid to ask the question everyone is thinking, and (3) to conduct each discussion as if I were never going to interview that person again.

Before an interview, my producers and I write up a series of questions based on research. Some journalists save the uncomfortable questions for the end of an interview, but I tend to lead with those. As tech journalist Eric Newcomer once observed in "An Ode to Code": "Swisher has a unique talent for coming off as simultaneously affable and hostile to her interview subjects. She's willing to undercut them and bring up old embarrassing answers. But she also keeps things moving along and seems to want her guests to come off well."

I think this is true, and I have always chafed at the idea that I was too "tough," although I did laugh when someone described my interview with comedy legend Jon Stewart as "casually cruel." Stewart joined me on my *Sway* podcast for the *New York Times*, where I spent four years as an opinion columnist, and I asked if he was still relevant. Frankly, it was a good question and he seemed to love answering it. (And, yes, the answer is that he is still relevant.)

While white tech dudes were my specialty, I began to vary my repertoire, especially at Code. One interview received pushback from the audience before it was even conducted. In that 2014 interview, I told my guest onstage, "When we announced that we were going to have Kim Kardashian at our conference, we got a lot of interesting reactions on Twitter, like why we would do this? Everyone has different opinions and some of them are not so nice, but I just want to give you some statistics: Kardashian has 20.5 million followers on Instagram, 24.8 million followers on Twitter, 24 million followers on Facebook. At the time, her mobile game was one of the top games on iPhone, garnering tens of millions of dollars in profit for her and the company Glu. She had clearly figured something out about the mobile area."

Obviously, Kardashian deserved to be interviewed as a business leader and as a social media genius, but when she called me she was surprised that anyone would be interested in her thoughts. "Kim," I told her, "you are the Olympics of oversharing."

In a weightier Code interview, I spoke with Maria Ressa, CEO of *Rappler*, who had alerted me years before to the proliferation of misinformation online. Like me, Ressa loved tech in spite of the damage caused by propaganda on social media. Because of her outspokenness, Ressa was under constant threat of imprisonment in the Philippines. Still, Ressa pressed her case: "The idea behind *Rappler* was, we're going to use this new technology and journalism to build communities of action. We live in a country that has endemic corruption, where institutions are extremely weak, leadership is personalistic, and here are all these people who just want a better life. Why can we not use this technology to build communities of action?"

The young reporter Kara Swisher might have been bothered by the idea, since it sounds more like activism than journalism. As it has turned out, especially as the dangers of the tech world and its endless power have only grown larger, the much older Kara Swisher now agrees.

CHAPTER 16

Come With Me If You Want to Live

Think of yourself as dead. You have lived your life. Now, take what's left and live it properly. What doesn't transmit light creates its own darkness.

—MARCUS AURELIUS, *MEDITATIONS*

Speaking of living, my career was not the only thing that was constantly evolving. In the middle of my sixth decade, I utterly disrupted my analog, personal life as well, taking risks not unlike a lot of people I covered.

Since starting to date in seventh grade (boys!), I had moved from relationship to relationship quickly, with my longest stretch of solitude being only a few months. So, once my divorce from Megan was finalized and another relationship I had after my marriage ended, I promised myself that I would try to be alone for a year, focusing on my work and sharing custody of our two teenaged boys.

Since Megan had taken the job of chief technology officer in the Obama administration in D.C., which she richly deserved, I wound up spending a lot of time on airplanes. On one red-eye flight back to San Francisco, in what was a rare moment of contemplation, I started thinking about how deliberate I had been in my career choices, but in my personal life I was much more instinctual. I decided to make a Kara version of what tech execs call an OKR (objectives and key results). Thus, I made a list—on my iPhone, of course—of what I wanted and, really, *needed* in a relationship that I hoped would last for the rest of my life.

Kind
Generous
Emotionally available
Can compromise
Intuitive
Is kind to my kids
Likes/wants kids
Can share friends
Can share family
Copacetic career
Intellectually compatible
Conversations
Likes to travel
Flexible

It was a short list, but a very tall order.

Soon after, my friends Candy Feit and Lydia Polgreen arranged a party to set me up with the first of two people that Candy thought were "perfect" for me. I never met the second person because within minutes of meeting Amanda Katz, I realized she had checked all the items on my list. Amanda had worked at the *Boston Globe* in a variety of roles and was currently an editor in the CNN.com investigations unit, but what really made an impression on me was she suggested that we first meet at a Brooklyn bar ahead of the party. Why?

"Single people are like TV for married people," she told me.

I laughed out loud at that, and it was love at first wit, which should have been on the list, as well as the added benefit of her advanced degree in poetry. *Hot.* We became serious immediately, and she was happy when I did not flee after she told me that, following a breakup of her own, she was now trying to have a baby as a single person. Was I cool with that? Are you kidding? It was an OKR!

Among my handful of regrets in life, not getting pregnant more than once was the most significant. I had wanted many kids but had waited until I was thirty-nine to have Louie. Doctors dubbed it a "geriatric" pregnancy, which pissed me off. But as much as I loved being pregnant, the recovery from childbirth was indeed hard on my body and I never pushed to do it again. After two sons, I also wanted a daughter. Most of all, I liked spending time with my kids better than anyone else and wanted more of that.

In an interview, I was asked about my attitude on change at the time, and I explained, "When something bad happens at work, I'm like, 'I don't need *you* to like me. I have dogs. I have kids. I need *them* to like me.' If I fail at being a parent, I feel terrible, but if I fail at some work thing, I'm like, *Oh, well.* If something goes wrong, a lot of people are like, 'What are we going to do!?' And I'm like, 'Something else.'"

It was time for something else (and, for the record, my kids and dogs still like me just fine—most days).

Within a year, Amanda gave birth to Clara and we all moved to D.C. in the midst of the pandemic, to be closer to my older children. We got married in a small outdoor wedding—pandemic style with masks and distancing—in October of 2020. With all that chaos, I thought, what's a little more? So, Amanda got pregnant again in early 2021 and we had a son, Solomon, in November. She also soon took a job as an editor in the Opinions section at my old stomping ground, the *Washington Post*.

Moving to D.C. was actually fortuitous since a lot of the action around tech had moved toward politics and regulation (or the lack thereof). It became increasingly important for me to forge relationships with government officials, since I had hopes that they might finally try to rein tech in. I had a lot of thoughts on the many issues and was itching to find a heftier platform to make my case. I wanted to call out tech's acquiescence around a range of issues like immigration and disinformation, especially with Trump in office. In March of 2018, I attended SXSW in Austin and had a chance meeting with *New York Times*'s Sam Dolnick (who is also one of its owners and now deputy managing editor at the *Times*). Our discussion led to an offer for me to write a weekly column, which was exactly what I needed.

My foray began more like a sonic boom. Out of the gate, as I noted earlier, I called Facebook, Twitter, and Google "digital arms dealers" and kept going with strongly worded pieces on the warping of Twitter by Trump, the glacial panic of Hollywood when it came to digital, the need for an Internet Bill of Rights, and I had one of the earliest pieces talking about the dangers of Chinese Communist Party surveillance on TikTok (in which I said I loved it but that I used it on a burner phone). That was attracting a lot of controversy, but it was the good kind that got people thinking differently. I have always had the conviction that columnizing is a losing game over time, as ideas get thinner and thinner and pomposity gets fatter and fatter, so I gave myself four years tops to make a dent. In fact, I quit my *Times* gig in 2022, right on schedule. Until then, I knew I could maintain a lean and mean attitude while alerting a global audience about the growing dangers of tech and, now and again, some of its delights (ASMR videos—Google/Bing/DuckDuckGo it!).

With my move east, I was definitely becoming less of a chronicler of the Internet age and more of its cranky Cassandra. My tenure at the *Times* also overlapped with the Covid-19 pandemic, which I posited would be a huge boon to the tech industry. One of my columns outlined how a socially distanced populace would accelerate already existing trends around communications, commerce, education, workplace, and more. "If power tends to corrupt, and absolute power corrupts absolutely, how can we best describe the kind of power Big Tech will wield when the coronavirus crisis is over?" I wrote in May 2020. "How about this: The tech giants could have all the power and absolutely none of the accountability—at least all the power that will truly matter."

I was truly concerned about people I had come to know well, and leaving Silicon Valley behind physically is what did it. Over the years, I'd stood in the backyards of the tech gods. I'd argued with eBay CEO Meg Whitman over anti-gay marriage

Proposition 8 in Sheryl Sandberg's living room. I'd listened incredulously to newly rich techies bid $12,000 dollars in an auction just to cut off John Doerr's tie and even more to throw then analyst Mary Meeker in the pool. I'd ogled a fireworks display paid for by a small startup, over a Southern California beach, from a swanky hotel lobby with Mark Cuban, as we both declared that the bubble was at its peak in July of 2000.

That was work, but being embedded for too long always exacts its price. And despite the many scoops usually not in the best interests of techies and a reputation as a tough reporter, which I was, I started to realize that I had become too much a creature of the place. That was pointed out clearly in a 2014 profile in *New York* magazine by Benjamin Wallace that was oddly titled: "Kara Swisher Is Silicon Valley's Most Feared and Well-Liked Journalist. How Does That Work?"

However clever the juxtaposition, that description stuck and became an annoyance to me. But one observation by Wallace stayed in my head: "What's most curious about Swisher's role in the Valley is not whether her connections and conferences compromise her—beyond grumbling about her Google conflict, not even her rivals can name a big story she's pulled up short on, and she's broken more big stories in the industry than anyone else—but how she's managed to elevate herself into Silicon Valley royalty by writing about Silicon Valley royalty, often acerbically."

He was dead right—while I had not become them, I was part of the scene in a way that was starting to feel uncomfortable. I had been a camera, at times an eviscerating one, but it was long past time to use all that knowledge I had gained to finally tell people what that photo actually showed. And while I was hardly an amanuensis, I had already started thinking my role needed to change much earlier, in fact. I said so at a SXSW panel that year, which the article quoted: "More and more, as I've thought about our new endeavor, at some point, we're going to have to start pissing people off more. And I think about that a lot. Sometimes I see people and I think: 'Soon, I'm going to screw you.' I do, I think that a lot more. . . . Things are going to have to start to get a little tougher."

That was me manifesting where I wanted to head—just like my perfect wife list. I even inked this intent on my body, adding two more tattoos on my wrists, right alongside the first letters of my children's first names in hearts. I boiled the premise down to the symbols for entropy and syntropy, which are arrows pointing outward and inward, basically representing chaos and order. I had covered the chaos—break things!—and now I wanted to know what the tech powers were going to do to put things back in order.

When I started covering the nascent sector in the 1990s, I had truly believed in tech's ability to transform the world, to solve problems that had plagued us for centuries and allow us to finally see our commonality over all our differences. My belief that everything that can be digitized would be digitized turned out to be true. The Internet, which others had mocked, had become nothing short of miraculous. And, as it turned out, also disastrous.

The dire situation had been aggravated by elected officials who, a quarter century into the Internet age, had managed to pass exactly zero legislation to protect anyone. Democratic institutions that we hold dear had crumbled in the face of what all this digital engagement has wrought: no privacy protections, no

updated antitrust laws, no algorithmic transparency require-
ment, no focus on addiction and mental impact. It is breathtak-
ing to think that there are no significant guidelines governing
these areas. However flawed, there are laws for everything *but*
tech companies.

You'd never know it, though, from listening to thin-skinned
techies, too many of whom have resisted any legitimate criticism, while also becoming weirdly media obsessed. They can't
stop talking about how much they think the press is irrelevant and have tried to do an end run around journalists once
the tongue baths they regularly got (and sometimes still do)
ceased. The truth is that media is complex and it sometimes
fails. It is also not particularly lucrative anymore, unless it's a
movie blockbuster or a hit TV show, and even that has come
under huge economic disruption due to digital technologies
like streaming. But most techies now dabbling in media are arrogant amateurs who think that because they excel in one area
they are masters of all domains, when what they really are is
just incompetent at giving any insight or illumination beyond
their own narrow self-interests. Do we want to know what
some loudmouthed VC with no expertise thinks about Covid
or Ukraine or the tragedy unfolding in the fall of 2023 in Israel,
without any self-reflection of their own role in cheapening discourse? Take a seat, boys.

Unfortunately, because I started to articulate this simple
truth out loud, there are many who now consider me a tech
hater. One recently called me the most "vitriolic voice" in the
sector. Others think I can be too negative about these fabulous
Silicon Valley innovations that we should be thankful for. To

some, I'm a "bummer." A few even view me as an enemy of the new digital world order. After I interviewed Yoel Roth at the 2023 Code, Musk tweeted that he was "pure evil" and that my heart was "seething with hate." (Check notes: After Roth quit Twitter, Musk falsely insinuated he was encouraging pedophilia, which resulted in Roth getting death threats and having to sell his home after being doxed.)

And, for the record, my heart is not seething with anything, especially since just after my sixtieth birthday I finally had the small hole that had caused my stroke plugged. It was a twenty-minute procedure that previously would have required open-heart surgery, so I obviously love innovations in tech even more than most people. Still, Musk and many of his enabling minions persist in framing me as a hater. It's just codswallop. What I hate is persistent puerile behavior and lack of care about the pain it causes, qualities too often tinged with odd personal grievance and deep-seated insecurity. These are grown men, who use excuses to dismiss the damage they create.

It's not hard to see why some of them then attack people like me (and there are many). I suppose they thought I was one of them, even though I was *never* one of them. I was there to cover them. My job was to point out how important it is to anticipate the consequences of invention. And to argue that safety and innovation do not have to be at odds. And to suggest that all this online rage might just impact the real world. And to posit that, worst of all, some of the world's richest and most powerful people may have become professional trolls for whom the rules do not apply, diminishing social discourse with their toxic adult-toddler antics (actually, my youngest children behave better, except sometimes Sol, but he's two). And more: I noted that power had become far too concentrated in a small group of homogeneous people and that money had done its usual job of corrupting.

Those culpable should be able to take it, since they certainly can dish it out. And while I can get pointed, it's definitely not personal.

Actually, it's a tiny bit personal. My two kids in college talk about how dispiriting the world can seem as they're flooded 24/7 with information that's both silly and dead serious, which creates problems that seem insurmountable and rancor that seems unsolvable. It's hard to deny their concerns about where this is all headed as we move to a world more digitized and sur-veilled and where data is the ultimate power. And young people are the ones who will be impacted the most.

That is why I tell them and anyone else who will listen that it is ever more urgent that we take back control, because what happens next will be due to the choices we make now. When it comes to continuing the tech tsunami that has blown down so much already, people like me hardly matter, because we are not the ones who will endure the weight of what is coming and we are not the ones who will be impacted the most. What worries me most is apathy in the face of all this Internet convenience. The deluge of digital, which is both necessary to participate in society while also increasingly addictive, makes it harder for anyone to act. It's heartbreaking to see so little energy put into fighting back. But as Allen Ginsberg said so eloquently: "It isn't enough for your heart to break because everybody's heart is bro-ken now."

Despite the heartbreak, we must act. And we must do it quickly to push technology toward its potential for positive impact. Digital is everything and *everywhere*, and like water, without any dams to stop it, it flows. Moreover, increasingly powerful technologies have capabilities far beyond what has come before, as we move to another Cambrian explosion, this time in the tech space around generative artificial intelligence. It has actually been around for a while, more commonly called machine learning, and everyone I interview now who knows what they're talking about agrees we are at an important inflection moment for good *and* bad.

So will machine learning be employed to discover new drugs that will solve cancer in a fraction of the time and for a fraction of the price? Will we use AI to put substantive health information into the hands of those who have long been denied it? Will we turn to it to turbocharge education across the globe? Will we design social media to bring voters together on what they agree on rather than what they do not, and jettison the noisy and malevolent people poisoning political discussion? Will we direct future tech to disperse power to more people rather than fewer? Will we lean on machine learning to come up with new ways to solve the climate crisis? Will we ban killer robots? Will we marry nice ones?

This is all possible with the even more powerful AI technology that is coming, which is why I am intent on making people realize that all this information that is now digitized is actually us—tech companies have scraped from us a database of human intentions, as well as our hopes and dreams and knowledge and, most of all, our questions about our world. And in fact, we bought and paid for the Internet at its beginning, but largely tech companies have benefited from it. It is rightfully ours to own and use to better humanity rather than cheapen and deaden it. Will we use it to warm our house rather than let those who did not care enough burn it down? As George Sand said, "It is high time we had lights that are not incendiary torches."

Which brings us to the question, "Will AI kill us?"

I can only answer at this moment now that I'm not as afraid of AI as I am fearful of bad people who will use AI better than good people. This requires that all of us think carefully about what gets made. Since it's hard to imagine what will come, my rule of thumb to innovators is: If you can imagine your invention in an episode of *Black Mirror*, then don't make it . . . unless it's a simulation where lesbians can meet because that episode—"San Junipero"—watch it!—was fantastic.

But back to death: Will the new iteration of AI eventually become self-aware and kill all of humanity because it's the logical thing to do? I am sorry to report that the short answer is yes. Or no. Maybe. Probably. All kidding aside, anything I write in the fall of 2023 about AI will be irrelevant already in the spring of 2024, except that we need to be talking constantly with all parties involved as it evolves, something I have been doing for a decade. In fact, Elon Musk was the first to alert me to the implications of advanced machine learning and the first to express worry.

Musk mentioned AI in every interview we did, because of his enthusiasm for its potential but also because he wanted to grapple with its dangers. That's why he said he was an early investor in OpenAI, which would introduce the groundbreaking ChatGPT in 2023. He thought that we needed to keep up with the fast-developing technology and use embedded brain tech to aid the "meat" that encased and hindered us.

In one discussion, Musk referenced Terry Bisson's radio play *They're Made Out of Meat*, about a pair of computer-based aliens, made out of bits and bytes, who have just visited Earth. "These creatures are the only sentient race in the sector and they're made out of meat," says one alien to the other, astonished that our viscera held together by muscles and encased by epidermis could makse a machine. Musk, when he was in his charming prankster mode, as he used to be more often, began to call our lips "meat flaps" and our throat a "meat tube." His salient point was that we needed to adapt for the coming revolution in artificial intelligence. His solution was to start a strange company called Neuralink to create a chip implant to improve the brain's bandwidth and be upgradable. It's an interesting and unproven gambit and also controversial for many reasons, including disturbing reports around its treatment of animals in testing.

Musk has been insistent that this enhancement could unlock human potential and thinks it is necessary to move fast since he believes AI will eventually plow over us like a highway construction machine rolling over an anthill. It was an apt metaphor, and on my *Sway* podcast, I asked him to dig deeper. "I was just pointing out with the anthill analogy that AI does not need to hate us to destroy us. In a sense, that if it decides that it needs to go in a particular direction and we're in the way, then it would without hard feelings, it would just roll over us. We would roll over an anthill that's in the way of a road. You don't hate ants. You're just building a road. It's a risk, not a prediction. So, yeah. I think that we really need to think of intelligence as really not being uniquely confined to humans. And that the potential for intelligence in computers is far greater than in biology. Just far, far greater."

Musk was right then and is right now. The point was underscored by OpenAI CEO Sam Altman, who broke with Musk about the future of the company over issues of control and direction. That included accepting increasing slugs of investment from Microsoft. Musk and OpenAI parted ways, but he would continue to attack it, especially after it accepted a $10 billion investment in 2023 and also created a "capped profit" entity along with the nonprofit one. The computing cost of expanding ChatGPT was enormous, so the move made sense. After insulting it as "woke," Musk announced his own AI company. Oh, the irony.

While I see his point, I certainly trust Altman more than Musk (low bar!). I have come to know and like the young entrepreneur since I met him in 2005. He was just nineteen years old then and had cofounded Loopt, a social networking location app that blew through $30 million in venture funding before being sold for parts later. He moved on to other endeavors, including running the popular startup accelerator Y Combinator. Over those years, I have spent many hours talking to Altman about the downsides of AI that were never brought up by the early Internet pioneers. Like them, Altman was often far too sunny, noting to me in a 2023 interview that AI "is going to elevate humanity in ways that we still cannot fully envision, and our children, our children's children, are gonna be far better off than the best of anyone from this time. And we're just gonna be in a radically improved world. We will live healthier, more interesting, more fulfilling lives. We'll have material abundance for people."

I pointed out that he sounded alarmingly like the early Internet people I'd met twenty-five years ago, when Altman was just twelve. Finally, I got him to admit: "We are messing around with something we don't truly understand." Thankfully, he has leaned into this message more in public, although some distrust the effort since the sector is still resisting any meaningful regulation.

That resistance came into sharp relief in November of 2023 when Altman was suddenly fired by OpenAI's non-profit board for the unspecified issue of not being "candid." Essentially, they were calling Altman a liar, without explaining at all what it meant. While there was a lot of noise about a holy tech war between those who supported AI acceleration versus deceleration, in reality, the board had gotten far too small after some departures and was dominated by AI pessimists who simply took their shot at reining in Altman and failed. Without going into all the odd twists and turns that happened over a weekend, Altman was restored to his job quickly with the support of the company's major investor, Microsoft, and most of its employees who threatened to quit over the board's move. The first AI power play thus over, the real race to dominate the sector is now on with numerous players like Google, Amazon, and, of course, Elon Musk, vying for hegemony. We'll see who prevails, but I can assure you the machines will not become self-aware and extinguish humanity. Yet. And if or when that happens, it will be because the enemy is actually and always us.

I more often prefer the attitude of Tristan Harris, a tech ethicist and cofounder and executive director of the Center for Humane Technology. A former Google design ethicist (yes, it's a job), Harris used that experience to later alert the public to tech's dangers, first about social media and now with AI. He described the landscape to me starkly in a 2023 interview:

> The places that I think people are landing include what we call pre-tragic, which is when someone actually doesn't want to look at the tragedy—whether it's climate or some of the AI issues that are facing us or social media having downsides. We don't want to metabolize the tragedy, so we stay in naïve optimism. A pre-tragic person believes, humanity always figures it out. Then there's the person who stares at the tragedy and gets stuck. In tragedy, you either get depressed or you become nihilistic.

Harris correctly sees another path:

> There's a third place to go, which is what we call post-tragic, where you actually accept and grieve through some of the realities that we are facing. You have to go through the dark night of the soul and be with that so you can be with the actual dimensions of the problems that we're dealing with and you're honest about what it would take to do something about it.

I hope more people in tech embrace that post-tragic stance. It would be a departure since most entrepreneurs are pre-tragic, passionately believing in themselves to the point of complete delusion. It's part of the Silicon Valley ethos that is both necessary and fatal: They feel like they have to say everything is right and there's nothing wrong with the product in order to succeed. As someone who has created many innovative journalism businesses, I understand, but it is also a stubborn attitude that too often brings peril to the rest of us.

Especially when, of course, there is something really wrong with the product. I'll never forget learning that lesson at a launch party for Google Glass, arguably the first major iteration of augmented reality. The company had rented a New Orleans riverboat, which sailed into the San Francisco Bay with me aboard along with a buffet table piled high with huge prawns. Everyone on the boat who worked at the company—so, not me—was given a pair of Google Glass smart glasses to wear, which were activated with the words "Hello Glass." The problem was that when someone tried to wake up their own Google Glass, they inadvertently woke up everyone else's in earshot. It became impossible to have an uninterrupted human interaction, so I sat in front of that mountain of prawns and thought to myself, "This is the end times," and, also, "Delicious shellfish!" It was, as they say, a moment, because what these techies were doing without any realization was utterly dystopian and they were ignorant that they were doing it in real time.

Pointing out these failings has remained my calling card, and I'm aware that me telling smart people to think smarter comes off as rude at times. I am not someone who apologizes a lot, and I try to behave so I don't have to. This has been perhaps one of the distinguishing characteristics of my success over the years. Other attributes: Obnoxiousness. Persnicketiness. A distaste for lies. A proclivity to call out nonsense, no matter the power of the person uttering it. In fact, *especially* if the person is very powerful. That is most commonly called "speaking truth to power," and it's much easier to do in a democratic country like the U.S. Many others do not have this unique privilege, so if you can, I highly recommend that you take advantage of it. While speaking out can be risky, the rewards are both psychic and, sometimes, financial. At least, that's been true for me. I have basically made a career of stepping out of line and did so when I gave up my path to power on the political beat at the *Washington Post* to start covering a nascent industry very few believed in.

The journey started out as a love story and, despite my many disappointments, remains one. I still love and breathe tech. If that sounds naïve after all I've said here, I get that, but despite division and no rules and screaming and reductiveness and anger and time-wasting and insurrection, tech remains a vast canvas of promise. Also, the cat videos are still good.

At least now we know the problems. This is why I increasingly focus on the adults in the room who can grok this. That included the people I invited onstage in 2022 for the last Code that I ran and hosted. As a bookend, I wanted to end the conference with a reflection of our first-ever guest: Steve Jobs. I sat down with his widow Laurene Powell Jobs, famed designer Jony Ive, and Apple CEO Tim Cook to discuss Steve's legacy.

Laurene talked about how if Steve had lived, "he would be very disappointed in the political climate . . . he would be speaking out easily and often." Cook noted that "we don't sit around and say, 'What would Steve do'; he told us not to do that." And Ive reminded the audience that Jobs' "understanding and reverence of the creative process was extraordinary."

No, Steve Jobs was in no way perfect. But what I was trying to invoke was a time when leaders made, or at least *tried* to make, better choices. Which is why I think we still have time to do it differently now—a do-over, if you will. If that sounds like a cop-out, fine, but it's pretty much our only hope. I have no real idea where any of it is going. Most of my thoughts on the future of [fill in the blank] would be just guesses. Streaming? Here to stay and necessary, even though a lot of pioneers will die on the new trail. Autonomous vehicles? I love them, and after all of them being tested for two decades, they are reaching a point of true utility, though we have to rethink whether more cars are the answer if we are not willing to remove humans as drivers. Jobs? Vast swaths of work will be gone, across information industries this time, but it will open up the avenue for humans to focus on what is creative. Longevity? We will all be living longer and better, Larry Ellison willing (he has been a big investor in these technologies).

I could go on and will, as it's all in flux. But I am certain that where tech goes depends on who makes the decisions. If it remains a small group of out-of-touch tech billionaires, I would say I am worried; if it's a diverse group of voices who are willing to listen and compromise, I am more optimistic. The only certainty I can offer for those of us with meat flaps is that everyone's analog life will end at some point, even if your digital presence will endure into the ages hence. This was, of course, the most important lesson I learned at a young age when my father died so suddenly. He thought he was headed for the big time and then he just fell over one day, and that has informed everything I've done since. Which is to say, I don't have time to wallow. You don't have time, either. Nobody has time.

In the interests of time, then, I thought about employing the stunt of asking ChatGPT how to end this book. My prompt: "Write a conclusion to a memoir in the style of Kara Swisher about her life as a reporter covering the Internet." What it spit out in about five seconds was exactly what you might expect—treacly and reductive and painfully anodyne—so, I asked for a redo that was less sunny, for which the AI took no umbrage. That also took five seconds and was marginally better, but still awful, which I render below, in part.

Title: "Wired Reflections: Navigating the Digital Currents"

In the tapestry of my life, the threads of technology have woven a narrative both bright and shadowed. The Internet, a sprawling expanse of opportunity and complexity, has been my canvas, my subject, and my challenge.

In "Wired Reflections," I've sought not only to chronicle the ascent of the digital age, but also to grapple with its complexities. From the dawn of connectivity to the present crescendo of virtual voices, I've borne witness to the power of human ingenuity, as well as its potential for misdirection.

Oh dear, that was unfortunate. And that was definitely not *Burn Book*. Be glad I spared you many paragraphs more. But what I can assure you from watching the last twenty-five years is that AI will get better and better over time, even as I get worse and worse. And yet, on this bright fall day, flawed, slow, analog me will try my hand at doing just a little better using my tiny and slightly broken brain.

Picture this: My desk at home overlooks my backyard, and the cold weather is clearly coming as the plants start to wither. Still, there is one stubborn riot of bright orange chrysanthemums that have grown from a tiny patch that I shoved into a pot in the spring without much hope of anything happening. Now the flowers overwhelm the pot, and I am strangely encouraged by their jaunty confidence and obvious fortitude. I have recently begun to garden more—although I am not good at it—because that is what a person who decided to have more children at an advanced age does, find quiet where I can. And, because I love a metaphor, I have come to find that gardening is the perfect encapsulation of both the digital and physical worlds in ways that are sometimes hard to see in real time.

In the poem, "A Gathered Distance," Mark Tredinnick articulates this well. He writes:

> *A garden is never*
> *Finished, and nor are you: Become, I think, a garden again,*
> *And never, like a garden, cease.*

This is the kind of advice that will serve us as we move on from where we are to go to the next thing and then the next thing after that. Life is a series of next things, and you'd do well to be ready for that. And that's why I say with great hope: I now leave you to your own devices—and I mean devices, like my longtime best friend, my iPhone, and also my AirPods and my AirPods Max and my Apple Watch and my iPad. Okay, obviously don't be me.

But please indulge me and take one more gentle suggestion— as someone who has forgotten more about those devices and what they mean than most people will ever know—that you maybe hit pause and put them down more often.

And, of course, *always* look up.

Notes

I'll keep this simple. There will be no footnotes, citations, or a bibliography for this book. Why? Because I'm not Bob Woodward. Okay, fine, because the information in this book is largely based on my three decades of reporting, including hundreds of interviews and reported stories that I have done for the *Washington Post*, the *Wall Street Journal* and *All Things Digital*, the *New York Times*, and at Vox Media's *Recode* and *New York* magazine. While I reference some other news articles in the memoir and cite those sources directly in the text, the book is primarily based on my own work, in print, onstage at the *D: All Things Digital* and Code conferences, and on podcasts. It is also based on conversations and encounters that I have had with many of tech and media's most famous and important players. To be clear, these are *my* recollections of these experiences, and I have sometimes recreated dialogue to the best of my memory, and I have also gone back to my stories and notes, or the people involved, to check them. Where we differ, I note it. I also make use of extensive emails and texts I have kept. Most of all, these are my unvarnished opinions about the companies and people I have seen up close, and the book reflects that. In other words, if you don't like what I think about Mark Zuckerberg or Elon Musk or Steve Jobs or any number of people I have covered over the years, *well*, go read a hagiography. There are plenty of them, and *this* is definitely not that.

Acknowledgments

Oh man, am I dreading this since I am sure I will forget someone, who will then, at some book party in 2024, give me the fisheye, which I will try my best to ignore. For those people, I ask that you give me a big break—I have up to five podcasts a week, four children (more on them later!), and a whole lot of other stuff too numerous to mention. Suffice it to say: I am sorry.

That said, some particular people deserve calling out and they include all the characters—both worthy and not—whom I have met in my many years of covering tech and Silicon Valley. I shall name none of them, though, because I just wrote a book about many of them. As the saying goes, I won't let the door hit me on the way out.

Now to the real deal:

First, Walt Mossberg, to whom this book is dedicated. I was lucky enough to get the best mentor and partner in the world at a young age, and his impact on my life, my career, my journalism, and my soul has been profound.

In that vein, I have been privileged to work for and with some of the finest people in media, including at the *Washington Post*, the *Wall Street Journal*, the *New York Times*, and especially at Vox Media. Of particular note is Jim Bankoff, who has been the kindest of bosses, a stand-up guy in a world that sits down far too much. So, too, the amazing people who have worked for of all my various entrepreneurial concoctions over the years, from *D: All Things Digital* to *Recode* to *Sway* to *On with Kara Swisher* and *Pivot*. I am not going to name all the names, but if I don't put Scott Galloway in, I'll never hear the end of it on the podcast.

Thanks, too, to my various and sundry agents at UTA, including Charlotte Perman, Marc Paskin, and Pilar Queen, all of whom give agents a good name. A great name, in fact, and they've been worth every percent. (Well, *almost* every percent.)

There is only one editor in existence who could have pulled me back into the book writing game: Jon Karp. He's now the big cheese at Simon & Schuster, with fancy private equity partners, but he was but a young editor when he put me—a young reporter—on the publication path. His impeccable judgment has been a constant boon to me. I owe him one more book, so at my pace, we will know each other until the end of our lives. So, too, Stephanie Frerich, whose last nerve I am sure I have gotten on, given how late I am on this book, but who always moved it in the right direction with taste and talent. She is a treasure of an editor.

Also from Simon & Schuster, thanks to: Brittany Adames, Priscilla Painton, Stephen Bedford, Julia Prosser, Elizabeth Herman, Aileen Boyle, Amanda Mulholland, Lauren Gomez, Zoe Kaplan, Navorn Johnson, Meryll Preposi, Beth Maglione, Samantha Cohen, Mikaela Bielawski, Paul Dippolito, Jackie Seow, Emma Shaw, Tom Spain, Ray Chokov, Nicole Moran, Marie Florio, Mabel Taveras, Lyndsay Brueggemann, Winona Lukito, Irene Kheradi, and Carolyn Levin. Also, I love a fact-check, and Kristina Rebelo did an amazing job under a tight deadline. And thanks to Asa Mathat and Rick Smolan for the wonderful photos of my interviews over the decades.

The process of writing a book does take a lot of folks (see

ACKNOWLEDGMENTS

above), but if I had to pick only one person who was the most critical, it would be Nell Scovell. As my editor, my sounding board, my idea factory, and now my good friend, her humor and deep knowledge of and insight into the tech industry has made my work easy and it has also made this book manifest. Without her drive, enthusiasm, and energy, it would imply not exist. She is also so funny, I never forgot to laugh.

Now to the Friends of Kara (FOK!) section. I have been blessed to have so many great ones over the years, and they have always been there on my long journey to here and have made it a lot more fun. I will not get to everyone, but I would like to specifically thank: Brooke Hammerling, Stephanie Ruhle, Lisa Dickey, Quincy Smith, Joanne Bradford, Meredith Levien, Tammy Haddad, Karen Friedman, Lauren Goode, Hilary Rosen, Maggie Haberman, as well as long-suffering comms pros for whom I have huge respect and to whom I have been a huge annoyance, including Alex Constantinople, Brandee Barker, Shannon Stubo, Frank Shaw, Jessica Powell, and Rachel Whetstone. And special thanks to Megan Smith, who has been one of the shining lights of the Internet age (and a terrific mom to ousr sons, too).

My family has also been a huge support to me and has encouraged all my schemes over the decades. My brothers, Jeff and David, are the best of that genre, along with their families. And my mom, Lucky, is a unique spirit in a world that needs more of them and has pushed me to become the person I am today.

So, too, my wife, Amanda Katz, who has been a spectacular partner in life, an amazing mother, and a superb editor and giver of book-writing advice. My 436 jobs, as well as this endless book, have put a lot of weight on her able shoulders, and she deserves a medal of some sort for her patience and equanimity.

ACKNOWLEDGMENTS

Her family, especially the world's best listener of my pods, Ann, has also been so kind.

But of all the people I want to thank, I'd have to say that my four children—Louie, Alex, Clara, and Sol—have been pretty much perfect and are the best things in my life. As rich as it has been, it pales in comparison to what they have given me. Which is, of course, endless joy.

Index

There is *no* index, people. So, you have to read the whole book all the way through to see if you're in it. I'll be honest—most of you are not. Still, read it all, even though it's hundreds of pages. Think of it like doom-scrolling Twitter—Ex, X, Q, *whatever*, Elon, you ceaseless drama diva. In any case, I believe you all can still pay mind for more than fifteen seconds, especially since you'll be alternately amused, horrified, repulsed, and ultimately, in violent agreement with me. You know I am, so enjoy the ride.